1,001
AFRICAN
NAMES

1,001 AFRICAN NAMES

FIRST AND LAST NAMES FROM THE AFRICAN CONTINENT

JULIA STEWART

A CITADEL PRESS BOOK
Published by Carol Publishing Group

In memory of Jeff Butler

Interior illustrations by Todd H. Schaffer

A Citadel Press Book
Published by Carol Publishing Group
Citadel Press is a registered trademark of Carol Communications, Inc.
Editorial Offices: 600 Madison Avenue, New York, N.Y. 10022
Sales and Distribution Offices: 120 Enterprise Avenue, Secaucus, N.J. 07094
In Canada: Canadian Manda Group, One Atlantic Avenue, Suite 105, Toronto,
    Ontario M6K 3E7
Queries regarding rights and permissions should be addressed to Carol
Publishing Group, 600 Madison Avenue, New York, N.Y. 10022

Carol Publishing Group books are available at special discounts for bulk
purchases, sales promotion, fund-raising, or educational purposes. Special
editions can be created to specifications. For details, contact: Special Sales
Department, Carol Publishing Group, 120 Enterprise Avenue, Secaucus, N.J.
07094

Manufactured in the United States of America
10 9 8 7 6 5 4 3 2 1

Library of Congress Cataloging-in-Publication Data

Stewart, Julia.
    1,001 African names : first and last names from the African continent /
Julia Stewart.
        p.   cm.
    "A Citadel Press book."
    ISBN 0-8065-1737-9 (pbk.)
    1. Names, Personal—African—Dictionaries—English.   2. Names,
Personal—Africa—Dictionaries—English.   I. Title.
CS2375.A33S73   1996
929.4'08996—dc20   95-49286
                                                         CIP

CONTENTS

v

Ceremonial mask, Ivory Coast

k

The
Libr
cou
sou
an

Co
ta
(l
a
F
C
a

Nigerian mask

ACKNOWLEDGMENTS

The majority of research for names in this book was done at the Library of Congress in Washington, D.C. However, the picture could not have been complete without the help of African sources and friends who verified information, added much, and assisted with the pronunciation of names.

Many warm thanks are due all those people in Kenya, Columbus, Ohio, and Washington, D.C., Chicago who facilitated this project over the past few years. They are my in-house (literally) illustrator and reader Todd Schaffer; Francis Hillman and Almaz Tecle of Nairobi and Tek Beyene of Columbus who provided a wonderful collection of Eritrean names; Modupeola Olajumoke Ajose of Columbus for help with Nigerian Yoruba and Muslim names; John Tawia Akrobettoe and his many friends in Columbus, once again, for contributing West African names—particularly Aminu Yakubu who took the time to assist with Hausa names; Joy Buseruka of Nairobi for supplying interesting Baganda and Kinyarwanda names and Juvens Ntampuhwe of Cyangugu, Rwanda, Chicago for Kinyarwanda names; Duncan (Dan) Omondi Oburu for an excellent compilation of Luo of Kenya names; Lamin Sillah of Columbus for aiding with names from Sierra Leone; Dr. Hillary Kelly for enthusiastic assistance with Oromo names; Tim Leyland for helping with southern Sudanese names; Joellen Lambiotte for help with West African names; Dave Thomas for Mozambican names; Prudence Nkinda for Meru of Kenya names; Mary McVay for West African names; and Lynn Thomas for Kenyan names.

Many thanks go to Mounir Adhoum, John and Tracy Gillis, and Mike Cornell for accommodation and support while in Washington, D.C. Appreciation is due the helpful staff at the embassies of Angola, Chad, Cote d'Ivoire, Egypt, Ethiopia, Kenya, Lesotho, Mali, Namibia, Nigeria, Senegal, South Africa, Tunisia, Uganda, Zaire, Zambia, and Zimbabwe. Special thanks also to Allan J. Wilson, my editor at Carol Publishing.

PART I
INTRODUCTION AND BACKGROUND

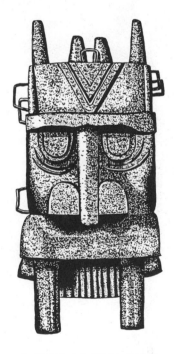

Otobo mask, Kalabari. Water spirit mask with Hippo and human features.

TRADITIONAL AFRICAN NAMING PRACTICES

The Name is the Spirit.
Lala of Zaire

Indigenous African names, evolved over many generations, abound with history and meaning. While Western names are generally chosen for their aesthetic value alone, African names are selected taking additional factors into consideration. Some names represent important observations of the parents, others reflect certain characteristics of the people bestowing them. Names, taken as a whole, can provide insight into what is important to a family and a community. The fact that a great portion of Igbo of Nigeria names relate to God and deities begs a conclusion that the Igbo are a highly religious people. Yoruba names, which challenge others to live up to the moral standards established by the society, indicate that the Yoruba value healthy relationships within the community.

Despite Africa's immense cultural diversity, when it comes to traditional naming practices many common threads can be traced. This is not to say all African societies adhere to identical principles when naming children. Nor do all groups have endless supplies of expressive personal names. In fact, African names range from fairly strict collections to wide selections, depending upon the culture. The Kikuyu of Kenya customarily name children after close relatives, thus recycling names within one family and resulting in a relatively small pool of names within the society.

Customarily, Kikuyu parents name their first son after the father's father, their first daughter after the mother's mother, their second son after the mother's father and their second daughter after the father's mother. The remaining children are

3

named after the parents' siblings or, lacking those, the grand-parents' siblings.

At the other end of the spectrum are the Ishan of Nigeria who tend to individualize every child's name, often relaying specific messages to other people in the family or community, and seldom employing the practice of namesakes. Ishan names laden with significance include ADOGHE (the gratitude of all the good things God has done to me is in my bosom), AJERIAKHILI (this smiling is to mask vengeance), AHATAJANALE (there will be no end if I talk of all we have been through), and AJAKOTA (let's plan together for the good of our family). One source alone has identified over 9,000 Ishan names, illustrating the Ishan talent for constructing unique appellations.

> *Each thing has its moment.*
> Bambara of West Africa

One custom that appears in numerous African societies is naming of children for the day of the week on which they were born. Swahili people of the east coast of Africa, for instance, name females born on Monday MWATATU, those born on Tues-day MWANNE, and males born on Friday JUMA—names derived from the Kiswahili words for those days of the week. In West Africa, the Bambara name boys born on Friday GUEIDIOUMA and those born on Saturday SIBIRI, while a Hausa boy born on Friday would be called DANJUMA and one born on Saturday becomes DANASABE, all names related to the day of the week in their respective languages.

Naming children according to the time of day they were born, or the season in which they are born, is also a convention of many African cultures. An Ovimbundu of Angola baby girl born at dawn may be called NGULA, which is derived from the expression *ongula yomele* meaning "the color of morning." Across the continent, an Oromo of Ethiopia and Kenya girl born at night is named DUKAN, meaning "darkness," and a Swahili child born at night becomes CHAUSIKU, literally "of the night."

The Luo of Kenya quite regularly name their children after

the time of day or season born. Luo time of day names are so specific as to differentiate between children born late in the morning on a sunny day and those born late in the morning on a hazy day. Luo seasonal names are OKOMO and AKOMO (born during the planting season), ODOYO and ADOYO (born in the weeding season), OKEYO and AKEYO (born during the harvest season), and so on. Other examples of seasonal names include AKARIKA, an Ibibio of Nigeria name meaning "harmattan," used for male and female children born during that season marked by dry, dusty desert winds, and the Tonga of Zambia name MWAJANANZALA, meaning "you have found hunger," given to a child entering the world during the traditional period of hunger preceding the harvest season. (See name charts at the back of this book.)

Children born on market days, during festivals, and around the time of religious holidays receive special names to mark these special occasions. EDET is an Ibibio and Efik of Nigeria name for males born on the market day of the same name. The Igbo sometimes label a girl born when the market was at its busiest and loudest UDEAFO, meaning "noise of the market." The Ebira of Nigeria call a child born during the Ekuechi festival ONDEKU and the child born during the Eika festival ADEIKA. Muslim parents in both East and West Africa might select the name HAJI for a boy born during the Islamic month of Ramadan, at which time devout Muslims make a pilgrimage to Mecca, called the *hajj.*

> *A child is hard to come by.*
> Igbo of Nigeria

The precise location of a child's birth frequently dictates the name selected by African parents. An Igbo of Nigeria mother who gave birth while out in the bush near some air roots named her child NWAOGA, "child of the air roots." CHIMBWALI is a Tonga of Zambia name meaning "sweet potatoes," given to a child born while the mother was in the sweet potato field, and CHIKOCHI is a Tonga name bestowed on a baby "delivered in a scotch cart."

Children are the pleasure of the earth.
Yoruba of Nigeria

A common practice among African societies is to name children according to the order in which they were born, known as serial naming. Swahili first born children are MOSI, second born become PILI, and third born are named TATU, which are the respective Kiswahili words for "one," "two," and "three." Serial names frequently reach up to ten or more, reflecting the fact that African mothers have traditionally given birth to large numbers of children. Twi of Ghana names BADU and BADUWA are used for tenth males and females, respectively, and the name ADEBEN is reserved for twelfth-born sons. The Tonga of Zambia engage the name TWAMVULA around the eighth child. Twamvula means "to abound, to be too much" in reference to the family's throng of offspring.

Do not sew a dress for the baby before the child is born.
Tanzania

Names describing conditions of the birth are also found throughout the continent. The Yoruba of Nigeria will name a child born after the normal nine-month gestation period OMOPE meaning "it is late." A Yoruba child born face downward is named AJAYI and one born breech, or feet first, is called IGE. The Banyoro of Uganda name KAIJABWANGU means "it came quickly," and would be used for a child born without complications. ELUMBU, an Ovimbundu of Angola name meaning "mystery," is used for a child born prematurely whose survival may have been in question for some time.

The man who stumbles on riches names his son
Olaniyonu ("riches entail problems").
Yoruba of Nigeria

Circumstances of the family and the community, and major events or natural calamities of the period are frequently expressed through African baby names. A Ghanaian child born when the family or village is prospering might be called ABAYIE (you have come in good times). In a good year for a Hausa community some male children might be named YALWA or MAIWADA (born in the midst of plenty). Should conditions be reversed, the Ghanaian child could be dubbed ANTUBAM (you did not come to meet good conditions) and the Yoruba child given the name ODUNEWU (year of danger).

The Sotho of Lesotho male name KGOTSO (peace) indicates that the family is experiencing smooth relations with friends, relatives, and neighbors. Sotho males born when the family has been affected by some kind of accident are commonly called KOTSI (danger) or TSIETSI (accident). The Tonga of Zambia name CHISONZI (locusts) is used for male children born during a locust invasion and HAAZITA (to attack) for children begat during times of war. MONYYAK, a Dinka of southern Sudan name meaning "man of drought," is appropriately assigned to boys born during a drought.

> *The state of the house must be considered*
> *before naming a child.*
> Yoruba of Nigeria

The Tutsi and Hutu of Rwanda and Burundi and the Banyoro of Uganda agree with the Yoruba proverb above. They routinely select names for their children that indicate the parents' state of mind or the household's status at the time of birth. A problem-ridden Rwandan family could choose the name FATUKOBIRI (take it as it is) as a way of encouraging themselves to endure their troubles. An impoverished Banyoro family might pick the name BASIMAKI (what have they to be thankful for?), while a more optimistic poor family might opt for the name TIBEITA (people do not kill themselves on account of poverty).

> *Many births, many burials.*
> Kikuyu of Kenya

Statistics show African nations retain some of the world's highest infant and child mortality rates in the world. This explains why so many African cultures have developed a slew of personal names related to infant death. One method of fighting off evil entities believed to cause death is to allot children ugly or deceptive names. For example, a Vai mother of Liberia who has watched other children die might choose the unattractive name WONYE—meaning a large ant—to make her baby less appealing to deadly forces. A Sotho mother would name her child MOSELE, which means "tail of the dog," for the same reason. Occasionally Ethiopian parents who have had sons die in the past assign female or unisex names to their male newborns believing that evil spirits may be targetting the males of the household.

Makonde mask, Mozambique

The Yoruba believe that spirits of children who have died are likely to be reborn in other babies. One source describes these as "wandering spirits of children given to the prank of entering into pregnant women, being born only to die for the sheer relish of the mischief." Yoruba parents whose previous children have died select names that will trick the reincarnated child into staying in the world of the living this time around. Examples of this type of name are AKISATAN meaning "no more rags (to bury you with)," KOSOKO meaning "no more hoe (to dig the ground for your burial)," and TIJU-IKU (be ashamed to die). Otherwise these parents opt for names that flat out insult the mischievious spirit, such as UDENE (vulture) and NKPAKUGHA (dustbin). These insult names are considered so foul that the child's friends in the spirit world wouldn't even want him to come back.

They despise the unsightly woman,
and she brings forth a splendid little boy.
Baganda of Uganda

It is not only otherworldly spirits that concern African parents when naming babies—they must occasionally ward off the evil schemings of the living as well. The Banyoro of Uganda sometimes allocate foreboding names to their children as a way of informing their enemies that they are aware of plots brewing to harm them—probably through sorcery. To openly accuse someone of witchcraft is a grave action, especially if the accuser is not one-hundred-percent sure who is the source of the evil. To notify real or imagined enemies in a subtle manner that they have caught on to their evil machinations, Banyoro parents give their newborns names such as BANOBA (they hate), MPABAISI (I give this child to the killers), or BALYESIMA (they will be pleased if the child dies). If someone had, in fact, been intending to harm the family, the belief is that now they will think twice.

The Yoruba and Igbo of Nigeria also employ this sort of warning name, challenging enemies to refrain from doing harm. Yoruba examples include EMENE (don't do) and IWEOBI (anger of the heart). These names are used by mothers who fear that other women harbor jealousies which might lead them to harm the child. ABOKA—an Igbo name derived from the proverb *aboka atunyeisi* meaning "If we revenge too much we throw our head in"—was selected by a very beautiful woman who had many suitors competing to win her hand in marriage. The successful husband was much resented by the other men, so the wife hoped to dispel their bitterness by choosing this name. The Igbo name NWAGBOGU sends a more direct message with its meaning "may a child bring an end to the quarrel." Other Igbo names of this ilk, are IROEGBUNNE (hatred does not kill a mother), MADUEKWENJO (men should not consent to evil) and CHIEGENTI (God does not listen to the enemy).

A child comes only as a gift from God.
Igbo of Nigeria

In numerous African cultures, the local word for God is applied as a prefix or suffix to names. *Mana*—Kinyarwanda for God—is a popular suffix for personal names in Rwanda. Cases include UWIMANA (belongs to God) and NAHIMANA (God will decide).

The Igbo words for God *Chi* (for the spirit guardian) and *Chukwu* (the name of the Great God) are found in names like AMARACHI (God's grace), IHECHI (light of God), and ELOCHUKWU (God's plan). One Yoruba word for God, *Olu*, appears frequently in personal names, as in OLUSOLA (God does me honor), OLUFEMI (God loves me), and OLUMOROTI (it is only with God that I stand). A contemporary survey of 4,421 Igbo names found that 25 percent of them contained God and deity components.

The Ovimbundu of Angola also have a set of names containing their word for God, *Suku*. Ovimbundu examples include SUKUAKUECE, derived from the proverb *Suku a ku ece, imbanda vi lipande*, which translates "May God free you, then the doctors may boast," and CAIMBASUKU from the proverb *ca imba Suku lomue omunu o patala*, meaning "the will of God is inescapable."

> *One is born, one dies; the land increases.*
> Oromo of Ethiopia

In some African societies children are named almost exclusively after the deceased, others honor only the living in this way, and some follow both courses. Naming children after the dearly departed is in part due to widespread belief in reincarnation. The Ibibio christen children with the names of late family members as a way of honoring the deceased and, sometimes, to help welcome their spirits back.

The Luo of Kenya name children after someone who passed away near the time of the child's birth, or after a prominent living person. Naming a child after the current chief, for instance, is a good way to improve your standing with the headman. Only on rare occassions do the Fulani of West Africa name children after living relatives because they believe only the dead can inhabit the soul of a child. Exceptions to this rule occur when a living person is deemed to have an enormous enough personality that it can be shared with children, such as a very old chief or a grandfather.

Some peoples routinely name children after tribal ancestors and utilize clan names. The Ebira of Nigeria praise name

OZIANIVASSA means "the son of Bassa" and recalls the clan of the same name. According to the Kikuyu of Kenya legend, the Kikuyu tribe was founded by a man named Gikuyu and his wife Mumbi. The couple begat ten daughters who founded the ten Kikuyu clans (they are sometimes referred to as the nine clans, reflecting a traditional aversion to counting living things). The names of Gikuyu and Mumbi's daughters—WANJERI, WANJIRU, WAMBUI, WANGUI, WANGECHI, WAMBURA, WANJIKU, WANGARI, WAMUYU, and WAIRIMU—are the most common female names used by the Kikuyu; even to this day.

A child is a source of blessings.
Igbo of Nigeria

It surprises Westerners how easily Africans can rattle off the definitions of indigenous names, especially when most of us find it difficult to explain the meanings of even a few European names—and the definition of our own names are sometimes unknown to us. One reason behind these effortless translations is the fact that most indigenous African names are rooted in the person's own language.

The majority of traditional names from Ethiopia and Eritrea are derived from words, or combinations of words, commonly used in the local languages. For instance, the Amharic word *wark*, which means "gold," is found in AFEWARK (golden mouth), ENGEDA WARK (the new arrival is gold) and TERUWARK (pure gold). The word *geta*, meaning "lord," appears in GETAHUN (be a lord), GETACHAW (their lord) and GETANAH (you are a lord).

Applying everyday words as names is practiced in virtually every African country and culture. SERAME is both a Sotho of Lesotho noun and male name meaning "cold," and LEFU is a Sotho word and male name for "death." Prefixes and suffixes are routinely attached to words to create gender specific names. The Luo of Kenya female name AOKO—used for females born before the mother arrives at the hospital for delivery—originates from the Dholuo word *oko* meaning "outside" preceded by "a," the prefix commonly used for Luo female names. OOKO is the name for a male child born under the same circumstances, the initial "o" being the most common prefix for Luo male names. The Sotho name TLALANE is slightly altered from the word *tlalana* (meaning "small famine") to make a female name, while MAHLOMOLA is a Sotho male name stemming from the verb *hlomola*, meaning "to grieve."

He who has said "I" has distinguished himself from others.
Somalia

Words describing some quality or feature of the person frequently serve as personal names. Characteristic-based names don't appear to be too widespread for newborns, considering the difficultly in determining in advance what traits a child will have. Exceptions include the Igbo name EZELAOBA—used for a baby girl who seems very healthy and strong at birth and which means "getting a good stock"—and HUSO, an Ovimbundu of Angola name meaning "the feigned sadness of a bride" given to a child who resembles another family member in some slight way.

Most characteristic names are reserved as nicknames for children and adults or are used as initiate names for those undergoing rites of passage into adulthood. The selections from this genre of names can be limitless. Quite often they are positive names, or praise names, intended to boost the child's ego, such as the Sotho female name SEPONONO meaning "the pretty one" and the male name MOHLALEFI meaning "the wise one." The Yoruba name ADUMADAN refers to a girl who is very dark-skinned and beautiful. There are also many names in this category that are more frank in their assessment of the person's personality or physical appearance. For example, the Ovimbundu name KAMEKE, derived from the word *omeke* which means "blind person," is applied to a person with small or squinty eyes. The Tonga of southern Zambia name MULANGU means "a bell" and is used for a loud or talkative person; CHIBEKWABEKWA, meaning "precious," can be tagged on a child who is spoiled by the parents; CHILWALO, which means "sickling," is given to a person who is always ill; and someone always on the move might be named SUNTWE, meaning "hyena."

Proverbs are the daughters of experience.
Sierra Leone

Despite the fact that most Africans, if asked, could provide a long list of indigenous names and their meanings, the definitions of just as many names have slipped away. It is certainly understandable that meanings get lost, diluted, and muted over time, as a seemingly plain African name can be imbued with complex underlying significance. For example, the Ishan of Nigeria name EWIE—which to the uninformed simply means "morning"—stems from the admonition *ewewie ede aye* which translates as "it is only morning so don't judge or laugh at me so soon." While the Ishan name ILUNMUN, which on the surface means "grass," is derived from the proverbial statement *ilunmun ison bheje eni eva da khonlen*—"grass will never grow where two elephants have fought"—and might have been chosen by a husband whose wife was always trying to pick fights with him.

Such names are classified as proverb names. The Ovimbundu of Angola are a source of numerous proverb names. Samples include MBUNDU derived from the proverb *ombundu yokombaka ombela yokonano*, which means "the mist of the coast is the rain of upland" (customs differ), and NJAKUPITI taken from the proverb *onji ku piti ku ka yi saike o vanja*, signifying "do not prevent others from following a course because you yourself do not adopt it."

He who does not travel will not know the value of men.
Berber of North Africa

African children, as well as adults, occasionally draw their personal names from places. A Banyoro of Uganda child born in Baganda territory might be called KABAGANDA. The Nigerian boy born while his parents were on a pilgrimage to Mecca could be named MAKAWIYYU. Nigerians from the north of the country customarily adopt place names as surnames, such as MOMOH SOKOTO and ABUBAKAR KANO—Sokoto and Kano being cities of northern Nigeria. Similarly, a Somali man named ABDI who is working away from home might be dubbed ABDI BAIDOA because he originates from the town of Baidoa. In Zaire it is not unusual for individuals to be known by the name of their former village. In turn, the names of these villages are frequently derived from the personal names of village headmen or chiefs.

Big-cheeked mask, Cameroon

TERMS OF ENDEARMENT, NICKNAMES, TWIN NAMES, AND NAMES FOR LATER IN LIFE

In the eyes of its mother, every beetle is a gazelle.
Morocco

Many African cultures set aside special names as terms of endearment or praise to be used primarily by close relatives and friends. These names, known as attributive names, can relay how others see the child or express the parent's hopes for what the child will become. The Yoruba call these *oriki* names, while the Igbo call them *aha agu*. Examples of Yoruba oriki names are ADUKE (one whom many compete to pet) and AJANI (one who possesses after a struggle). Igbo animal nicknames falling in the aha agu category include ICHOKU (parrot) for a talkative person, AGWO (snake) for a sly and mischievious child, and ELE (antelope) for a good runner. Some common Ibibio attributive names for boys are UKO (courage, the brave one), IKID (tortoise, the clever one), and IKPE (young lad). Ibibio girls might be dubbed MBOPPO (maiden), EDIMA (loved one), or NNEYEN (pretty child).

Twi-speaking peoples of Ghana bestow *Kra* names, or names given to the soul of a child. A Kra name is used only when praising or thanking the person for something they have done. The praise is directed towards the individual's Kra, considered a higher-being, acting through the body of the person. Twi Kra names follow day-of-the-week patterns (see name charts at the back of this book). Some Bantu tribes of Zambia also bestow spirit names on newborns because every child is considered the inheritor of a deceased person's spirit. These names, although commonly known to a person's family and neighbors, are not readily shared with outsiders for it is

15

believed that such openness exposes the person's spirit to witchcraft.

People are wonderful and strange.
Igbo of Nigeria

The Mashona of Zimbabwe traditionally take a second name at the age of twelve or thirteen. These Mashona names often reveal an individual's character and obsessions. For instance, MUSHOSHOMU derived from the verb "to be talkative" is applied to a nonstop talker, MUTEYE from the related verb meaning "to catch animals in a trap" is used for a person who likes hunting, and MATAKAIRA, derived from the verb *ku nekaira* which means "to walk to and fro," is assigned to one who is continually running around.

A profusion of characteristic names are used as nicknames by the Ovimbundu of Angola. KOSALE, for example, means "the one who goes there and back in a day" and implies an energetic or sprightly person. CAPUKULUA, means "it's neglected" and is given to a poor, thin, or poorly treated child, and KANJONJO, which means "humming bird," is applied to a probing or an interfering person. Another people of southern Africa, the Khoisan, assign every baby a pet name to be used exclusively by the parents until the child matures. Names of this nature commonly refer to physical peculiarities or some event associated with the child. Khoisan nicknames include EIBARAB (boy with the long face), GAXUB (the tall one) and AMGOSEB (the one with pointed lips).

The Dinka of southern Sudan will also allot children nicknames according to physical description, common examples being to call a very black child DINKA and a light-skinned child ARAB. One relief worker reports that Somalis love to use nicknames. In this case the sobriquets, being determined by some physical defect or peculiarity, often verge on the derisive. For example, a left-handed colleague was called GURE, or "lefty." Another was labeled FAHRU, "hairlip," and a man whose nose was sheared off was dubbed SANKA, "the nose." If these seem cruel, consider the local epithet used for a female aid worker who didn't shave her underarms—in translation her nickname meant "the woman with vaginas all over her body."

A mother of twins must have a belly.
Kundu of Cameroon

It is common in many African cultures to find special names designated for twins and those children following or preceding twins. The Tonga of southern Zambia name a child born after twins NSANZYA which means "cleansing" and reflects the Tonga belief that babies born after twins have a purifying effect on the womb. The Yoruba name for a first born twin of either sex is TAIWO or TAIYE, short for *to-aiye-wo* which means "have the first taste of the world." KEHINDE is the Yoruba name for the second twin, meaning "he (or she) who lags behind." The Yoruba child following twins is named IDOWU and is regarded as a willful child. In fact, Idowu children are considered so stubborn that if a mother doesn't bear this child after having twins, it is believed the unborn Idowu will invade her head and cause her to go insane.

It is a child that gives the parents the highest status.
Igbo of Nigeria

As there are special names designated for twin children, there are also specific bynames for the parents of twins and triplets. A mother of twins among the Ovimbundu of Angola becomes NANJAMBA, which literally translates as "mother of twins," and the mother of triplets is called NELONGO, "mother of triplets." According to the Baganda of Uganda, if a husband and wife have twins, they become known as SSALLONGO and NALONGO, respectively. If this same couple has a second set of twins, they are renamed SSABALONGO and NABALONGO.

*Everyone knows the old woman's name, yet everyone calls
her great-grandmother.*
Mamprusi of Burkina Faso

As with the parents of twins, many African parents adopt new names after giving birth to children. Throughout Africa, it is quite common for a mother to be referred to by the name of her first born son. In Kenya, for example, if a woman's first born boy is named HIJI, the mother becomes known as MAMA HIJI. The same holds true in Egypt where the friends of a couple who have given birth to a son named AHMAD might affectionately refer to them as UM AHMAD (mother of Ahmad) and ABU AHMAD (father of Ahmad). Likewise, Ibibio parents with a child named IME would be shown respect by being called EKA IME (mother of Ime) and ETE IME (father of Ime).

> *You can't change your destiny.*
> Aja-fon of Benin

Although the Aja-fon may like to repeat the above expression—like various other African peoples—they are not opposed to giving the old college try in an attempt to influence fate. An adult of the Aja-fon or the Ovimbundu of Angola who falls upon misfortune or illness may take a new name in hopes of reversing his or her luck. An Aja-fon can adopt a clandestine name to fool enemies who might be channelling evil thoughts and spirits through the original name. They may also rename a child whose birth name foretold a negative future. The Ovimbundu may change their name at the age of about sixteen should their birth name be unappealing to them.

Those who have experienced some profound transformation in life, or have entered periods of distress or despair, sometimes select new appellations to express their changing fortunes. In one case, an Ovimbundu man named MUKAYITA who repeatedly fell ill decided to take the new name KATAHALI (he who has seen trouble), while a sickly man who was cured opted to become KAIHEMBA (one who lives by medicine). Cases of Ovimbundu despair names are VATUSIA (they leave us behind) applied by someone whose relatives or friends have died, TUAYUNGE (in times of plenty we had friends, in hardship they do not share), and HULILAPI (I grow where?)—the lament of a woman whose life is so restrictive that she is unable to express herself.

AFRICAN NAMING CEREMONIES

When a person is given a name, his spirits accept it.
Ibo of Nigeria

Traditional African naming ceremonies range from simple to elaborate and the time of naming also varies widely amongst tribes. Whereas their Kikuyu name their newborn within hours, the Ishan of Nigeria traditionally wait until the child is three months old. While the Hausa name children after two weeks, the Yoruba of Nigeria customarily name female children on the seventh day, twins and Muslim children of both sexes on the eighth day, and males on the ninth day. The Igbo wait twenty-eight days, during which period the child is known simply as *omo ofu* (new child).

It is children that make relations.
Igbo of Nigeria

On the appointed day for naming Yoruba children, friends and family gather to see the child brought into public view for the first time. As a type of baptism, a container of water is thrown upon the roof of the house while the baby, cradled in the arms of a nurse or elderly female relative, is positioned to catch the runoff. The baby is expected to cry, receiving shouts of joy from those assembled. Parents and elders then name the child, and festivities commence including presenting gifts to the child.

An Igbo naming ceremony likewise involves a gathering of relatives from both sides of the family. Both the mother's and the father's families choose names for the child, but one of these names will supercede the other as the child grows. Sometimes even three or four names may be chosen at the ceremony, depending on the wishes of influential relatives which must be granted.

Ishan naming ceremonies also involve a joyous gathering of relatives and friends. At this occasion, the family patriarch throws the child into the air and calls out a name. If the crowd accepts the name they will cry out in approval, "he will live long with the name." If not, the patriarch tries again. During the day's festivities the child is passed around to give friends and relatives an opportunity to bestow their own pet names on the child, and through these names to send subtle messages to the parents.

The Ga of Ghana carry out naming rites on the eighth day after birth. At the presentation ceremony the eldest person from the house where the event is taking place recites the following prayer to bless the newborn child:

Oyez! May the Gods pour their blessing upon us!
Oyez! May the Gods pour their blessing upon us!
Oyez! May the Gods pour their blessing upon us!
A child has been presented; we have formed a circle
    round to view it.
Whenever we dig may it become a well full of water: and
    when we drink out of the contents thereof may it be
    the means of health and strength to us!
May the parents of this child live long!
May it never look at the place whence it came!
May it be pleased always to dwell with us!
May it have respect for the aged!
May it be obedient to elders, and do what is right and
    proper.
May many more follow, full of grace and honor!
May the families always be in a position to pay respect
    and regard to this child, and out of his earnings may
    we have something to live upon!
May it live long and others come and meet it!
As a Ga person does not speak at random, so may this
    child be careful of his words and speech,

and speak the truth so that he may not get into trouble
   and palavers!
Oyez! May the Gods favor us with their blessing!

   The day that the newborn's naval cord falls off is the day
that a child from several tribes of Zambia receive its name.
Traditionally the infant's maternal grandmother presides over
the ceremony, with her side of the family determining whose
spirit the baby has inherited. This might be done through long
discussions, including questioning the mother and father about
which deceased persons they dreamt of during the wife's
pregnancy. Alternatively, an elder can directly ask the baby if it
is a certain ancestor. If the baby smiles the elder might exclaim
that he's found the correct name. If the baby cries throughout
that night, another name may be selected the next day, and the
next day again, until finally the child passes a night peacefully.
In the event that the child becomes ill, it is sometimes believed
that the wrong spirit name was chosen and another one is given
at that juncture.

Jokwe dance mask, Central Congo

SUPERSTITIONS ASSOCIATED WITH NAMES AND BABIES

A bad name is ominous.
(Bitso lebe ke seromo.)
Sotho of southern Africa

Many African societies believe that names can affect a person's destiny. This is not an antiquated theory, rather it is alive and well. The Ibibio expression *anyin asisop owo* (a name sometimes influences the character and personality of the bearer) was reaffirmed in a pop song by contemporary Ibibio musician Basco Bassey who warns "If you have a child don't call it: 'I don't rejoice' or a name such as NDOTONYI, 'I have no hope,' or MFON NKPANA, 'the good ones die.'" The Yoruba saying, "a child's name influences its behavior," shows that they concur with this superstition. A American form Dagara child given the name MALIDOMA (be friends with the stranger) is expected to travel or live among foreigners. Similarly, the Sotho postulate that a child named MOTSAMAI (the one who travels) will be a keen traveller or will enjoy visiting.

Give birth to children, you'll be pregnant with worries.
Ovambo of Namibia

Twin children can be a blessing or a curse, but rarely is the birth of twins viewed as a neutral event. The Nuer and Dinka of southern Sudan posit that twins are the reincarnated spirits of birds. In Benin the spirits of twins are believed to dwell in the forest and are worshipped. The Bassari of Togo used to so abhor the arrival of twins that the cursed infants were thrown to their death inside an anthill. One Yoruba woman described twins as

22

"God-like" and explained that they are so highly praised in Yoruba society that many women prefer not to have them to avoid bearing such a lofty responsibility.

The Fulani of West Africa consider bearing twins a negative and ominous event. If both twins survive to puberty the parents have much to fear, for superstition says that one of the parents will die. On the other hand, if one of the twins dies in infancy, it is believed this dead child can harm the mother unless she handles it with utmost respect. This she does by making a doll or image of the deceased, dressing it in children's clothing and treating it with the same care as the living twin until the dead child's sibling is weaned. The first born Fulani twin is considered the junior child because, from its initial moment, it showed inferiority by agreeing to go first to prepare the way for the superior child.

The Sotho of southern Africa regard the arrival of twins as a positive event although an element of anxiety still exists. Twin babies are deemed a gift from the ancestors, a sign that the spirits look favorably upon the parents. But the common conception that twins are more fragile than other children, and that rarely will both survive to adulthood, lends the element of fear to an otherwise joyous event. The Ovimbundu of Angola also view twins as a mixed blessing; they are welcomed and cherished, and at the same time are regarded as prodigies requiring special care.

> *Time causes remembrance.*
> Efik of Nigeria

Just as we say "Monday's child is full of grace," some African cultures also attribute characteristics to children according to the day of the week they were born. The Aja-fon people of southern Benin believe:

Monday's child is lucky and will succeed in life with
   ease;
Tuesday's child is stubborn and may be exposed to
   injury;

Wednesday's child is unlikely to gain anything more
   than mediocre successes;
Thursday's child is friendly and nice;
Friday's child is stubborn, strong, and combative;
Saturday's child is unlucky and vengeful; and
Sunday's child is generous.

The Aja-fon find these characteristics to be fluid; a person born closer to the hour of the preceding or following day may be influenced by that neighboring day. And, of course, the nature of the parents and ancestors also sways the behavior of the child.

> *To bear a girl is to bear a problem.*
> Tigrinya of Ethiopia and Eritrea

There are numerous other miscellaneous beliefs related to children. For example, ancient Egyptian custom held that a child carried high was a girl and, the reverse, one carried low was a boy. Egyptian superstition also said that if the mother dreams of a head scarf the baby will be a girl, and if she dreams of a handkerchief it will be a boy. The Dinka of southern Sudan assert that if a woman is grumpy with other women while she is pregnant the child will be female, and if she is grumpy towards men it will be a male. The Bari of southern Sudan maintain that first and last born children are the most self-reliant and that first born sons inherit all the brains of the family. The Akan of Ghana belief that nine is a magic number extends to children, giving ninth-born children special status in a family.

    Some peoples of Benin contend that children born with six fingers or six toes are blessed with good luck and are fated to become rich. Children with only four digits may go either way, so a priest must be consulted to determine whether the child is destined for riches or for the poorhouse and to ascertain what the parents can do to affect the outcome. Despite modern influences, most Aja-fon of Benin are reported to still believe that childen who do not undergo traditional naming rituals will later develop physical or mental handicaps.

MODERN NAMING TRENDS

When the music changes, so does the dance.
Hausa of West Africa

Africans are adept at straddling divergent traditions, especially when it comes to nomenclature, changing names like hats, according to the social situation. One Kikuyu of Kenya woman goes by the name Irene (her Christian name) in the workplace, Wanjiru (her Kikuyu name) among Kikuyu friends, and Mama Hiji (Hiji being the name of her firstborn son) in her neighborhood.

Nowadays, in non-Muslim African societies, the majority of citizens, especially city dwellers, bear both indigenous African names and Christian or European names. Simply by skimming lists of African presidential cabinets, one can deduce that in virtually every African country western first names are in use. The Botswana presidential cabinet has members named Festus, Patrick, Raymond, and Archibald, and in Burkina Faso, cabinet members have gone by the names Herman, Juliette, Marc, Alice, and Vincent.

In Zaire, the biblical name Mary is so common that one

Basonge dance mask, Congo

Zairean authority offered the tongue-in-cheek speculation that of the country's fifteen million women, twelve million are called Mary. Mary is also one of the most frequently heard European names in East Africa, along with Joyce, Rose, Lucy, and Theresa. Popular Christian names for men in East Africa include Francis, John, and Peter, among others. Because Ethiopia is home to some of the earliest Christians, many of these names have historically been part of their regional name pool. Currently, popular Christian names in Ethiopia and Eritrea include HANA, HELEN, MARTHA, ARON, DANIEL, and EPHREM. The European name NATASHA (meaning "born at Christmas, child of Christmas") is reportedly quite popular among the Swahili peoples of East Africa, despite the fact that they are predominantly Muslims.

> *The custom of a country embarrasses the King.*
> Amharic of Ethiopia

Just as their ancestors named children after important events of the times, twentieth-century Africans continue to name children after contemporary personalities, events, and items. In Nigeria, some men born during World War II bear the name ITILA, a corruption of the name Hitler, certainly not as any sort of admiration for Hitler but simply to convey the fact that these males were born during the War of Hitler. Likewise, following a state visit to Nigeria made by the Queen of England in the 1950s, some Nigerian female children were given the name KWINI, a local twist on the word Queen.

One source, dated from the 1960s, found an Ethiopian man named MILLIYON, a derivation of the English word million, while another study noted that the madman of one particular Hausa village had been dubbed AIRPLANE. It is not unusual to find a Kenyan man born in the early 1960s with the name KENNEDY after American President John F. Kennedy. In South Africa a boy was named FRANCE because he was born around the time that his uncle had returned from France during a war. A woman living in Takaba, a remote village in northeastern Kenya, named one of her daughters PARIS after a bottle of Yves St. Laurent perfume of the same name. Most recently, a

Rwandan woman who gave birth to a child while she was in jail named the child INNOCENT.

> *To observe the taboos is to be alive.*
> Igbo of Nigeria

In the past it would have been completely inappropriate for an African to bear a twin name, order of birth name, time of day born name, season name, etc., that did not fit the actual circumstances of birth. Nowadays, it is more common to find Africans with inapplicable first names and surnames. One example is a Luo man named DAN OPIYO. Dan is not a firstborn twin, as his second name indicates. Rather, he is the son or grandson of a man who was a firstborn twin. As the standard-ization of last names began to take hold in Africa, this relative's name was adopted as the family surname. Likewise, the growing practice of using namesakes finds children being named after their father, mother, or other relative, with names that reflect the namegiver's circumstances of birth rather than the child's.

Swahili earring, Paté Island

AFRICAN NAMES FOR AFRICAN AMERICANS

However far the stream flows, it never forgets its source.
Yoruba of Nigeria

Records show that numerous African names were retained by African slaves and colonialists in early America. The name BATHSHEBA (an Abyssinian name meaning "daughter of the oath") appears in documents from the colonial era. West African names, such as MINGO and CONGO for men and the female names ABAH, CUMBA, and JUBA, were also used in America in the late seventeenth and eighteenth centuries.

In the late 1800s, Africans living in the West Indies bore day of the week names paralleling those found in West Africa. For example, Jamaican names for females born on Friday included PHIBBA and FEEBA which are related to the Agni and Efe of Togo and Benin name AFIBA. Names for male children born on Friday included CUFFEE and COOFEE which correspond to the Agni and Twi name KOFI currently used for Friday-born males.

Researchers studying Gullah speakers living in parts of the coastal southeast United States have found African names retained into recent times. It has been noted that these Americans, like their contemporary counterparts in Africa, use Christian names for interaction with outsiders and names of African origin when socializing amongst themselves.

Go back and fetch what was left behind.
Akan of Ghana

Just as the names of Africans who inhabited early America were altered to fit the new environment of a land situated an ocean away from their origin, it is likely that the African names becoming popular in America today will take on their own shape and character. Much of this is due to language differences which makes pronunciation sometimes difficult for non-native speakers. Another factor will be the way the names are received, shortened, and translated.

Prominent African-Americans who underwent name changes include the writer Rolland Snellings who became ASKIA MUHAMMAD TOURE, the teacher and writer LeRoi Jones who became IMAMU AMIRI BARAKA, and anthropologist and educator NIARA SUDARKASA who was born Gloria Marshall Clark. In an article titled "Outta My Name," poet MALAIKA ADERO narrates her experience of selecting an African name:

> ...I heard Roberta Flack sing a song about telling Jesus can she change her name, and I asked my Mama if she would change mine. And like Jesus, she said, "be all right"...she got right with the task, talking to some friends from home—Tanzania and Somalia—and came back to me with choices. Without knowing the meaning of the names she wrote on a piece of paper, I was attracted to one— Malaika....We chose the surname from a book. Adero—it means, one who comes to make things better. It was our new family name, not just mine. Malaika means my angel, fitting from a mother to her first-born.

> *If you find the locals frying their eyes, fry yours also.*
> Nyanja of Malawi

Many contemporary African-Americans have looked to Muslim names for purposes of ethnic identification, such as prizefighter Cassius Clay who adopted the Muslim name MUHAMMAD ALI and pro-basketball player Lew Alcindor who became KAREEM ABDUL-JABBAR. There is no doubt that Islamic names are extensively used in Africa and Africans played a major role in the development of Islam. At the same time, there are probably more Africans bearing Christian names than Muslim names. Africans were also represented in the early days of Christianity. Some historians have submitted that Mary, Jesus, Moses, and Solomon were originally portrayed with negroid features until European revisionists came on the scene and represented them as Caucasians. In any case, modern Africans primarily assume Christian and Muslim names to express their religious preference.

Islam was brought to Africa through an Arab incursion and resulted in widespread adoption of Muslim names. With the spread of Christianity, biblical names also began to appear in Africa, in some locations—such as Ethiopia—well before the growth of Islam. It was the advent of colonialism in the 1800s that ushered in the broad use of Christian names. Whether Arab invaders or European invaders, they were both non-indigenous influences. However, it must be recognized that with time and history these so-called outside influences have become part and parcel of the very cultures themselves.

It should be recognized that a Muslim name does no more to pinpoint a person's geographic heritage than does a Christian name. If an article appears about someone named Ahmad, there are multiple mental pictures a reader could draw up of this man—he could be from Somalia, Saudi Arabia, or from Bosnia, he could be an Arab from North Africa or a Muslim from Chechnya, or he might be an African-American. On the other hand, call him Kwame and one thing is fairly certain—that he is either a man from Africa or of African descent.

This observation is not meant in any way to denigrate Muslim names, only to point out that if one's goal in choosing a name is to express geographic and ethnic heritage, an indigenous African name—or at least a distinctly African version of a Muslim name (many of which are found in this book)—may be the better option. Of course, Muslim names are usually very charming and may be highly desirable for purely aesthetic reasons—which is reason enough to select a name from any culture or religion.

It is worthwhile to give serious thought to the name you choose for your newborn or yourself. Take time to research an appropriate and meaningful name—as they say in Nigeria, *a name does not get forgotten.*

BACKGROUND TO MAIN ETHNIC GROUPS REPRESENTED IN THIS BOOK

Although names from all parts of Africa are included in this book, the bulk of names are drawn from the ethnic groups or languages described below.

Baganda   The Baganda inhabit southern Uganda and are one of the country's most powerful ethnic groups. The Baganda kingdom, which was established in the twelfth century, became one of the regions largest kingdoms. Although the Baganda kingship was abolished in 1967 by the newly independent government, the *Kabaka*, or king, has recently been restored as a figurehead in Uganda. The Baganda traditionally made cloth from the bark of trees, and prior to the turmoil that marked the 1970s in Uganda, they were successful cotton and coffee farmers. Today bananas remain their main food crop.

Basotho   The various Basotho peoples compose one of the most sizable ethnic groups of southern Africa. They include the Suto of Lesotho, the Tswana of Botswana, and the Pedi of the Transvaal, South Africa. Traditionally the Basotho were farmers who also kept cattle and goats; however today many Basotho men are migrant workers in South Africa's towns, mines, and farms. Their language, Sesotho, is one of Africa's primary literary languages. Many works of poetry, fiction, and nonfiction, as well as one of Africa's oldest vernacular newspapers, have been published in the Sesotho language.

Hausa   One of Africa's largest ethnic groups, the Hausa comprise the main population of southern Niger and the Muslim emirates of northern Nigeria. Traditionally the Hausa have been farmers and traders. They are also renowned as craftsmen, especially for their cotton cloth, leather goods, mats, and pottery. Their Chadic language, also called Hausa, is indigenous to Nigeria and Niger, but is spoken widely in West Africa as a trade language.

Kinyarwanda Kinyarwanda is the official language of Rwanda. It is similar to Kirundi, the language of the neighboring country of Burundi. Rwanda is a tiny country in East Africa in which three main ethnic groups reside: the Tutsi, Hutu, and Twa. The majority of the population farm the country's fertile hillsides and raise cattle.

Luo The Luo live mainly in western Kenya on the eastern shore of Lake Victoria. Traditionally they are fishermen and farmers, primarily cultivating maize, millet, cassava, and sesame. One of Kenya's main ethnic groups, they speak a Chari-Nile language called Dholuo.

Mashona The Mashona are a cluster of peoples in eastern Zimbabwe and central Mozambique. The main sub-groups are the Zezeru, Karanga, Kalanga, Manyika, Tonga-Korekore, and Ndau. Their Bantu language, called Shona, is spoken by about three-quarters of the population of Zimbabwe. The Mashona are primarily farmers who also keep cattle. They are traditionally renowned for their iron-working, cloth-weaving, pottery, and beer making.

Oromo The Oromo are one of Africa's largest ethnic groups. They live in Ethiopia and northern Kenya, and include the Borana, Arusi, and other sub-groups. In literature they are often referred to as the Galla, but this is considered a derogatory term and is no longer acceptable. Traditionally the Oromo have been pastoralists, a lifestyle which most southern Oromo still adhere to, while the northern Oromo have become farmers. Their society is arranged under democratic elections of chiefs and sub-chiefs. They speak a Cushitic language also called Oromo.

Ovimbundu The Ovimbundu, also called the Mbundu, are a Bantu-speaking people living in southern Angola. They are one the country's chief ethnic groups. Historically organized under a king, the Ovimbundu were avid long-distance traders who covered great swaths of central Africa. They also engaged in farming and hunting, and are renowned in art circles for their wood carvings, particularly of miniature animal figures.

Swahili Compared to the widespread use of their language, the Swahili themselves are a relatively small ethnic group inhabiting the Indian Ocean islands and coastal areas of Kenya and Tanzania. As early as 2,000 years ago, merchants from the Middle East and the Mediterranean began plying the East Africa coast and later embarked on expeditions inland. Eventually these traders mixed with Bantu-speaking Africans to create a unique Swahili culture which embraced Islam and was centered around Arabic-style cities. The Swahili cultivate bananas, maize, millet, cassava, coconut, and cloves, and fishing is also an important activity. Swahili craftspeople are famous for their intricate wood carvings and patterned mats. Their language, called Kiswahili, is one of Africa's best-known and most widely spoken languages. Kiswahili serves as a *lingua franca* for people from hundreds of different tribes, and is heard throughout Kenya and Tanzania and in parts of Uganda, Rwanda, Burundi, eastern Zaire, southern Somalia, and northern Mozambique.

Tigrinya This Semitic language is the main indigenous language of Eritrea, and is also spoken in parts of Ethiopia and Sudan. Related to Amharic, the official language of Ethiopia, both languages are rooted in Ge'ez, an ancient language of Ethiopia.

Tonga The Tonga are a cluster of Bantu-speaking peoples of southern Zambia, Zimbabwe, Malawi, and Mozambique. They are Zambia's largest ethnic group. Primarily maize farmers and cattle herders, the Tonga have historically lacked strong centralized authority.

Yoruba The Yoruba reside primarily in southwestern Nigeria and are one of Nigeria's most prominent ethnic groups. While the Yoruba have customarily been farmers, growing maize, yams, cassava, and other crops, they also boast a history of urban living. The Yoruba city of Ibadan was the largest precolonial city in sub-Sahara Africa. Although many Yoruba have adopted Christianity and Islam, their indigenous religion is still widely practiced. Their language is also called Yoruba.

GUIDE TO PRONUNCIATION

The names in this book are followed by their pronunciation enclosed in parentheses. The phonetics used are intended to make pronouncing the names as easy as possible for an English-language audience. Several African languages contain sounds unfamiliar to English speakers, such as the clicking sounds in various tongues of southern Africa, the gutteral sounds used in Arabic and languages influenced by Arabic, and the tonal variations of Yoruba. The Yoruba word *awo* illustrates the complexities of that language. Depending on the tone used, *awo* can mean a dish, a crash, a fishing net, a guinea-fowl, or a secret.

People from different regions also pronounce words and names distinctively. For example, the Ovimbundu of Angola pronounce names and words differently depending on whether they live inland or along the coast. One region pronounces *maikulu*, the term for grandmother, as mah-KOO-loo, whereas the other says migh-KOO-loo. Accents also may vary depending on who is speaking or in what context the name is used.

Although attempts have been made to ensure that the pronunciations given are authentic, some names will inevitably be said with an English bent to them. Readers should consider these pronunciations as a guide only. Should a reader select a name, they are advised to check with a native speaker to listen carefully for any nuances. This might be accomplished by locating specialists in African languages, African students or professors from a local university, or contacting the embassy of the country from which the name originates.

The following is a list of the symbols found in the book followed by examples of the sounds used in American English words. The stressed syllable in each name is indicated by small capital letters, such as BAH-tah.

34

Symbols	Example	Symbols	Example
ah	father	or	for, nor
a	pat	ow	now
ay	pay	aw	paw, brawl
uh	about, gut	oy	toy, noise
air	care, air	u	look, put
eh	met	ur	batter
ee	bee	s	salad
i	fit	j	jelly
igh	high	dj	education
eer	pier	g	go
oh	toe	z	zoo
o	hot	th	thing
oo	boot, fruit	zh	vision

Festival mask, Nigeria

PART II
THE NAMES

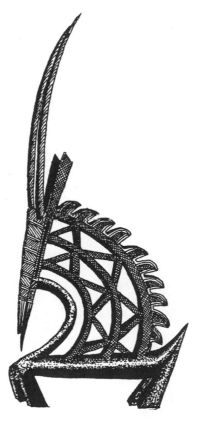

Crown of a headdress of the Bamana, Mali.

A

Chamin Asis
May the sun smile upon you.
Kalenjin of Kenya blessing

FEMALE

Abadeet (*ah-bah*-DEET)   Eritrean female name meaning "comforter."

Abnet (*ahb*-NEHT)   Eritrean female name meaning "example."

Abiba (*ah*-BEE-*bah*)   Like Iyabo and Yetunde, this Yoruba of Nigeria name is used for a female child born soon after her grandmother has died.

Abiona (*ah-bee*-OH-*nah*)   Yoruba of Nigeria name meaning "born by the wayside" used for children born while the mother was on a journey.

Ade (*ah*-DAY)   Yoruba of Nigeria unisex name meaning "crown, royal." It is commonly used in compound names such as Adenike.

Adenike (*ah-deh*-NEE-*kay*)   Yoruba of Nigeria female name meaning "crown is loving, affectionate."

Adila (*ah*-DEE-*lah*)   This Swahili female name means "just, fair" and is derived from *adili*, a Kiswahili word of the same meaning.

Adita (*ah*-DEET-*ah*)   Luo of Kenya female name referring to a round basket with high sides. This is one of many traditional "basket names" used by mothers who have previously lost children. The newborn child is symbolically taken away by an honorary mother who then returns the child in a basket to the real mother. The names reflect the type of basket used to perform this ritual.

Aduke (AH-*doo*-KAY)   A Yoruba of Nigeria female oriki name meaning "one whom many compete to pet, much loved." Pet is used here to mean to stroke or touch a person as in admiration. Oriki names are special names given to a Yoruba child in addition to his or her official name. They are used within the immediate family and among close friends as terms of endearment, and are positive names intended to bolster the child's ego. (Note when pronouncing this name that the second syllable dips lower than the other two syllables. Readers are advised to check with a Yoruba speaker to hear the proper pronunciation.)

Adumadan (*ah*-DOO-*mahah*-DUHN)   Yoruba of Nigeria female oriki name (see Aduke) for a girl who is dark-skinned and beautiful.

Afishetu (*ah-fee*-SHEH-*too*)   A Nigerian variation of the Muslim name Hafsah, which means "young lioness" and refers to a wife of the Prophet Muhammad. Other variations of this same name include HAFUSATU (*hah-foo*-SAH-*too*) and HAFUSA (*hah*-FOO-*sah*).

Ahorishakiye (*ah-hoh-ree-shah*-KEE-*yay*)   Kinyarwanda of Rwanda name meaning "whenever it wants (it happens)." This name is used when parents have a child after many years of infertility. Short forms could be RISHA or SHAKIYE.

Aini-Alem (IGH-*nee-ah*-LEHM)   Tigrinya of Eritrea and Ethiopia female name meaning "eye of the world."

Akech (AH-*kaych*)   Luo of Kenya name used for females born during a famine. It is derived from the Dholuo word *kech* which means "hunger."

Akili (*ah*-KEE-*lee*)   Swahili female name meaning "wisdom" and Kiswahili word meaning "intelligence, clever idea."

Akippi (*uh*-KIP-*ee*)   The word for "water" in the Toposa language. MORU AKIPPI means "place of water" and is a location in southeastern Sudan.

Akoko (*ah*-KOH-*koh*)   This Luo of Kenya female name is derived from the Dholuo word *koko*, which roughly translated means "boogie man" or "monster," referring to a scary creature during childhood.

Akuji (*ah*-KOO-*jee*)   A Yoruba of Nigeria name for a child born after the mother has had other children die. It means "dead and awake." Because the Yoruba traditionally believe in reincarnation, if a child dies it is believed that he or she will come back with the birth of the mother's next child. Names selected for these reincarnated children are meant to encourage them to stay alive this time.

Akwe (AH-*kway*) Luo of Kenya female name that means "peaceful one."

Alake (*ah*-LAH-*kay*) Yoruba of Nigeria female oriki name (see Aduke) meaning "one to be petted (if she survives)."

Alemash (*ah-leh*-MAHSH) Tigrinya of Eritrea and Ethiopia female name meaning "made it green."

Alima (*ah*-LEE-*mah*) A Nigerian variation of the Muslim name Halimah, which means "clement, humane." Halimah was the wet nurse who raised the Prophet Muhammad.

Almaz (*ahl*-MAHZ) Ethiopian and Eritrean female name meaning "diamond." In Arabic this name is pronounced ahl-MAHS. The Swahili version is ALMAZI (*ahl*-MAH-*zee*).

Amadika (*ah-mah*-DEE-*kah*) An uncommon name of the Mashona of Zimbabwe that is derived from the verb *ku dikana*, which means "to be beloved."

Aman (*ah*-MAHN) A popular Somali version of the Muslim female name Aminah, which means "trustworthy."

Amoke (*ahm*-OH-*kay*) Yoruba of Nigeria female oriki name (see Aduke) meaning "whom to know is to pet."

Ana (AH-*nah*) Word meaning "where" in the Wolof language of West Africa.

Anana (*ah*-NAH-*nah*) Kiswahili word meaning "soft, gentle."

Ananda (*ah*-NAN-*duh*) This name of Indian origin is used by females in Mauritius. It comes from Sanskrit and means "happiness, bliss."

Anisa (*ah*-NEE-*sah*) A Kiswahili word meaning "joy, pleasure."

Anukis (*uh*-NOO-*kis*) The name of this water goddess of ancient Egypt means "to embrace" and refers to the Nile River waters flooding and fertilizing the land. Anuki is depicted as a woman wearing a feather headdress.

Anyawu (ahn-YAH-*woo*) This Igbo of Nigeria name meaning "sun" is often used as a surname. As a first name it can infer "one who is as beautiful as the rising or setting sun." A short form could be ANYA.

Anywaa (*an*-YWAH) The name of an ethnic group living in the

Upper Nile region of southern Sudan. Also called the ANY-
UAK (*an*-YWAHK), their name is derived from the Dholuo word
nyak, which means "to share."

Aoko (*ah*-OH-*koh*)   Luo of Kenya female name used when the
mother doesn't arrive at the hospital in time for the baby's
delivery. The name is derived from the Luo word *oko*, which
means "outside."

Aola (*ah*-OH-*lah*)   The Aola are a clan of the Luo-Abasuba
people of Kenya living on islands in Lake Victoria. The name
means "double-crossers" in Dholuo language.

Apeke (*ahk*-PAY-*kay*)   Yoruba of Nigeria female oriki name (see
Aduke) meaning "call to be pet."

Apinke (AHK-*pin-kay*)   Yoruba of Nigeria oriki name (see
Aduke) meaning "everyone pets her." Apinke might be given
to a firstborn girl because people tend to make a fuss over
firstborn children.

Aponbepore (AH-*pohn*-BAY-*por*-AY)   Yoruba of Nigeria oriki
name (see Aduke) used for women who have light skin and
are beautiful. One source says this name is used for "one who
is reddishly beautiful as good palm oil." (Note that the p's in
this name are somewhat explosive sounding.)

Arawet (*ahr-ah*-WEHT)   A Kalenjin of Kenya word meaning
"moon."

Asabi (*ah*-SAH-*bee*)   Yoruba of Nigeria female oriki name (see
Aduke) meaning "one of select birth."

Asha (AH-*shah*)   A Swahili variation of the Muslim female
name Aishah which means "living" and refers to Aishah, the
chief wife of the Prophet Muhammad. It is related to the
Kiswahili word *maisha*(*mah*-EE-*shah*, MIGH-*shuh*) which means
"life" and is sometimes used as a name. Nigerian variations
of this name are AISHATU (*ah-ee*-SHAH-*too*), AISHETU (*ah-ee*-SHEH-
too), and AYESHATU (*ah-ee*-SHAH-*too*).

Ashietu (*ah-shee*-EH-*too*)   A Nigerian variation of the Muslim
name Asiyah, which means "console." Ashietu was the wife
of a Pharaoh during the time of the Prophet Musa (Moses)
who was known for being a godly woman.

Asli (AHS-*lee*) Tigrinya of Eritrea and Ethiopia female name
meaning "original, pure."

Aster (AH-*stair*)   Ethiopian and Eritrean version of the biblical name Esther, which means "star."

Atiti (*ah*-TEE-TEE)   Edo of Nigeria generic name for baby girls. This name is given to all female newborns for their first three months until a permanent name is selected.

Atonga (*ah*-TOHNG-*ah*)   Luo of Kenya traditional basket name (see Adita) referring to a large round basket with high sides.

Audi (OW-*dee*)   Hausa of West Africa name for a female born after the father has died, which signifies "last daughter."

Awero (*ah*-WAIR-*oh*)   Yoruba of Nigeria female oriki name (see Aduke) that means "one to be washed and dressed up."

Awiti (*ah*-WEE-*tee*)   Luo of Kenya female name that means "sent away" and refers to the ritual of symbolically sending newborns away in a basket (see Adita).

Ayashe (*ah*-YAH-*shee*)   Common female name of the Hausa of West Africa meaning "throw away."

Ayodele (*ah*-*yuh*-DEH-*lay*)   Yoruba of Nigeria name meaning "joy enters the house."

Ayoka (*ah*-YOH-*kah*)   Yoruba of Nigeria female oriki name (see Aduke) meaning "one who causes joy all around."

Ayondela (*ah*-*yohn*-DAY-*lah*)   Ovimbundu of Angola female name derived from the proverb *Okoti ka yumbi yombi; vohi tua yondela Kaluga*, which means "A little tree bends and bends; we all bend toward death."

Azana (*ah*-ZAH-*nah*)   South African name meaning "ultimate."

Azuka (*ah*-ZOO-*kah*)   Igbo of Nigeria female name meaning "support is paramount" and "our past glory."

MALE

Abadi (*ah*-BAH-*dee*)   Tigrinya of Eritrea and Ethiopia male name meaning "comforter."

Abaloni (*ah*-*bah*-LOH-*nee*)   Oromo of Ethiopia and Kenya male name meaning "owner of cattle." This would be used for men who possess a lot of livestock, a sign of prosperity in Oromo society (see Abaracha).

Abaracha (*ah*-*bah*-RAH-*chah*)   Oromo of Ethiopia and Kenya male name meaning "owner of frogs." This teasing nickname would be used for a man who doesn't own livestock (see Abaloni).

Abashe (*ah*-BAH-*shay*)   Common male name of the Hausa of West Africa meaning "throw away."

Abay (*ah*-BIGH)   This popular male name of Ethiopia and Eritrea is the local name for the Blue Nile River. Also spelled ABBAY, it signifies "something that never ends" and "someone who doesn't give up easily."

Abbare'e (AH-*bah*-RAY-*ay*)   Oromo of Ethiopia and Kenya male name meaning "born near a place with many goats." A variant spelling is ABAREA (*ah-bah*-REE-*ah*).

Abdellatif (*ahb-dehl-lah*-TEEF)   A Muslim male name popular in North Africa that means "the pleasant one." It is a combination of the name ABDEL, meaning "servant of," and LATIF, one of the 99 names of Allah which means "pleasant, gentle, gracious."

Abiodun (*ah-bee*-OH-*duhn*, *ah-bee-oh*-DOON)   Yoruba of Nigeria name for children born around the time of Christmas and New Year. A variation of this name is ABODUNDE (*ah-boh*-DOON-*day*) and popular short forms are BIODUN and BODI.

Abraha (*ah-brah*-HAH)   Eritrean and Ethiopian name of Ge'ez origin meaning "he lit (what was gloomy)."

Abu (AH-*boo*)   This is the Arabic word for "father" and is a popular Muslim name in North Africa. It is also a popular name in Sierra Leone used for firstborn boys.

Abubakar (*ah-boo*-BAH-*kahr*)   A Nigerian variation of the Muslim name Abu Bakr ibn Abi Quhafah, which refers to the first Khalifa (secular and religious head of Islam) after the death of the Prophet Muhammad. Bakar by itself means "young camel" and "firstborn" while Abubakar means "father of the camel." Other Nigerian versions of this name include BAKARI (bah-KAHR-*ee*), BUBAKAR (BOO-*bah-kahr*), BUBA (BOO-*bah*), BUKAR (BOO-*kahr*), and ABU (AH-*boo*).

Adamu (*ah*-DAH-*moo*)   The Swahili version of the biblical name Adam, which means "red earth." This is related to the Kiswahili word BINADAMU (*been-ah*-DAH-*moo*), which translates literally as "son of Adam" and means "human being."

Adedapo (*ah-deh*-DAH-*poh*)   Yoruba of Nigeria male name meaning "royalty unites the people."

Adekunle (*ah-day-*KOON-*lay*)   Yoruba of Nigeria male name meaning "the crown remains in this house." KUNLE is a short form of this name.

Adem (*ah-*DEHM)   Ethiopian and Eritrean version of the biblical name Adam, which means "red earth."

Adeniji (*ah-dehn-*EE-*jee*)   Yoruba of Nigeria name meaning "the crown has a shadow." It is mostly a surname, but traditionally males of the royal family used it as a first name. Adeniji has its own oriki name (see Ajamu), which is APATA, meaning "rock." Thus, ADENIJI APATA translates as "a rock that casts out its shadow."

Adesina (*ah-day-*SHEE-*nah*)   This Yoruba of Nigeria male name means "my coming opens the way" and is used by women who have been infertile. Short forms of this name are ADE and SINA.

Adetutu (*ah-day-*TOO-*too*)   Yoruba of Nigeria male name that means "cool crown, peaceful reign."

Adiel (*ah-dee-*EHL)   This Luo-Abasuba of Kenya male name is probably derived from the word *diel*, which means "goat" in Dholuo.

Afewerki (*ah-feh-*WURK-*ee*)   This Eritrean name of Ge'ez origin literally means "golden mouth" and refers to someone who doesn't speak badly of things.

Agu (*ah-*GOO)   Igbo of Nigeria nickname meaning "lion" and signifying a strong or powerful person.

Agyemang (*ah-jee-*MAHNG)   Twi of Ghana unisex name meaning "savior of the nation." This is mostly used as a surname. (Note the final "g" is very closed, almost like cutting your voice off halfway through the letter.)

Ajamu (*ah-jah-*MOON)   Yoruba of Nigeria male oriki name meaning "one who seizes after a fight." Oriki names are special names given to a Yoruba child in addition to his or her official name. They are used by the immediate family, and among close friends, as terms of endearment and are positive names intended to bolster the child's ego.

Ajani (*ah-*JAH-*nee*)   Yoruba of Nigeria male oriki name (see Ajamu) meaning "one who possesses after a struggle."

Akinyele (*ah-kin-*YEH-*lay, ah-keen-*YEH-*lay*)   Yoruba of Nigeria male name that means "a strong one befits the house." Short forms of this name are YELE and AKIN—itself a male name meaning "warrior, hero, brave man."

Akway Cam (AH-*kway* CHAHM)   This is the name of an early twentieth-century king of the Anyuak people of the Upper Nile region of southern Sudan. His full name was Nyeya Agada Akway Cam Gilo.

Alamako (*ah-lah-mah-*KOH)   Malinke of Guinea unisex name meaning "God bless (this child)."

Alasan (*ah-lah-*SAHN)   A Nigerian variation of the Muslim name Hasan, which means "handsome" and refers to a grandson of the Prophet Muhammad from his daughter Fatimah.

Alatanga (*ah-lah-*TAHN-*gah*)   Kikumu of Tanzania male name meaning "God will help us."

Algi (AHL-*gee*)   Oromo of Ethiopia and Kenya male name that refers to a fibrous plant that grows wild in dry areas and is used for making mats, ropes, and roofing.

Alem (AH-*lehm*)   Tigrinya of Eritrea and Ethiopia unisex name meaning "world." The Amharic version of this name is ALAM. It is often used in compound names such as ALAM SAGAD (the world bows down), ALAM SELASSI (world of the Trinity), ALAMAYYAHU (I have seen the world), and ANDU ALAM (this one is a world).

Alhaji (*ahl-*HAH-*jee*)   This Muslim name meaning "the pilgrim" is popular in Islamic regions of Africa. It is bestowed on boys born during the Muslim holy month of Ramadan, the time at which devout Muslims undertake the *hajj,* a pilgrimage to Mecca. A man may also adopt this name upon returning home from the *hajj.* A variation is ALHAJA (*ahl-*HAH-*jah*).

Amandla (*ah-*MAHND-*lah*)   Zulu of South Africa male name meaning "power."

Amini (*ah-*MEE-*nee*)   Swahili version of the Muslim male name AMIN (ah-*meen*), which means "trustworthy, honest."

Amiri (*ah-*MEER-*ee*)   The Swahili version of AMIR and AMEER (*ah-*MEER), a Muslim male name meaning "prince."

Amun (AH-*muhn*)   An Egyptian name meaning "what is hidden." Amun was the ancient Egyptian god of air and wind.

Amwendo (*ahm-*WAYN-*doh*)   This Giriama of Kenya name

means "the going" and was used as the name for a generation of people born during a period of migration.

Ande (AHN-*day*)   Tigrinya of Eritrea and Ethiopia male name that means "pillar." This old-fashioned name was often used as a prefix, as in ANDE MARIAM (MAHR-*ee-ahm*), meaning "pillar of Mary." Although originally the name connoted "strong, unwavering, sturdy," these days Ande is more often used to tease someone who—borrowing words from American author Toni Morrison's book *Song of Solomon*—just stands around and sways.

Antankara (*on-tahn*-KAHR-*ah*)   A people living in the extreme north of the island country Madagascar. The name means "the people of the rock." This name could be shortened to ANTAN or KARA.

Anwar (AHN-*wahr*)   This Muslim male name is popular in North Africa and means "the brightest, the most illuminated." Anwar el-Sadat was president of Egypt from 1970 until he was assassinated in 1981. He received the Nobel Peace Prize in 1978 along with Israeli Premier Menachem Begin.

Arianhdit (*ahr-ee-ahn*-DIT)   The name of a religious prophet of the Dinka people of southern Sudan who died in 1948. Arianhdit refers to the name of a Dinka spirit.

Asis (*ah*-SEES)   Kalenjin of Kenya word meaning "sun."

Asubonteng (AH-*soo-bohn*-TEHNG)   Twi of Ghana male name meaning "big river."

Atum (AH-*tuhm*)   One of the oldest gods of ancient Egypt, Atum was the first god of Heliopolis. He is depicted as a man wearing a double crown. Also called TUM and ATMU, his name is believed to mean "the accomplished one."

Avongara (*ah-vohn*-GAHR-*ah*)   Name derived from the words vo meaning "to tie," and ngara, a man's name. Ngara was a southern Sudanese king who was hated by his people, but no one was able to depose him because of his impressive physical strength. Finally, a young man fought the king, defeated him and tied him up. This young man became the new king named Vongara, "tied up Ngara." The descendants of King Vongara are called avongara and make up the Voyol clan of the Azande tribe of southern Sudan.

Awacho (*ah*-WAHCH-*oh*)   This word means "I have said" in the
Dholuo language of Kenya. Awacho is also the name of a
medicinal tree found in northeastern Kenya. One village in
this region is called AWACHO SAMBUR (*sam*-BOOR) after an old
man named Sambur who climbed an Awacho tree.

Baga rice harvest mask, Guinea

B

It takes a whole tribe to raise a child.
Dagara of West Africa proverb

FEMALE

Bahatisha (*bah-hah-*TEE-*shah*) Kiswahili word meaning "to guess, to take a chance." This could be shortened in several ways, including TISHA, itself a Kiswahili word meaning "to threaten," BAHATI, the Kiswahili word for "luck," or HATI, the word for "document."

Bakundukize (*bah-koon-doo-*KEE-*zay*) Kinyarwanda of Rwanda name meaning "they like the rich." This name is used if some members of the parents' family don't like them because they are poor. It shows that the relatives only respect those who are wealthy. A short form could be KIZE.

Bamporiki (*bahm-por-*EE-*kee*) Kinyarwanda of Rwanda name meaning "why do they betray me?"

Baramousso (*bah-*RAH-*moo-soh*) Bambara of West Africa female name meaning "cherished one, favorite one," used by a man for his favorite wife, which is typically the youngest one. This name could be shortened to BARA, MOUSSO, or RAMOU.

Barayagwiza (*bah-rah-yah-*GWEE-*zah*) Kinyarwanda of Rwanda name meaning "they have a lot to say." It is used when someone is telling bad stories about the parents. Parents give their child this name to show that no matter what is said, it can't discourage them.

Barke (BAHR-*kay*) Swahili female name meaning "blessings." A variation of this name is BARAKA (*bah-*RAH-*kah*).

Bashasha (*bah-*SHAH-*shah*) A Kiswahili word meaning "smile, good cheer."

Bast (*bast*) Also BASTET, the name of an ancient Egyptian

49

goddess of pleasure. Bast is depicted as having a woman's body and a cat's head and represents the sun's beneficial powers. The name means "she of the city of Bubastis." Bubastis is pronounced byoo-BAS-tuhs and is the modern-day city of Tell Basta.

Baturiya (*bah-*TOOR*-ee-ah*)   Hausa of West Africa nickname for girls who are light-skinned.

Bayavuge (*bah-yah-*VOO*-gay*)   Kinyarwanda of Rwanda name meaning "let them say what they want." This name, like BARAYAGWIZA, is used when people are gossiping about the parents. It is given to show that the parents are sorry the others say such things.

Belaynesh (*behl-igh-*NEHSH)   Eritrean and Ethiopian female name meaning "you are above all, you are superior."

Besma (BEHS*-mah*)   Muslim female name heard in North Africa that comes from the Arabic word meaning "smile." BASMA is a Somali version and BASEEMAH and BASIMAH are Muslim variations meaning "the smiling one."

Betsileo (*beht-si-*LAY*-oh*)   A people of Indonesian descent living on Madagascar's southern plateau. Betsileo means "the invincible people." This name could be shortened to BETSI.

Beyla (*bay-*LAH)   A town in southeast Guinea in the interior highlands. Its name is believed to come from the Arabic exclamation *billah*, meaning "by God!"

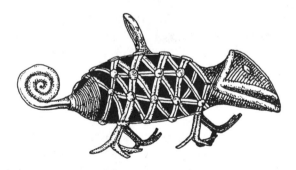

Chameleon pendant. Brass jewelry of the Tikar people (Cameroon).

Bikita (*bee*-KEE-*tah*)   A village in southeastern Zimbabwe. The name comes from the local word for "anteater," an animal once commonly found in the area.

Bilen (*bee*-LEHN)   Tigrinya of Eritrea and Ethiopia female name meaning "pupil of an eye."

Bilki (BIL-*kee*)   This is a Nigerian variation of the Muslim name for the Queen of Sheba, Belkis. Other Nigerian variations of this name include BILIKISU (*bee-lee*-KEE-*soo*), BILI (BEE-*lee*) and BILQIS (BIL-*kees*). The name Sheba means "oath."

Bissirat (BIS-*i-raht*)   Tigrinya of Eritrea and Ethiopia female name meaning "congratulations, good news."

Bosede (*boh*-SAY-*day*)   Yoruba of Nigeria name for females born on Sunday. It means "good tidings." A popular short form is BOSE (BOH-*say*).

Bukene (*boo*-KAY-*nay*)   Kinyarwanda of Rwanda name meaning "poorness."

Bukoko (*boo*-KOH-*koh*)   Tonga of Zambia unisex name meaning "beer." This name would be used, for example, for a child whose mother liked to drink beer while she was pregnant.

Bunze (BOON-*zi*)   Bakongo of west-central Africa unisex name meaning "unripe fruit."

MALE

Baba-Ile (*bah-bah*-EE-*lay*)   This Yoruba of Nigeria term means "head of the household, master of the house." BALE (BAH-*lay*) is a short form of this term.

Babangida (*bah-bah-n*GEE-*dah*)   Hausa of West Africa male name meaning "father of the house."

Babarimisa (*bah-bah-ree*-MEE-*sah*)   This Yoruba of Nigeria name means "father fled at my approach" and may be selected if the father died before the child was born. Because this name can also connote "my father fled when he saw me" it is not especially popular. Short forms could be BABA or RIMISA.

Bagule (BAH-*gool*)   Mende of Sierra Leone name for a male with a reddish complexion. Another version of the same name is KABAGULE (*KAH*-BAH-*gool*).

Bahari (*bah*-HAHR-*ee*)   Swahili and Muslim male name meaning "seaman" and the Kiswahili word for "sea."

Bakano (*bah*-KAH-*noh*)   Hausa of West Africa male name meaning "inhabitant of Kano, from Kano." Traditionally, Hausa men who travelled frequently would add such a name to their first name to indicate their country of origin. For example, SIDI BAKANO indicates Sidi from Kano. (See Dan Kano.)

Bakau (*bah*-KOW)   This Senegalese town is located on the west-facing coastline not far from Banjul. The name means "big place."

Balogun (*bah-loh*-GOON)   Yoruba of Nigeria male oriki name (see Ajamu) meaning "war general." It is also used as a surname.

Bamuthi (*bah*-MOO-*tee*)   Ndebele of Zimbabwe and South Africa name that means "he of the tree."

Bangamwabo (*bahn-gah*-MWAH-*boh*)   This Kinyarwanda of Rwanda name means "they hate themselves." It is used if some members of the family do not like the parents. The parents use this name to show their relatives that they are wrong.

Banji (BAHN-*jee*)   Tonga of Zambia unisex name meaning "many," used for the second born of twins.

Banjoko (*ban*-JOH-*koh*)   Yoruba of Nigeria name meaning "sit down, or stay, with me." This is mostly used as a surname.

Banyangiriki (*bahn-yahn-gee*-REE-*kee*)   Kinyarwanda of Rwanda name meaning "why do they betray me?"

Barake (*bah*-RAH-*kay*)   Swahili male name meaning "God's blessing."

Barmani (*bahr*-MAH-*nee*)   Hausa of West Africa unisex name meaning "leave me this one," used when previous children have died.

Bash (BAHSH) and **Bashiru** (*bah*-SHEER-*oo*)   Nigerian variations of the Muslim name Bashir or Basheer. This is one of the names of the Prophet Muhammad and means "precursor, forerunner."

Bashiri (*bah*-SHEER-*ee*)   This Swahili male name means "bringer of good tidings" and is derived from the Kiswahili word of the same spelling, which means "to predict, bring news."

Bata (BAH-*tah*)   Swahili name and Kiswahili word that means "duck."

Batiraishe (*bah-teer-*AH-EE-*shay*)   Mashona of Zimbabwe male name meaning "to work for the Lord." Short forms of this name are either BATI (BAH-*tee*) or BATIRAI (*bah-teer-*AH-EE).

Beenzu (BAYN-*zoo*)   Tonga of Zambia unisex name meaning "guests," used for a baby born just after visitors have come.

Belay (*behl-*IGH)   Eritrean and Ethiopian male name meaning "above, superior."

Bem (*behm*)   Tiv of Nigeria male name meaning "peace."

Benhazin (*bay-*UH-*zeen*)   According to legend, this powerful king of Dahomey (now Benin) had female archer bodyguards who cut off their right breasts to improve their shooting ability. (Note the pronunciation given is an attempt to show a French accent; check with a native of Benin to hear the exact pronunciation of this name.)

Berkane (*bair-*KAHN)   A town in northeastern Morocco named after Aberkane, a Muslim holy man. The name Aberkane comes from a Berber word meaning "black."

Bes (*behs*)   A mythological god of ancient Egypt. Bes is a god of pleasure and the guardian of the home. His power and dancing protects mothers and newborns from harm. He is usually depicted as a cherubic little man wearing a leopard skin tied around his shoulders and an ostrich feather in his hair.

Bina (BEE-*nah*)   Nigerian variation of the Muslim name Bilal, which means "moisture, freshness." Bilal was a black slave in Mecca who was freed by the first Khalifa Abu Bakr and who became Islam's first Muezzin (one who calls the faithful to prayer).

Biton (*bee-*TOHN)   Bambara of West Africa male name meaning "born after a long wait." BITON COULIBALY (*koo-lee-*BAH-*lee*) was a king of the Bambara Empire.

Bizimana (*bee-zee-*MAH-*nah*)   Rwandan male name meaning "only God knows."

Borbor (BOH-*boh*)   In Sierra Leone this is a generic name used for small boys.

Braima (BRAH-*ee-mah*)   A Mende of Sierra Leone variation of the Arabic name Ibrahim, itself a form of the biblical name Abraham, which means "father of a multitude." Another Mende variant of this name is BOIMA (BOH-*ee-mah*).

Bukar (BOO-*kahr*) A short form of the Muslim male name
Abubakar. (See Abubakar.) Zanna Bukar Dipcharima was a
prominent Nigerian politician from the 1940s through the
1960s. He is the namesake of a popular and distinctive
Nigerian embroidered skullcap called the *zanna bukar*.

Bulus (BOO-*loos*) Hausa of West Africa version of the biblical
name Paul, which comes from a Latin word meaning "little."

Bundu (BOON-*doo*) Mende of Sierra Leone
name for a male with a dark-brown
complexion.

Bunzi (BOON-*zee*) This is the Bavili of central-west Africa name for the southeast
wind. It means "deep in nerves" and is
considered "the messenger."

Burahimu (*boo-rah*-HEE-*moo*) A Swahili version of the biblical name Abraham. Other
Swahili variations are ABRAHAMU (*ah-
brah*-HAH-*moo*) and IBRAHIMU (*ee-brah*-HEE-
moo). The name means "father of a
multitude."

Buzi (BOO-*zee*) East African name and word
meaning "goat, kid."

Byago (*bee*-YAH-*goh*) Kinyarwanda of
Rwanda name meaning "sorrow."

Byukusenge (*byoo-koo*-SAYN-gay) Kinyarwanda of Rwanda name meaning "wake up
and pray."

Stylized bronze pendant of a pregnant
woman, worn by the Abron of the Ivory
Coast.

C

Brown Baby Cobina, with his large black velvet eyes,
His little coos of ecstasies, his gurgling of surprise,
With brass bells on his ankles, that laugh where'er he goes,
It's so rare for bells to tinkle, above brown dimpled toes.

Brown Baby Cobina is so precious that we fear
Something might come and steal him, when we grown-
ups are not near;
So we tied bells on his ankles, and kissed on them this charm—
"Bells, guard our Baby Cobina from all devils and all harm."
Gladys May Casely Hayford, Ghanaian teacher and poet

FEMALE

Caimile (*chah-ee-*MEE-*lay*) An Ovimbundu of Angola woman
might give herself this name of despair after losing all of her
children. It is derived from the proverb *ca imile li loluka; epata li
citiwe li kunduka*, which means "that which is born falls; a
family is born and perishes." This can also be roughly
translated to mean "a tree bears fruit and the fruit falls to the
ground; a family has children and they all die."

Capopia (*chah-poh-*PEE-*ah*) Ovimbundu of Angola female name
derived from the proverbial saying *ca popia Suku si patala*,
which means "it says God I do not dispute."

Ceyavali (*chay-yah-*VAH-*lee*) Ovimbundu of Angola female
name derived from the words *ceya vali* that mean "it has come
again." This name is used when other children have died and
the family is not terribly optimistic about the survival of this
child; they are basically saying "here we go again."

Chandamukulu (*chahn-dah-moo-*KOO-*loo*) The traditional title
of mothers of kings of the Bemba people of northeastern
Zambia. This name could be shortened to CHANDA.

Chausiku (*chah-oo-*SEE-*koo*)   Swahili name for females born at night. It literally means "of the night."

Cheche (CHAY-*chay*)   Swahili female name and Kiswahili word meaning "small thing, small piece."

Chilala (*chee-*LAH-*lah*)   Tonga of Zambia unisex name meaning "sleeping." It might be used, for example, by a woman who previously had several children and then was unable to conceive for a very long time.

Chililabombwe (*chee-lee-lah-*BOHM-*bway*)   This mining town in northern Zambia has a local name that means "croaking frog."

Chimpati (*cheem-*PAH-*tee*)   Tonga of Zambia unisex name meaning "cattle kraal." This name might be chosen if the baby was born while the mother was in the cattle kraal (a livestock enclosure).

Chinaza (*chee-*NAH-*zah*)   Igbo of Nigeria unisex name that means "God answers (prayers)."

Chipei (*chee-*PAY-*ee*)   A female name of the Mashona of Zimbabwe that means "to give."

Chitanga (*chee-*TAHN-*gah*)   This unisex name of the Tonga people of Zambia is derived from the word *matanga*, which means "pumpkin." It is used either as a nickname for someone who likes to eat pumpkins or for a baby whose mother craved pumpkins while she was pregnant.

Chivodzi (*ch*ǝ*e-*VOH-*dzee*)   Mashona of Zimbabwe female name meaning "the bad-maker."

Cilanga (*chee-*LAHN-*gah*)   Tonga of Zambia unisex name meaning "drought." A variation of this name is CILALA (*chee-*LAH-*lah*).

Cilingohenda (*chee-leen-goh-*HAYN-*dah*)   Ovimbundu of Angola name meaning "it is a pity."

Cilombo (*chee-*LOHM-*boh*)   Traditionally one of the two most common names for women among the Ovimbundu of Angola. Cilombo literally means "roadside camp" and is said to mean "a sight for sore eyes." The other most common female name is NGEVE (*n*GAY-*vay*), a name derived from the word *ongeve*, which means "hippopotamus" and which is also used as the name for the third born of triplets. CILOMBO-COKU-UNJUKA, meaning "Cilombo the gentle," and NGEVE-YESUNGA, "Ngeve the good," are characters in a popular folktale.

Cinakavali (*chee-nah-kah-*VAH-*lee*)   This Ovimbundu of Angola female name is derived from the proverb *cina ka va li asosa, ka va yungi ka va teleka*, which translates as "since they do not eat brambles they neither pick nor cook them" and means "work should be done for a useful end." This name could be shortened to CINA.

Cinawendela (*chee-nah-wayn-*DAY-*lah*) Ovimbundu of Angola female name derived from the proverbial saying *ocina wa endela ca ku nyeha onduko*. Literally this translates as "the thing you went for took away your name" and means that when a person goes away from home to work they find themselves among strangers and in that environment the person must make a name for himself or herself without relying upon their former reputation.

Cisanganda (*chee-sahn-*GAHN-*dah*) This Ovimbundu of Angola female name is derived from the proverb *ci sia la la nganda ocimbanda*. This saying translates as "the fee is left with the doctor" and means "the one who does the work is the one to receive the pay."

Cisengu (*chee-*SAYN-*goo*) Female children of the Ovimbundu of Angola may be given this name, which means "a small bird with a long tail."

Citalala (*chee-tah* LAII-*lah*) Ovimbundu of Angola female name derived from the proverb *ci talala ka ci pui kusenge; ciwa ka ci pui komanu*, which translates as "greenness is never wholly absent from the woods and goodness is never wholly absent from people."

Cokovenda (*choh-koh-*VAYN-*dah*) This Ovimbundu of Angola female name means "a thing pertaining to a shop." It is one of many place names that begin with *coko*, meaning "a thing of," and is combined with the place.

MALE

Caungula (*kah-uhn-*GOO-*luh*) This Angolan title for a chief means "leader of the people." A town in northern Angola bears this name.

Cetewayo (*seht-eh-*WIGH-*oh*, said properly there is a clicking sound in the initial syllable) This nephew of Chaka—the founder of the Zulu nation—was the last ruler of the independent Zulu kingdom. Cetewayo became king in 1872 and held his royal residence at Ulundi (which means "the high place"). In the Anglo-Zulu War of 1879, Cetewayo's forces were defeated at Ulundi, which was then burned. Following this defeat, Cetewayo was awarded only limited powers by the British and by 1897 Zululand became part of Natal, South Africa. Also spelled CETSHWAYO, his name means "what are we planning?" and refers to the royal family's master plan of seeing Cetewayo ascend to the throne of the Zulu kingdom.

Chadamunda (*chah-dah*-MOON-*dah*) Common name of the Mashona of Zimbabwe that means "loves to farm." It is derived from the verb *munda*, which means "garden."

Chamucima (*chah-moo*-CHEE-*mah*) Tonga of Zambia male name meaning "short-tempered."

Cheelo (CHAY-*loh*) Tonga of Zambia unisex name meaning "animal, meaningless, ghost." A mother who has watched previous children die might give her baby this non-name to convey her feelings of resignation and to express the futility of choosing a real name since there is a chance the child might die anyway.

Chumba (CHOOM-*buh*) Kalenjin of Kenya name meaning "white person." Used, for example, when a child is born at the time a relative returns from a missionary station or town, where white people are known to reside.

Chi (CHEE) Igbo of Nigeria name meaning "God, Creator." It is usually used in combination with other words to create compound names such as ADACHI (daughter of God), CHIAKU (God of wealth), IHECHI (light of God), and CHIKE (God of strength).

Chilili (*chee*-LEE-*lee*) Tonga of Zambia unisex name meaning "garden." This name would be given to a baby born while the mother was working in a field or in the garden.

Chimelu (*chee*-MEHL-*oo*) Igbo of Nigeria male name that means "made by God."

Chimiwenda (*chee-mee*-WAYN-*dah*) An uncommon Mashona of Zimbabwe name derived from the verb *ku wenda*, which means "to walk."

Chipego (*chee*-PAY-*goh*) Tonga of Zambia unisex name meaning "gift." A woman might choose this name, for example, if she had been unable to conceive for a long time, or if she had a chain of children of the same sex and this one was of the opposite sex.

Chipo (CHEE-*poh*)   Popular name in Zimbabwe that means "a gift."

Chishale Shale (*chee*-SHAH-*lay* SHAH-*lay*)   Male name of the Bemba of Zambia meaning "a thing that is left behind." It is used as a nickname for an old man whose contemporaries have all died.

Chitimukulu (*chee-tee-moo*-KOO-*loo*)   The traditional title of kings of the Bemba people of northeastern Zambia. It means "the great tree." A common short form of this name is CHITI.

Chiyobeka (*chee-yoh*-BAY-*kah*)   Tonga of Zambia male name meaning "noise maker." This name might be given to a child born when there is much quarrelling or noise in the village. A short form could be YOBEKA.

Choolwe (CHOHL-*way*)   Tonga of Zambia unisex name meaning "lucky."

Chuks (CHOOKS)   Popular nickname for people bearing Igbo of Nigeria names such as CHUKWUDIELU (God is great), CHUK-WUBUNNA (God is fatherly), CHUKWUJAMMA (May God bless) and IKECHUKWU (God's power).

Chukumeka (*choo-koo*-MAY-*kah*)   Igbo of Nigeria name meaning "God gives me."

Citonkwa (*chee*-TOHN-*kwah*)   Tonga of Zambia male name meaning "to be pushed or urged." It might be given to a child whose father is known for encouraging others to do something good, or in the case of a mother going into labor far from a village and being urged to keep moving until she arrives at a village where she can deliver the baby.

Ciwake (*chee*-WIGH-*kay*)   This Hausa of West Africa male name could be given to a boy born when his parents were eating beans, or may be used as a nickname for a child who loves to eat beans.

D

And when they name you, great warrior,
Then will my eyes be wet with remembering.
And how shall we name you, little warrior?
See, let us play at naming.

Didinga of Sudan song on child naming

FEMALE

Dada (DAH-*dah*) Yoruba of Nigeria unisex name for a child born with curly, dreadlock style hair. This is also a common surname.

Dara (DAH-*rah*) Yoruba of Nigeria female name meaning "good." (See also Omodara.)

Dekat (DEH-*kaht*) For the Bari people of Equatoria Province in southern Sudan, this is the word for "stories."

Delu (DAY-*loo*) Hausa of West Africa name for a female born after several sons, implying "the only girl."

Denhere (*day*-NAIR-*ay*) A common female name of the Mashona of Zimbabwe derived from the word *denere* meaning "thicket." An older version of this name is KADENERE (see entry under K).

Diketi (*dee*-KEH-*tee*) Oromo of Ethiopia and Kenya female name meaning "small." (See also Hadiketi.)

Dina (DEE-*nah*) Common Mashona of Zimbabwe name that means "a nice shelter place."

Djibola (*djee*-BOH-*lah*) An uncommon female name from Zaire meaning "to open."

Dupe (DOOP-*ay*) Yoruba of Nigeria female name meaning "thanks." It is usually used in combination with other words to create compound names, such as MODUPEOLA (*moh*-DOO-*pay-oh*-LAH), which means "I thank God (I have done well)."

MALE

Dambudso (*dahm*-BOOD-*soh*)   A common unisex name of the Mashona of Zimbabwe that means "trouble."

Dandu (DAN-*doo*)   The name of this village in Takaba Division of northeastern Kenya means "paths."

Dan Kano (*dahn* KAH-*noh*)   Hausa of West Africa male name meaning "son of Kano, from Kano." Dan means "son of" in Hausa. (See Bakano.)

Dan More (*dahn*-MOR-*ay*)   This male name of the Hausa of West Africa means "son of enjoyment." Traditionally Dan More was a title for the favorite person of a king or a chief. Now it is used primarily as a nickname equivalent to "my favorite son."

Dapo (DAHP-*oh*)   Yoruba of Nigeria male name meaning "brings together," usually used in compound names such as ADEDAPO (*ah-deh*-DAHP-*oh*), which means "the crown brings the people together."

Daraja (*dah*-RAH-*jah*)   Swahili male name and Kiswahili word meaning "a bridge, steps, rank."

Daren Tuwo (DAH-*rayn*-TOO-*woh*)   Hausa of West Africa male name signifying "born at night during supper." *Dare* means "night" and *tuwo* is the name for a traditional Hausa dish of ground grains made into a thick porridge. This name was chosen by a mother who was preparing *tuwo* at the time her labor pains began.

Davu (DAH-*voo*)   Male name of northern Kenya meaning "beginning."

Diallo (*dee*-AH-*loh*)   Male name of Guinea, Mali, and Niger meaning "bold."

Diata (*dee*-AH-*tah*)   Malinke of West Africa male name that means "lion."

Didinga (*di*-DIN-*guh*)   This name of an ethnic group living in southern Sudan means "heavy."

Dikko (DEE-*koh*)   This Hausa of West Africa male name for the first child in a family is very popular, especially around the city of Katsina, Nigeria, the heart of Hausa culture.

Dingiswayo (*din-gi*-SWIGH-*oh*)   This Zulu male name means "the banished one" and was the name of a famous Zulu warrior.

Diwani (*dee*-WAH-*nee*)   Swahili name and Kiswahili word meaning "councilor, mayor."

Djito (DJEE-*toh*)   An uncommon male name from Zaire meaning "heavy, big."

Dogo (DOH-*goh*)   Hausa of West Africa common male name meaning "long, tall, lanky." This is also a Swahili male name and Kiswahili word meaning "small."

Dogon Jakada (DOH-*gohn jah*-KAH-*dah*)   Hausa of West Africa male name meaning "the tall messenger."

Duah (DOO-*yah*, DOO-*ah*)   Twi of Ghana male name meaning "tree."

Dufu (DOO-*foo*)   Oromo of Ethiopia and Kenya common male nickname meaning "fart." Surprisingly, this name is often used for important and powerful men who are secure and gracious enough that they don't mind the name's playful implication. This is not unlike our expression "the old fart."

Duka (DOO-*kah*)   Hausa of Nigeria male name meaning "all." Also, a female name of the Hamar people of southwest Ethiopia and a Kiswahili word meaning "shop, store."

Duke (DOO-*kay*)   This Samburu of Kenya male name is also the name of a village in northeastern Kenya, which means "field of salt."

Dumi (DOO-*mee*)   According to the Bavili people of central-west Africa, this is the name of the northeast wind, considered "the inspirer."

Ibeji statuette. Ibeji is a statuette used when one twin dies. The Ibeji is treated like a living child; it is fed and washed as such. Yoruba, Nigeria.

E

I have lived in the redness of the stones that mark a path
through my blood; I am the descendant of a forgotten race,
but I carry in my hands the remnants of their fire.
Mohammed Khair-Eddine, Moroccan novelist and poet

FEMALE

Ebun (*eh-*BOON)   Yoruba of Nigeria female name meaning "gift."

Efunsetan (*eh-foo-*SHAY-*ton*)   Yoruba of Nigeria female name meaning "Efun (a deity) has done it (by granting the child)."

Ehobib (*ch* IIOII *bib*)   Hottentot of South Africa place name that means "found beautiful."

Ekuva (*ay-*KOO-*vah*)   This female name of the Ovimbundu of Angola refers to the axe a king uses to behead subjects. The keeper of this axe is an old witch who is also called Ekuva.

Elumbu (*ay-*LOOM-*boo*)   Ovimbundu of Angola name for a female child born prematurely and whose survival was uncertain. It is derived from the word of the same spelling, which means "mystery."

Erin (AIR-*in*)   The Yoruba of Nigeria word meaning "elephant."

Erinle (*air-*IN-*lay*)   The name of a Yoruba of Nigeria deity.

Esenje (*ay-*SAYN-*jay*)   Ovimbundu of Angola female name derived from the proverb *esenje liwa ka li moli ofule; onyima yiwa ka yi moli omola*. Literally this translates as "A good stone does not see the pounding of maize; a good back does not see a child." This is both a lament of women without children and a general expression meaning "that's the way things go."

Ezenma (*ay-*ZAYN-*mah*)   Igbo of Nigeria name meaning "queen of beauty."

MALE

Ehioze (*eh*-HEE-*oh*-ZAY)   Benin and Nigeria male name meaning "I am above jealousy."

Ekundayo (*eh*-KOON-*dah-yoh*)   Yoruba of Nigeria male name meaning "sorrow becomes happiness."

Ellema (*ay*-LAY-*mah*)   Popular Oromo of Ethiopia and Kenya male name meaning "one who is milking a cow."

Embaye (*ehm*-BIGH-*ay*)   Tigrinya of Eritrea and Ethiopia male name meaning "my fort, my mountain."

Enobakhare (*eh-noh-bah*-KAH-*reh*)   Benin and Nigeria male name meaning "the king's word."

Entebbe (*ehn*-TEH-*bay*)   A town in southern Uganda on the shores of Lake Victoria and site of Uganda's international airport. This name means "chair" in a local Luganda dialect.

Enyama (*ayn*-YAH-*mah*)   Ovimbundu of Angola name for males and females derived from the word *enyamahuti*, which means "hawk." According to traditional beliefs, when the shadow of the hawk falls upon the mother it bewitches her child while in the womb, causing a paralysis.

Ephrem (EHF-*rehm*)   The Eritrean and Ethiopian version of the biblical name Ephraim, which means "doubly fruitful." Another spelling is EFREM.

Ewansiha (*eh-wan-see*-HAH)   Benin and Nigeria male name meaning "secrets are not for sale."

Ezenwa (*ay*-ZAYN-*wah*)   Igbo of Nigeria name meaning "the most kingly among children."

F

What have you been eating, you're swelling up like an okra!
Perhaps it's sweet potatoes you've been eating.
Allah preserve us till harvest
And let us see how the okra swells up!
Hausa of West Africa song for girls who
become pregnant out of wedlock

FEMALE

Fabunni (FAH-*boo-nee*)   Yoruba of Nigeria unisex name meaning "Ifa (a deity) has given me this." This is mostly heard as a surname.

Farafenni (*fah-rah*-FEHN-*yay*)   A town located on the Gambia River in The Gambia. The name of this rural business center is derived from the Mandingo words *farro*, meaning "riceland" and *fennyo*, meaning "the tail;" thus, the name means "the tail end of the rice lands or rice fields." This name could be shortened to FARA or FENNI.

Fatimetu (*fah-tee*-MEH-*too*)   A Nigerian variation of the Muslim name Fatimah, which means "weaned" and refers to one of the daughters of the Prophet Muhammad. Swahili variants of this name include FATMA (FAHT-*mah*) and FATUMA (*fah*-TOO-*mah*).

Fauziya (*fow*-ZEE-*yah*)   A Swahili version of the Muslim name Fauzia, which means "victorious, successful."

Folasade (FOH-*lah*-SHAH-*day*)   Yoruba of Nigeria female name meaning "honor bestows a crown." Soul singer **Sade** (SHAH-*day*) was born in Ibadan, Nigeria, with the name Helen Folasade Adu. Another short from of this name is FOLA, which means "honor."

Freweynee (*fruh*-WAY-*nee*)   Tigrinya of Eritrea and Ethiopia female name that means "seed of a grape."

Fumane (*foo*-MAH-*nee*)   Basotho of Lesotho female name meaning "the found one."

Furaha (*foo*-RAH-*hah*)   Swahili female name and a Kiswahili word meaning "glad, happiness."

MALE

Fahru (*fuh*-ROO)   Somali nickname meaning "hairlip."

Fanus (FAH-*noos*)   Tigrinya of Eritrea and Ethiopia unisex name that means "a bright light, a lantern."

Fatiu (*fah*-TEE-*oo*)   A Nigerian version of the Muslim name Fatih or Faatih. It is one of the names of the Prophet Muhammad and means "liberator, opener."

Fatukobiri (*fah-too-koh*-BEER-*ee*)   Kinyarwanda of Rwanda name meaning "take it as it is." This name is used when the family is having problems at the time of the child's birth. It is intended to reassure the family that they can endure their problems.

Fianarantsoa (*fyahn-ahr-ahn*-TSOH-*uh*, *fyahn-ahr-ahn*-TSOO-*uh*)   The name of this town in southeastern Madagascar means "a place where one learns what is good" in the Malagasy language. This name could be shortened to FIAN or ARAN.

Fisseha (*fi-seh*-HAH)   Eritrean and Ethiopian male name of Ge'ez origin that means "happiness, joy."

Frezghi (FREHZ-*gee*)   Tigrinya of Eritrea and Ethiopia male name meaning "fruit of God."

G

My life is but a dirty penny
that is only valued because
it is the only one
My life is but a ten rand note
that can be used only because
there may be change.

Zindzi Mandela, daughter of Nelson and
Winnie Mandela, from *Black As I Am* (1978)

FEMALE

Gakee (*gah*-KEE)   One of the most common female names of the
Meru people of Kenya, this name means "the one who grinds
the millet very well for making porridge."

Genet (*gch*-NEHT)   Female name of Eritrea and Ethiopia that
means "Eden (garden of)." The name Eden means "pleasure." A variation of this name is GANNAT.

Ghiday (*gi*-DAY)   Tigrinya of Eritrea and Ethiopia female name
meaning "my share, my turn." Also spelled GIDAY, this
protection name might be chosen by a woman who had
previously lost a baby to signify "it's my turn for one to live."

Ginikanwa (*jee-nee*-KAHN-*wah*)   Igbo of Nigeria female name
meaning "what is more precious than a child?" This name
could be shortened to GINI.

MALE

Galadima (*gah-lah*-DEE-*mah*)   The Hausa of West Africa term
for a prince.

Gamada (*gah*-MAH-*dah*)   Borana of Kenya male name meaning
"glad, pleased," used by parents who have waited a long
time for a child and are happy with the arrival.

Gamaembi (*gah-mah*-EHM-*bee*)   Balese of Zaire name meaning "the man without a chief."

Gasigwa (*gah*-SEEG-*wah*)   Kinyarwanda of Rwanda name used when one of the parents dies at the time of the child's birth before the baby has been named.

Gavivi (*gah*-VEE-*vee*)   Ewe of Ghana name meaning "money is sweet." This is mostly used as a nickname or surname for men who like money too much. Such Ewe nicknames are applied especially at times of festivals.

Gazali (*gah*-ZAH-*lee*)   A Nigerian variation of the Muslim name Abu Hamid al-Ghazali, who was a venerable Muslim theologian, jurist, mystic, and philosopher. Another Nigerian version of this same name is KASALI (*kah*-SAH-*lee*).

Gboli (BOH-*lee*)   Mende of Sierra Leone name for a man who has a light complexion. (Note that although technically the initial "g" is pronounced, it is nearly imperceptible.) Another version of this same name is GBORLI (BOHR-*lee*).

Gendeme (*jehn*-DEHM-*ee*)   Mende of Sierra Leone name for a short man. (See also Tumbui.)

Ghe'le (GEH-*lay*)   Tigrinya of Eritrea and Ethiopia male name meaning "strength."

Giigle (GEE-*glay*)   Somali nickname meaning "stutterer."

Gilo (GEE-*loh*)   The name of the founding father of the Anyuak people of southern Sudan.

Godana (*goh*-DAH-*nah*)   Oromo of Kenya and Ethiopia name for a male child born when the family was migrating.

goha (GOH-*hah*)   A famous character of Egyptian comic stories who is usually portrayed as a miser.

guban (*goo*-BAHN)   The Somali name for the country's torrid and barren coastal plain on the Gulf of Aden. It means "burnt."

Gumel (*goo*-MEHL)   The name of a Nigerian emirate (a territory ruled by an emir) lasting from 1749 to 1903 of which the modern town of Gumel was the capital. The name is derived from a Fulani word for a short-horned cow.

Gure (*goo*-RAY)   Somali nickname meaning "left-handed."

H

I have restored that
which is in ruins,
I have raised up that
which was unfinished.

inscription on a monument to Hatshepsut

FEMALE

Haazita (*hah*-ZEET-*ah*)   Tonga of Zambia unisex name meaning "a group of enemies want to attack." This might be given to a child born during wartime.

Habibuna (*hah-bee*-BOO-*nah*)   Swahili word meaning "our beloved."

Hada (HAH-*dah*)   The name of a village in Takaba Division of northeastern Kenya that means "salty place."

Haddas (HAH-*dahs*)   Tigrinya of Eritrea and Ethiopia female name meaning "new."

Hadiketi (HAH-*dee*-KEH-*tee*)   Oromo of Ethiopia and Kenya female name meaning "small." (See also Diketi.)

Hagodana (HAH-*goh*-DAH-*nah*)   Oromo of Kenya and Ethiopia female name for a child born when the family was migrating.

Hagosa (*hah-goh*-SAH)   Tigrinya of Eritrea and Ethiopia female name meaning "happiness, joy."

Hajanika (*hah-jah*-NEE-*kah*)   Tonga of Zambia name meaning "to be available, to be at hand."

Hajari (*hah*-JAHR-*ee*)   This female Swahili name is a version of the biblical name Hagar, which means "flight." Hagar was the mother of all Arabs.

Asante fertility doll, Ghana.

Hajunza (*hah*-JOON-*zah*) Tonga of Zambia unisex name meaning "tomorrow." This might be chosen by a mother who had repeatedly postponed a trip during which time the baby was born.

Hakunyo (*hah*-KUN-*yoh*) Oromo of Ethiopia and Kenya female name meaning "belly button," used for children whose umbilical cord drops off early.

Hanazullumi (*hah-nah*-ZOO-*loo-mee*) An uncommon Hausa of West Africa female name meaning "prevent worry." It is derived from the Hausa words *hana*, which means "to stop," and *zullumi*, which means "to whine, to complain."

Hanetu (*hah*-NAY-*too*) A Nigerian variation of the Christian and Muslim name Hannah, who was maternal grandmother of Jesus (called the Prophet Isa in Islam). The name Hannah means "grace."

Haracha (HAH-*rahch-ah*) Oromo of Ethiopia and Kenya female name meaning "frog." Parents who had a previous child die would use this negative name to ward off evil.

Hareena (*hahr*-EE-*nah*) Tigrinya of Eritrea and Ethiopia unisex name meaning "we have chosen."

Hashoba (*hah*-SHOH-*bah*) Oromo of Kenya and Ethiopia female name meaning "someone who is very pretty or fancy."

Hasweeka (*hah*-SWAY-*kah*) Unisex name of the Tonga of Zambia that means "getting lost." It might be used as a nickname for a child who gets lost often.

Hatshepsut (*hat*-SHEHP-*soot*) This Egyptian queen ruled from 1490–1469 B.C. during the eighteenth dynasty. Hatshepsut proclaimed herself Pharaoh (equivalent to King) and dressed as a man. She is considered one of the greatest female rulers ever. This name is also spelled HATSHEPSET (*hat*-SHEHP-*seht*).

Hattabari (*hah-tah*-BAHR-*ee*)   According to legends of the Otuho people of the Torit area of southern Sudan, Hattabari was a woman who created beer on the Itatok Mountains.

Hawakulu (*hah-wah*-KOO-*loo*)   A Nigerian variation of the name Hawwa, which is the Muslim name for Eve, the first woman and wife of Adam. The name Eve means "the urge primeval, life."

Hazina (*hah*-ZEE-*nah*)   A Kiswahili word meaning "treasure."

Heewan (*hee*-WAHN)   Eritrean and Ethiopian name for the biblical Eve, which means "the urge primeval, life."

Hija (HEE-*juh*)   A female name heard in African Muslim communities. It is derived from the Arabic word *hajj*, which means to make a pilgrimage to Mecca during Ramadan.

Hiwot (*hi*-WEHT)   Tigrinya of Eritrea and Ethiopia female name meaning "life."

Husna (HOOS-*nah*)   Swahili female name meaning "most beautiful."

Huso (HOO-*soh*)   Ovimbundu of Angola female name derived from the expression *ohuso yakai*, meaning "the feigned sadness of a bride."

Hypatia (*high*-PAY-*shuh, high*-PAT-*ee*)   A beautiful Egyptian philosopher of the fourth–fifth century who resided in the Greek city of Alexandria. Hypatia was stoned to death in the streets because of her pagan beliefs.

MALE

Haben (HAH-*behn*)   Tigrinya of Eritrea and Ethiopia male name meaning "pride."

Habibulai (*hah-bee-boo*-LAH-*ee*)   A Nigerian variation of the Muslim name Habibullah, one of the names of the Prophet Muhammad, which means "the beloved of God."

Habili (*hah*-BEE-*lee*)   The Swahili version of the biblical name Abel. Abel was the second son of Adam and Eve and was murdered by his brother Cain because of jealousy. The name means "breath, vapor."

Habimana (*hah-bee*-MAH-*nah*)   Rwandan male name meaning "there is God."

Habtom (*hahb*-TOHM)   Tigrinya of Eritrea and Ethiopia male name meaning "their wealth, riches." A similar Amharic name meaning "the rich one" is HABTAMU.

Habyarimana (*hahb-yahr-ee*-MAH-*nah*)   Kinyarwanda of Rwanda name meaning "it is God who makes someone have a child." It is used by parents who have gone a long time without bearing children and who have been looking forward to having another one. Juvénal Habyarimana served as president of Rwanda from 1973 until his death in 1994 when his presidential jet was shot down over Kigali, the capital city.

Hacempeta (*hah-chaym*-PAY-*tah*)   Tonga of Zambia male nickname for someone who likes to travel or roam. It means "traveller, wanderer."

Hadgu (HAHD-*goo*)   Tigrinya of Eritrea and Ethiopia male name meaning "his heir, someone to carry on his name."

Hadiimana (*hah-dee*-MAH-*nah*)   Male name of the Tonga of Zambia meaning "to become bent." It might be used for the child of a lame or elderly man.

Haile (HIGH-*lay*)   Amharic of Ethiopia name meaning "his power."

Hakankone (*hah-kahn*-KOH-*nay*)   Tonga of Zambia male nickname that means "sorghum husks" and is given to someone who likes making and eating sorghum porridge.

Halwiindi (*hahl*-WEEN-*dee*)   Tonga of Zambia unisex name meaning "shrine for rain." It would be given to a child born when villagers were praying to a shrine for rain. (See Lwiindi.)

Ham (HAM)   This biblical male name means "hot." Ham was the third son of Noah and the father of the Hamitic race. The Hamites inhabit north and northeastern Africa, and include descendants of ancient Egyptians, Berbers, Somalis, and some peoples of Ethiopia.

Hanyama (*hah-n*YAH-*mah*)   Tonga of Zambia male name that means "meat." It would be given, for example, to a child who was born while the father was away hunting.

Hanzila (*hah-n*ZEE-*lah*)   Male name of the Tonga of Zambia that means "road, path, way." This name might be chosen, for example, if the mother gave birth to the child while on her way to the hospital.

Haruni (*hah*-ROON-*ee*)   This Swahili male name is a version of the biblical name Aaron, which means "mountaineer" or "enlightener."

Hyksos (HIK-*sohs*, HIK-*sahs*)   An ancient Egyptian name believed to mean "the rulers of foreign lands" or "the princes of the eastern desert." The Hyksos, considered a barbaric people, ruled Egypt for 511 years forming the fifteenth and sixteenth dynasties. They made their capital at Memphis.

Hidi (HEE-*dee*)   Common male name of the Oromo of Ethiopia and Kenya derived from the word *hunde* meaning "root." HUNDE (HOON-*day*) has also been used as a variant of this name.

Hindolo (HIN-*doh-loh*)   Mende of Sierra Leone name meaning "male child."

Hirsi (HEER-*see*)   Somali name meaning "amulet."

Horus (HOR-*uhs*)   This ancient Egyptian sun god is son of Osiris and Isis and is represented as having the head of a hawk. The Latin name Horus is derived from the Egyptian name HERU, which means "hawk."

Spirit mask, Gabon

I

Everything bears both death and life. Rain brings down lightening and life-giving water, earth brings forth harvest and entombs the dead, the sun spreads light and drought; the years bring on old age and famine, children and Independence.

Ahmadou Kourouma, *The Suns of Independence* (1968)

FEMALE

Ife (*ee*-FEH) Yoruba of Nigeria female name meaning "love." This is also used in combination with other words to create compound names such as IFETAYO (see below).

Ife (EE-*fay*) The name of this city in southwestern Nigeria is a Yoruba word meaning "wide." According to Yoruba mythology, Ife-Ife is the sacred location where the first humans lived.

Ifetayo (*ee-feh*-TAY-*oh*) Yoruba of Nigeria female name meaning "love excels all."

Igbekoyi (*ig-beh*-KOH-*yee*) Yoruba of Nigeria name used for a child born after the mother has had other children die (see Akuji). It means "even the bush won't have this" and is meant to convince the child to stay alive. Short forms could be KOYI or IGBE.

Ige (EE-*gay*) Yoruba of Nigeria unisex name for a child born breech presentation (feet or buttocks first).

Ikoko (*ee*-KOH-*koh*) Lingala of Zaire female name referring to a small fish.

Ilega (*i*-LEHG-*uh*) Didinga of southern Sudan name used for girls born during the hunting season.

Ilori (*ee*-LOR-*ee*) Yoruba of Nigeria name for a child conceived during absence of menstruation.

Isabis (*i*-SAH-*bis*)   Hottentot of South Africa place name that means "something beautiful to see."

Iyabode (*ee-yah*-BOH-*day*)   Like Abiba and Yetunde, this Yoruba of Nigeria name is used for the first girl of the family to be born after the paternal grandmother has died. It means "mother returns." A common short form is IYABO (*ee*-YAH-*boh*). It could also be shortened to IYA (*ee*-YAH), itself the Yoruba word for "mother."

Iyakaremye (*ee-yah-kahr*-AYM-*yay*)   Kinyarwanda of Rwanda name that means "only the creator has power over me."

Izibili (*iz*-EH-*bee-lee*)   Ishan of Nigeria name for a very black child.

MALE

Idirisi (*ee-deer*-EE-*see*)   The Swahili version of the biblical male name Enoch, which means "dedicated."

Iggi (*i*-GEE)   Hausa of West Africa name for an only son.

Ikhnaton (*ik*-NAHT-*n*)   This Egyptian name means "it pleases Aton." Ikhnaton became Pharaoh of Egypt in 1372 B.C. He married his sister Nefertiti and worshipped only one god, Aton, the sun god. This name is also spelled AKHENATON (*ah-keh*-NAH-*t'n*).

Imamu (*ee*-MAH-*moo*)   Swahili male name meaning "spiritual leader" and Kiswahili term for "Mosque minister."

Imhotep (*im*-HOH-*tehp*)   Referred to as "the father of medicine," Imhotep was a black Egyptian of the third millennium.

Isayas (*i-say*-YAHS)   Also spelled ISSAIAS (*ee-sigh*-AHS), this is an Eritrean and Ethiopian version of the biblical name Isaiah, which means "salvation of Jehovah." Isaiah was the first of the great prophets who foretold the coming of Christ.

Issay (*i*-SAY)   Eritrean and Ethiopian version of the biblical name Esau, the eldest son of Isaac and twin brother of Jacob. The name Esau means "hairy." A variation of this name is ESSAW (*ay*-SOW).

Itieni (*ee-tee*-EHN-*nee*)   Maasai of East Africa word meaning "the thing which stands apart." At 8,244 feet (2,514 meters), Itieni is the highest peak of the Nyambeni Hills located near the town of Meru, Kenya.

Iyapo (*ee-yah*-POH)   Yoruba of Nigeria name meaning "many trials."

Iyoyo (*ee*-YOH-*yoh*)   Ishan of Nigeria unisex name meaning "don't think I am senseless or foolish."

Izefia (*i*-ZEH-*fah*)   Ishan of Nigeria name meaning "I have no child to disinherit." This name could be shortened to ZEF.

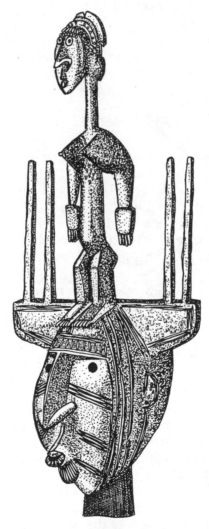

Children's secret society mask, western Sudan

J

*Our children may learn about heroes of the past. Our task
is to make ourselves architects of the future.*
Jomo Kenyatta, first president of Kenya

FEMALE

Janina (*zhuh*-NEE-*nuh*) Tunisian female name that means
"garden."

Jendayi (*jehn*-DAH-*yee*) Mashona of Zimbabwe name meaning
"give thanks."

Jengo (JEHN-*goh*) Mende of Sierra Leone name for a woman
with a reddish complexion. (See also Mamagule.)

Jira (JEER-*ah*) Tigrinya of Eritrea and Ethiopia female name
meaning "related by blood."

Juana (*joo*-AH-*nah*) A Kiswahili word meaning "to know one
another."

Julikana (*joo-lee*-KAH-*nah*) This Kiswahili word means "be
known."

Julisha (*joo*-LEE-*shah*) A Kiswahili word meaning "to make
known."

MALE

Jabilo (*jah*-BEE-*loh*) Dholuo of Kenya term for a medicine man.

Jafaru (*jah*-FAH-*roo*) A Nigerian variation of the Muslim name
Jafar, which means "brook, creek" and refers to a cousin and
companion of the Prophet Muhammad. Another Nigerian
version of this name is GAFARU (*gah*-FAH-*roo*). Ethiopian variations include JUFAR, GIAFAR, and JIFAR. ABBA JIFAR II was an
eighteenth-century Oromo (of Ethiopia) king who was carried everywhere by two servants, one under each arm, so
that his feet never touched the ground. (ABBA is an Ethiopian
name meaning "father" and is also used as a title.)

The top of a staff, in gold, West Africa.

Jakada (*jah*-KAH-*dah*)   Hausa of West Africa male name meaning "the messenger."

Jaramogi (*jair-uh*-MOH-*gee*)   Luo of Kenya male name meaning "traveller."

Jengo (JAYN-*goh*)   Swahili male name derived from the Kiswahili word of the same spelling that means "building." The name implies "strength."

Jiburili (*jee-boor*-EE-*lee*)   Swahili version of the biblical name Gabriel whose name means "man of God."

Jirgi (JEER-*gee*)   Hausa of West Africa nickname meaning "airplane" or "train," given to someone who is always moving fast or is always in a hurry. (The Hausa word *jirgi* is combined with other words to determine whether it is an airplane or a train, in the sense of "carriage of the sky" or "carriage of the rails.")

Jok (*jok*, pronounced staccato) Mostly used in the Bor area of southern Sudan, the name Jok refers to a Dinka spiritual God.

Jorj (*jorj*)   Ethiopian version of the English name George which means "the earthworker, farmer."

Juji (JOO-*jee*)   Hausa of West Africa male name meaning "rubbish heap," used by a woman whose previous children have died. Traditionally when such a child was born the grandparents would take the newborn and set it out by the trash pile to show that it is just as well to throw the baby away if it plans to follow the path of the other children. After this gesture to fate is finished, the mother runs out and reclaims her child.

Jumoke (*joo*-MOH-*keh*)   Yoruba of Nigeria name meaning "everyone loves him."

Junju (JOON-*joo*)   Junju was a *kabaka* (king) of the Buganda of Uganda who ruled from around 1764 to 1766. He was murdered by his younger brother Semakookiro after he killed Semakookiro's wife for having refused him.

K

Child, child, child,
love I have had for my man.
But now, only now,
have I the fullness of love.

Didinga of Sudan song

FEMALE

Kacela (*kah*-CHAY-*lah*) Tonga of Zambia unisex name meaning "hunter." This might be a nickname given to someone who is successful at hunting and who always brings back game, wild fruits, honey, etc.

Kadenere (*kah-day*-NAIR-*ay*) Female Mashona of Zimbabwe name derived from the word *denere* meaning "thicket." This would formerly have been used for a child born under a tree or in the bush. The more common modern version is DE-NHERE. (See entry under D.)

Kai (KAH-*ee*, *kigh*) Female name from northern Ghana meaning "lovable."

Kaikura (*kigh*-KOO-*ruh*) Mende of Sierra Leone name referring to a type of ground squirrel. A variation of this same name is KAIKULA (*kigh*-KOO-*luh*).

Kambundu (*kahm*-BOON-*doo*) Ovimbundu of Angola female name meaning "a little frog."

Kamiapiulu (*kah-mee-ah-pee*-OO-*loo*) Ovimbundu of Angola female name derived from the word *okamiapiulu*, which means "a little cinder." This belongs to a class of names used by women to express new experiences in life. In one instance, a girl who got lost from a caravan renamed herself this. This name could be shortened to KAMIA, MIA or PIULU.

Kande (KAHN-*day*) Hausa of West Africa name for the firstborn daughter after several sons.

Kapera (*kah*-PAIR-*ah*) Mashona of Zimbabwe female name derived from the verb *ku pera*, which means "to be finished, to come to an end." This might be chosen, for example, if many other children in the village had died near the time of the child's birth.

Karamojong (KAIR-*uh-muh*-JONG)   A Nilo-Hamitic cattle-raising people of northeastern Uganda. The name means "people who die of old age," referring to the fact that the Karamojong settled in an area that was conducive to raising animals without threat of many diseases. This name could be shortened to KARA.

Karikoga (*kahr-ee*-KOH-*gah*)   A common unisex name of Zimbabwe meaning "self-sufficient, he/she is on his/her own."

Karungi (*kah*-ROON-*gee*)   Usually given to girls, this Baganda of Uganda name means "beautiful."

Kateke (*kah*-TAY-*kay*)   Ovimbundu of Angola female name derived from the proverb *kateke tueya tua lia palonga; kaliye kalo peya oku lila povilindo*. This literally translates as "the day we came we ate off dishes; now it comes to eating off wooden bowls" and means that a person has worn out welcome. This name is used to describe persons who are well liked at first, but who become less popular after longer acquaintance.

Kavovo (*kah*-VOH-*voh*)   The local name for a devastating famine that occurred in Embuland in Kenya in the early 1900s. Kavovo is derived from the Kiembu verb *kuvova*, which means "to hate without reason," referring to the fact that people began to hate each other because of scarcity of food.

Kavuta (*kah*-VOO-*tah*)   Giriama of Kenya name meaning "the poor," which was used as the name of a generation born during a period of famines and epidemics.

Kazija (*kah*-ZEE-*jah*)   Swahili female name meaning "plenty of work."

Kazuri (*kah*-ZOOR-*ee*)   This word means "small and beautiful" in Kiswahili.

Kei (*kay*)   A river in eastern Cape Province, South Africa, which flows into the Indian Ocean. Its name comes from the Hottentot word meaning "sandy, white."

Kenda (KEHN-*duh*)   In both Kiswahili and the Kiembu language of Kenya this word means "nine." In the Kimeru language of Kenya, it is the word for "December."

Kendi (KEHN-*dee*) Female name of the Meru people of Kenya that means "the loved one."

Kerkenna (*kehr-keh*-NAH) A group of seven islands in the central Mediterranean Sea off the east coast of Tunisia. Also spelled KERKENNAH, the name is derived from its ancient form of Cercina. The name Cercina is related to the mythological figure CIRCE (SIR-*see*, KEER-*kay*), who, according to Greek legend, was an African witch who transformed the Greek troops of Odysseus into swine.

Kesho (KAY-*shoh*) Swahili name meaning "the future" and the Kiswahili word for "tomorrow."

Kia (KEE-*ah*) Dholuo of Kenya word meaning "hill."

Wooden spoon, Somalia.

Kiden (KI-*dehn*) Bari of southern Sudan name for a female born after three or more boys.

Kifunji (*kee*-FOON-*jee*) The name of a sister of Queen Nzinga of Angola (1583–1663). Queen Nzinga led her people in resisting Portuguese occupation, which resulted in Kifunji's capture. While being held prisoner, Kifunji managed to channel intelligence information to her sister. In October 1647, Kifunji was drowned by the Portuguese as they retreated following a defeat by Queen Nzinga's forces. (See Mukumbu for information on another of Queen Nzinga's sisters.)

Kirundu (*ki*-ROON-*doo*) Female name of the Luo of Kenya derived from the Luganda word *ekirundu*, which means "private garden."

Kisakye (*kee*-SAH-*chay*) Baganda of Uganda unisex name that means "grace."

Kitoko (*kee*-TOH-*koh*) Lingala of Zaire word meaning "beautiful."

Kizazi (*kee*-ZAH-*zee*) A Kiswahili word meaning "a generation."

Koda (KOH-*dah*)   Foula of West Africa unisex name for last born children. This child is usually considered the mother's pet.

Koko-Mwezi (KOH-*koh* MWAY-*zee*)   The name for a god of the Taveta people of Kenya that means "grandmother moon."

Kosenge (*koh*-SAYN-*gay*)   Ovimbundu of Angola name for a female child born in a field or in the woods. It is derived from the words *ka usenge*, which mean "the bush."

Koshi (KOH-*shee*)   Hausa of West Africa word and female name meaning "full, satisfied."

Kubi Ayana (KOO-*bee* ah-YAH-*nah*)   Name of a village in Takaba Division of northeast Kenya that means "the lucky hill."

Kudisan (*kuh*-*di*-SAHN)   Tigrinya of Eritrea and Ethiopia female name meaning "the blessed one."

Kunzi (KOON-*zee*)   Bavili of central-west Africa term for the northwest wind, considered an electric force.

Kush (*koosh*)   An ancient kingdom based in Sudan that has often been identified with Ethiopia. It is the country that was settled by the descendants of Ham. Also spelled CUSH, the name signifies "mysterious, powerful, and unknown."

Kususula (*koo-soo*-SOO-*lah*)   Tonga of southern Zambia unisex name meaning "eating," used for children born as the mother was preparing to cook a meal. This name could be shortened to SUSU or SULA.

MALE

Kabili (*kah*-BEE-*lee*)   The Swahili version of the biblical name Cain, which means "possession." Cain was the eldest son of Adam and Eve. *Kabili* is also a Kiswahili word meaning "to face toward."

Kafelo (*kah*-FAY-*loh*)   Baganda of Uganda name meaning "monkey."

Kaihemba (*kah-ee*-HAYM-*bah*)   Ovimbundu of Angola name that means "the one who lives by medicine." This name might be taken by someone whose life was saved by taking medicines.

Kajok-Koji (KAH-*jok*-KOH-*jee*)   The name of an early twentieth-century chief of the Kuku people of southern Sudan from whom the town of Kajo-Keji derived its name. Kajok means "calf" and koji refers to the fencing used for keeping the calves.

Kal'ab (*kahl*-AHB)   Eritrean and Ethiopian male name derived from Ge'ez that means "God's word."

Kalei (*kah*-LAY-*ee, kah*-LAY)   Ovimbundu of Angola male name meaning "one who works for the king."

Kambihi (*kahm*-BEE-HEE)   Unisex name of the Tonga of Zambia meaning "whirlwind." A baby born just after a whirlwind has passed might be given this name.

Kambundu (*kahm*-BOON-*doo*)   According to Ovimbundu of Angola tradition, a mother gives her baby this name if she bled at some time during her pregnancy. Such a child is believed to have been bewitched and requires special attention because the spirit is unstable and may separate from the body. The mother carries a rattle with her and shakes it at rivers and crossroads to prevent the child's spirit from wandering off.

Kame (KAH-*may*)   Swahili male name and Kiswahili word meaning "desolate, arid."

Kandimba (*kahn*-DEEM-*bah*)   Ovimbundu of Angola name meaning "the little hare."

Kangwe (KAHN-*gway*)   Ovimbundu of Angola male name meaning "the little leopard."

Kaniini (*kuh*-NEE-*nee*)   Tonga of Zambia male name meaning "small," used for babies who are small at birth.

Karan (KAH-*rahn*)   The name of a Yoruba of Nigeria tyrant king who is the source of the expression "As cruel as Karan."

Karanja (*kuh*-RAHN-*juh*)   Kikuyu of Kenya male name meaning "guide."

Kari Kai (KAH-*ree* KIGH)   Mandingo of Sierra Leone male name meaning "serpent man." KAI, by itself, is a common name among the Mandingo people.

Kasamba (*kah*-SAHM-*bah*)   Baganda of Uganda male name meaning "kicker," used for a baby who was active in the womb.

Kaseko (*kah*-SAY-*koh*)   Mashona of Zimbabwe male name derived from the verb *ku seka*, which means "to mock, to ridicule." It could be used, for example, by a woman who previously experienced trouble bearing children and had been taunted by village woman.

Kasim (*kah*-SEEM)   Swahili and Muslim male name meaning "the restrainer, the controller of anger."

Katafwa (*kah*-TAHF-*wah*)   Unisex name of the Tonga of southern Zambia meaning "death." It is used as a nickname for a person who is often sick.

Bush cow ring, bronze. Senufu, Ivory Coast.

Katahali (*kah-tah*-HAH-*lee*)   Ovimbundu of Angola name derived from the expression *ka tala ohali*, which means "he who has seen trouble."

Katito (*kah*-TEE-*toh*)   Ovimbundu of Angola name meaning "little."

Kaula (*kah*-OO-*lah*)   Tonga of Zambia male name meaning "buying." It would be given to someone who buys whatever he sees.

Kaura Namoda (*kow*-RAH *nah*-MOH-*dah*)   A town in northern Nigeria that bears the name of an early nineteenth-century Fulani warrior. Kaura is a Fulani title equivalent to "warlord."

Kazi (KAH-*zee*)   Swahili name meaning "hardworking man" and the Kiswahili word for "work."

Kazimuntu (*kah-zee*-MOON-*too*)   According to Rwandan legend, Kazimuntu is the common ancestor of all people (equivalent to Adam). His three children Gatutsi, Gahutu, and Gatwa are the founders of the three tribes of Rwanda, the Tutsi, Hutu, and Twa.

Keb (*kehb*)   Also GEB (*gehb*), this ancient Egyptian god of the earth was father of Osiris and Isis.

Keffi (KEH-*fee*)   The name of this tin-mining town in central Nigeria is believed to mean "stockade" in a local language.

Kenyi (KEHN-*yee*)   Bari of southern Sudan name for a male born after three or more girls.

Kerimu (*kuh*-REEM-*oo*)   A Nigerian variation of the Muslim name Al-Karim or Al-Kareem, one of the attribute names of Allah that means "the liberal, the generous."

Khedive (*kuh*-DEEV)   This title, used by Turkish viceroys who ruled Egypt from 1867 to 1914, is similar to the English title Lord.

Khensu (HEHN-*soo*, KEHN-*soo*)   A moon god of ancient Egypt. (Note that the initial consonant is pronounced with a guttural sound for which there is no English equivalent; the pronunciations offered are possible English interpretations of the sound.)

Kiambogo (KEE *ahm*-BOH-*goh*)   Kikuyu of Kenya place name meaning "the place of buffalo."

Kibarake (*kee-bah*-RAH-*kay*)   Swahili name meaning "little blessing."

Kibwana (*kee*-BWAH-*nah*)   Swahili name meaning "little man."

Kibwe (KEE-*bway*)   Male name from Central Africa meaning "blessed."

Kidane (*kee*-DAHN-*ay*)   An Ethiopian and Eritrean male name of Ge'ez origin that means "my vow, my covenant."

Kileken (*kil-eh-kehn*)   The Maasai of Kenya and Tanzania name for the planet Venus, the morning and evening star. It means "orphan boy."

Kinfe (*kin*-FAY)   Eritrean and Ethiopian male name meaning "wing." Variations include KENFU (his wing), KENFE (my wing), and KENFA GABREEL (Gabriel's wing).

Kione (*kee*-OH-*nay*)   Luo of Kenya male name meaning "someone who comes from nowhere." Kione was a legendary leader of the Luo people during the 1700s.

Kipkarren (*kip*-KAIR-*ehn*)   This Nandi of Kenya town name means "place of the spears." It can be shortened to either KIP for a boy, or KARREN for a girl.

Kirabo (*chi*-RAH-*boh*) Baganda of Uganda unisex name meaning "gift from God."

Kiros (KEER-*ohs*) Ethiopian and Eritrean version of the Greek name Cyrus, which means "the king."

Kiserian (*ki*-SAIR-*ee-uhn*) Maasai of Kenya and Tanzania word meaning "peace." It is also the name of a village near the town of Ngong in Kenya.

Kiwanuka (*kee-wah*-NOO-*kah*) Baganda of Uganda name meaning "he fell in the womb when the mother didn't know," referring to an unexpected pregnancy.

Kondo (KAHN-*doh*) Vai of Sierra Leone male name meaning "flying fox."

Kono (KOH-*noh*) A peoples of Sierra Leone. The name Kono means "left behind" in Mandinka language and refers to the fact that this group of people decided to remain in the eastern mountainous region of Sierra Leone during the migration of the Mandinka peoples through that country.

Kontar (KOHN-*tahr*) Akan of Ghana name for an only child.

Kosoko (*koh*-SOH-*koh*) Yoruba of Nigeria name for a child born after the mother has had other children die. (See Akuji.) It means "no more hoe (to dig the ground for your burial)" and it is meant to convince the child to stay alive.

Kotsi (KOHT-*see*) Basotho of Lesotho male name meaning "danger, accident." This might be given to a boy born around the time when an accident has occurred that has somehow affected the family.

Kulal (*koo*-LAHL) Samburu of Kenya place name that means "meeting place for the elders." Mount Kulal is a forested mountain in Kenya's northern frontier that stands 7,498 feet (2,287 meters) high.

Kunyo (KUN-*yoh*) Oromo of Ethiopia and Kenya male name meaning "belly button," used for children whose umbilical cord drops off early.

Kuron (KOO-*rahn*) The word for "thanks" in the Kuku language of southern Sudan.

Kuruman (KOO-*roo-mahn*)   A town, river, and hills in northern Cape Province, South Africa. The name means either "calabash," "tortoise," or "place where wild tobacco stands" in different local languages.

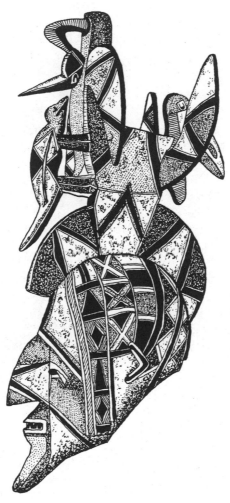

Helmet mask, western Sudan

L

With you I have refound my name,
My name long hidden 'neath the salt of distances.
David Diop, "With You," *Poundings*, 1956

FEMALE

Lakwena (*luh*-KWAY-*nuh*) Acholi of northern Uganda name and term meaning "messenger of the chief." It is also used as a surname.

Langazana (*lahn-gah*-ZAH-*nah*) Ndebele of Zimbabwe name meaning "Miss Earnest-Longing."

Laniyonu (*lah-nee*-YOH-*noo*) Mostly used as a surname, this Yoruba of Nigeria name means "honor is full of troubles." Short forms could be LANI or YONU.

Laoratu (*lah-oh*-RAH-*too*) A Nigerian variation of the Muslim and Swahili female name Ramlah, which means "divination." (See Remi.)

Lemlem (LEHM-*lehm*) Tigrinya of Eritrea and Ethiopia female name meaning "lush, green, fertile."

Lerato (*leh*-RAH-*toh*) Basotho of Lesotho female name meaning "love."

Lewa (LAY-*wah*) Yoruba of Nigeria female name meaning "beautiful." It is often used in compound names such as OMOLEWA. (See entry under O.)

Livanga (*lee*-VAHN-*gah*) Ovimbundu of Angola female name derived from the proverb *livanga oku soka ku livange oku lia*, which means "be first to think, do not be first to eat."

Loba (LOH-*buh*) Lingala of Zaire nickname that means "to talk."

Loiyengalani (*loy-ehn-guh*-LAH-*nee*) A town in Kenya whose name means "the place of many trees." This name could be shortened to LOI or LANI.

Lolonyo (*loh*-LOHN-*yoh*)   Ewe of Ghana female name meaning "love is beautiful."

Lolovivi (*loh-loh*-VEE-*vee*)   Ewe of Ghana female name meaning "love is sweet."

Lostris (LOH-*stris*)   Egyptian name meaning "daughter of the waters."

Luam (*loo*-AHM)   Tigrinya of Eritrea and Ethiopia female name meaning "peaceful, calm."

Lubna (LOOB-*nah*)   Swahili female name meaning "storax." Storax is an aromatic resin obtained from trees.

Lwiindi (LWEEN-*dee*)   Unisex name of the Tonga of Zambia that means "shrine for rain." This would be given to a child born when the villagers were praying for rain at a shrine. Another version of the name is HALWIINDI.

MALE

Ladipo (*lah*-DEEP-*oh*)   Yoruba of Nigeria name meaning "increase honor."

Laibon (*ligh*-BAHN)   Maasai of Kenya and Tanzania title for a prophet.

Lam (*lam*)   Common male name of the Shilluk of the Upper Nile region of southern Sudan.

Lamin (*lah*-MEEN)   This popular male name from Sierra Leone is a version of the Muslim name Amin or Ameen, one of the names of the Prophet Muhammad that means "honest, trustworthy." Nigerian variations of this name are LAMINU (*lah*-MEEN-*oo*) and AMINU (*ah*-MEEN-*oo*).

Lazizi (*lah*-ZEE-*zee*)   A Nigerian variation of the Muslim name Al-Aziz or Al-Azeez, one of the 99 names of Allah that means "the almighty, the powerful." Other Nigerian versions of this name include LASISI (*lah*-SEE-*see*), LAISI (*lah*-EE-*see*), and AZIZ (*ah*-ZEEZ).

Leeto (*lee*-EH-*toh*)   Basotho of Lesotho male name meaning "journey," used for a child born while the mother was on a journey.

Lehana (*lay*-HAH-*nah*)   Basotho of Lesotho male name meaning "one who refuses."

Lencho (LEHN-*choh*)   Oromo of Ethiopia and Kenya male name meaning "lion."

Lesiolo (*leh-see-*OH*-loh*)   Lesiolo is a mountain peak found in Kenya's northern frontier district that stands 8,123 feet (2,478 meters) high. The name is the Samburu word for a type of tree.

Lobi (LOH-*bee*)   Lingala of Zaire word that means both "yesterday" and "tomorrow."

Lodu (LOH-*doo*)   Bari of southern Sudan name for a second born male.

Lolega (*loh-*LEHG*-uh*)   Didinga of southern Sudan name for boys born during the hunting season.

(Bronze) Ife head of Olokun, Nigeria

Luanda Magere (*loo-*AHN*-dah mah-*GEH*-ray*)   A legendary warrior of the Luo peoples of western Kenya whose tale is reminiscent of the biblical story of Samson and Delilah. Luanda Magere married a beautiful princess from another tribe, the Lang'o, against the wishes and advice of Luo elders. His bride showered him with love and drink in order to learn the secrets of his extraordinary strength. She then abandoned him, taking his secrets back to her people.

Luk (pronounced like the English name Luke)   A common Dinka of southern Sudan male name and word meaning "gatherings."

Lusati (*loo-*SAH*-tee*)   Ovimbundu of Angola name for males and females born after the death of the father. It is derived from the word *olusati* that means "a stalk of maize" and could refer to maize stalks that remain in a harvested field.

Lusungu (*loo*-SOON-*goo*) Kibena of Tanzania male name meaning "mercy."

Lutu (LOO-*too*) Swahili version of the biblical male name Lot (Abraham's nephew), which means "veil."

L'uul (*lool*) Tigrinya of Eritrea and Ethiopia male name meaning "prince."

Lweendo (LWAYN-*doh*) Tonga of Zambia unisex name that means "journey." This name is bestowed upon the firstborn of twins, or it might be given to a child who was born while the mother was travelling.

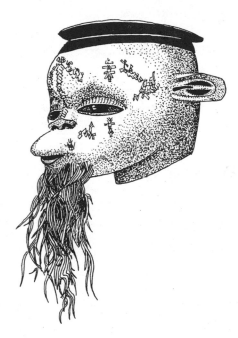

Makonde mask

M

Ewe malikiya   O my queen,
ulo na fahari   proud and glorious
ulo tukukiya   exalted
katika wazuri,   among beautiful women,
nitakuliliya   I will cry for you
mwisho wa umri.   till the end of my life.
first verse of "My Queen," a Swahili love poem.

FEMALE

Maat (*muh*-AHT, MAY-*uht*) Meaning "truth, law," this is the name of an ancient Egyptian goddess of justice, order, and righteousness. She is depicted as a woman with a feather protruding straight up from her head.

Macia (MAH-*syuh*) A village in southern Mozambique. Its name is believed to mean "orphan."

Magara (*mah*-GAHR-*ah*) Mashona of Zimbabwe female name derived from the verb *ku gara*, which means "to sit, to stay."

Maha (MAH-*hah*) Female name used in Muslim cultures in Africa that means "beautiful eyes."

Mahabuba (*mah-hah*-BOO-*bah*) Swahili term of endearment for females that means "loved one, sweetheart." A variation of this same word is MUHABA (*moo*-HAH-*bah*).

Mahajanga (*mah-hah*-JAHN-*gah*) A city and port in northwestern Madagascar. This Malagasy name is believed to mean either "healing one" or it may have come from the local word *mji-angaia*, which means "village of angaia" (a local flowering shrub).

Mahavavy (*mah-hah*-VAH-*vee*) A river in northwestern Madagascar. The name means "making a woman" in the Malagasy language and refers to men who are afraid of the river because of crocodiles. This name could be shortened to

MAHA, which means "capable of, able to" in Malagasy, or VAVY, meaning "woman."

Maikulu (*migh*-KOO-*loo*) Ovimbundu of Angola term meaning "old mother" that is used for grandmothers.

Makadisa (*mah-kah*-DEE-*sah*) Uncommon Mashona of Zimbabwe female name derived from the verb *ku disa*, which means "to like very much."

Makenna (*mah*-KEH-*nah*) Meru of Kenya female name meaning "happiness."

Makiadi (*mah-kee*-AH-*dee*) Bakongo of Zaire unisex name meaning "sad, sorrowful event."

Makula (*mah*-KOO-*lah*) Baganda of Uganda unisex name meaning "pearl."

Malikiya (*mah-lee*-KEE-*yah*) Swahili term meaning "my queen."

Mamagule (*mah*-MAH-*gool*) Mende of Sierra Leone name for a woman with a reddish complexion. (See also Jengo.)

Mandipedza (*mahn-dee*-PAYD-*zah*) Common female name of the Mashona of Zimbabwe that means "to finish." A mother might give a child this name, for example, if it is the last child she plans to bear. Short forms of this name are PEDZA or PEDZI (PAYD-*zee*).

Manica (*muh*-NEE-*kuh*) A province in west central Mozambique. The name Manica is derived from the name of an indigenous peoples of this region, the Nica.

Mariamu (*mahr-ee*-AH-*moo*) Meaning "rebellion," this is a Swahili name referring to the biblical Virgin Mary, the mother of Jesus. Ethiopian and Eritrean versions of this name are MARYAM and MARIAM (MAHR-*ee-ahm*).

Mariatu (*mah-ree*-AH-*too*) A Nigerian variation of the Muslim name Mariyah, which means "pure." Mariyah the Egyptian was one of the wives of the Prophet Muhammad. A variation of this name is MALIETU (*mah-lee*-EH-*too*).

Marka (MAHR-*kah*) Hausa of West Africa female name meaning "steady rain," given to girls born during the rainy season.

Mascara (MAS-*kuh-ruh*) A town in northwestern Algeria. The name is derived from Arabic and means "mother of soldiers." (Note: this name may be confused with the cosmetic of the same name.)

Mashava (*mah*-SHAH-*vah*)   A village in south-central Zimbabwe. The name means "red," in reference to nearby hills that have a reddish hue.

Masusu (*mah*-SOO-*soo*)   Tonga of Zambia unisex name that means "hair."

Matalai Shamsi (*mah-tah*-LAH-*ee* SHAHM-*see*)   According to Swahili legend, this is the name of a beautiful princess known as Princess Sunrise. This could be shortened to SHAM, itself the Kiswahili name for the country of Syria.

Mawu (MAH-*woo*)   According to the Ashanti of Ghana, Mawu is the queen of the universe and represents wisdom.

Mazila (*mah*ZEE-*lah*)   Tonga of Zambia unisex name meaning "road" and used for children born when the mother was travelling.

Mbarushimana (*mbah-roo-shee*-MAH-*nah*)   Kinyarwanda of Rwanda name that means "I am luckier than them." This is used by parents to show their adversaries that they won't be defeated because God loves them more.

Meaza (*meh*-AH-*zah*)   Tigrinya of Eritrea and Ethiopia female name meaning "tastes nice."

Medhin (*meh*-DEEN)   Eritrean and Ethiopian female name of Ge'ez origin meaning "my savior."

Melitte (*meh*-LI-*tay*)   Tigrinya of Eritrea and Ethiopia female name that means "full of grace."

Merhaweet (*mair-hah*-WEET)   Tigrinya of Eritrea and Ethiopia female name meaning "one who brings out of misery, out of trouble."

Meria (*mair*-EE-*ah*)   A Nigerian variation of the Christian name Mary and the Muslim name Maryam, mother of Jesus. The name Mary means "the rebellious one." Another version of the same name is MERIAMU (*mair-ee*-AH-*moo*).

Merkab (*mair*-KEHB)   Tigrinya of Eritrea and Ethiopia female name meaning "ship."

Milandu (*mee*-LAHN-*doo*)   Tonga of Zambia unisex name meaning "a case to answer." A child might be given this name if it was born during a time when the mother was involved in a court case or a dispute of some kind.

Miniya (*mihn*-EE-*yah*)   Tigrinya of Eritrea and Ethiopia female name meaning "I have much expected of her."

Misganna (*mis-*GAH*-nah*)   Tigrinya of Eritrea and Ethiopia female name meaning "gratefulness."

Miyanda (*mee-*YAHN*-dah*)   Tonga of Zambia unisex name meaning "roots." This name might be given if the mother used traditional roots to induce pregnancy, or in the case when a baby is born sickly and traditional roots and herbs are used to help it survive.

Mizan (*mee-*ZAHN)   Tigrinya of Eritrea and Ethiopia female name meaning "balance."

Modupeola (*moh-*DOOP*-ay-oh-*LAH)   Yoruba of Nigeria female name meaning "I thank God (I have done well)." Short forms of this name are DUPE, which by itself means "thanks," OLA, meaning "rich," and MODUPE, meaning "I am grateful."

Monafiki (*moh-nah-*FEE*-kee*)   Hausa of Nigeria name for a person who does mischief.

Monono (*moh-*NOH*-noh*)   Basotho of Lesotho female name meaning "prosperity."

Luba-Shankadi bowl, Zaire.

Mosele (*moh-*SAY*-lay*)   The diminutive form of the South African female name MOSELANTJA, which means "tail of the dog." Considered very ugly, this name is given to a baby when previous children with more attractive names have died. It is believed that the bad fortune will be stopped by selecting a disgusting name.

Mudiwa (*moo*-DEE-*wah*) Shona of Zimbabwe unisex name meaning "beloved." (See Mudikanwi.)

Mugesi (*moo*-GAY-*see*) Luo of Kenya female name. According to legend, Mugesi was the first rainmaker on Mfangano Island in Lake Victoria. She was selected for this honored position by the elders from the other world after she displayed fearlessness when they appeared to her with a blindingly bright light surrounding their forms.

Mugisha (*moo*-GEE-*shah*) Rukiga of Uganda female name meaning "luck."

Mukamutala (*moo-kah-moo*-TAH-*lah*) Kinyarwanda of Rwanda name meaning "she was born during the rule of King Mutala."

Mukamwezi (*moo-kah*-MWAY-*zee*) Kinyarwanda of Rwanda name meaning "she was born in the moonlight."

Mukumbu (*moo*-KOOM-*boo*) A sister of Queen Nzinga of Angola (1583–1663). Queen Nzinga led her people in resisting Portuguese occupation. During one battle in which the Portuguese were victorious, Mukumbu was captured. Queen Nzinga presented the Portuguese with 130 slaves in exchange for her sister's freedom. (See Kifunju for information on another of Queen Nzinga's sisters.)

Muleya (*moo*-LAY-*yah*) Tonga of Zambia unisex name that means "goat, animal." This is a praise name that might be given to a child belonging to a clan whose totem is a goat.

Muliinda (*moo*-LEEN-*dah*) This unisex name of the Tonga of Zambia means "twins" and is given to the second born twin if the firstborn twin dies.

Mumbeja (*moom*-BAY-*jah*) Baganda of Uganda royal title and name meaning "princess."

Munacitonkwa (*moo-nah-chee*-TOHNK-*wah*) Tonga of Zambia unisex name derived from the words *muna*, meaning "follower, subject of," and *tonka*, "to push, to urge." This name might be used for a person from Citonkwa village, or for a person who has been chased out of a village. It could be shortened to MUNA or CITONKWA.

Munashe (*moo*-NAH-*shay*) Common Mashona of Zimbabwe name meaning "the Lord is with you." A popular short form of this name is MUNA (MOO-*nah*).

Mushitara (*moo-shee-*TAH*-rah*) The Kiswahili name for the planet Jupiter. This name could be shortened to TARA or MUSHI.

Muteniteni (*moo-*TEH*-nee-*TEH*-nee*) Zairean nickname that means "firefly." This name could be shortened to MUTENI or TENI.

Muuka (MOO*-kah*) Tonga of Zambia unisex name meaning "insect, reptile." A woman who has had several miscarriages or whose previous children have died may name her baby Muuka.

Mwendalubi (*mwayn-dah-*LOO*-bee*) Unisex name of the Tonga of Zambia meaning "bad luck." This might be used when a baby is born around the time of a funeral.

Mwiinde (MWEEN*-day*) Tonga of Zambia unisex name meaning "to be passed, to be overtaken." A mother might name her child Mwiinde if while she was pregnant she was overtaken by many people while walking on a journey.

MALE

Mabbalani (*mah-bah-*LAH*-nee*) Tonga of Zambia male name that means "writer, court clerk." This name could be shortened to LANI.

Mabili (*mah-*BEE*-lee*) Name of the east wind, which is believed to have carried knowledge and religion to the Bavili people of central-west Africa. The name means "the princely one who calls people together" and "the inspired."

Macharia (*muh-*CHAHR*-ee-uh*) Kikuyu of Kenya male name meaning "lasting friend."

Mafuta (*mah-*FOO*-tuh*) Lingala of Zaire male name that means "fat." It is also the Kiswahili word meaning "oil, fat."

Mahabubu (*mah-hah-*BOO*-boo*) Swahili term of endearment for males that means "loved one, sweetheart."

Mahari (*mah-*HAH*-ree*) Tigrinya of Eritrea and Ethiopia male name derived from Ge'ez meaning "forgiver, one who gives mercy." It is also spelled MEHARI (*muh-*HAH*-ree*).

Mahdi (MAH*-dee*) This Sudanese name comes from the Arabic expression *Al-Mahdi*, which means "the expected one, the rightly guided one." Muhammad Ahmad ibn Abdallah al-

Mahdi (c. 1841–1885) was a Sudanese prophet who led his people against Turko-Egyptian rule in the early 1880s.

Mahu (MAH-*hoo*)   This unisex name of the Tonga of Zambia is considered a non-name. A mother would name her newborn Mahu if she had previous babies that died and she didn't want to undergo the effort of giving the child a person's name only to be disappointed again.

Mai Zaria (*migh-zah*-REE-*uh*)   This Hausa of West Africa term and nickname means "owner of Zaria (a town in northern Nigeria)." The chief or emir of any town or village might be referred to as such. A resident who bears the same personal name as the current chief or emir might also be referred to in this way.

Majambere (*mah-jahm*-BAIR-*ay*)   Kinyarwanda of Rwanda name meaning "he was born when they were developing the country." This might be shortened to BERE or JAMBERE.

Makalo (*mah*-KAH-*loh*)   Basotho of Lesotho male name meaning "wondering."

Makondo (*mah*-KOHN-*doh*)   Tonga of Zambia unisex name meaning "war," used for children born during a time of war or when there is much conflict within the village or family.

Malek (*mah*-LEHK)   A Dinka word used to describe a white bull that has many small black spots mainly around its neck. According to the Dinka of southern Sudan, this is the name of the river spirit.

Maliki (*mah*-LEE-*kee*)   Swahili male name meaning "king, owner" and referring to the angel Maliki, who, according to Swahili belief, is "guardian of the fire."

Malomo (MAH-*loh-moh*)   Yoruba of Nigeria name for a child born after the mother has had other children die. It means "don't go anymore" and is meant to encourage the child to stay alive this time. (See Akuji.)

Manani (*mah*-NAH-*nee*)   Swahili name meaning "the giver," in reference to God.

Mangi Mkuu (MAHN-*gee m*KOO)   Wachagga of Tanzania term for "big chief, headman."

Manjakaze (*mahn-jah*-KAH-*zay*)   The name of a village in southern Mozambique that means "power of blood."

Manyeleti (*mahn-yeh*-LEH-*tee*)   A game reserve in the Transvaal region of South Africa. Manyeleti means "the place of the stars."

Mapopwe (*mah*-POHP-*way*) Tonga of Zambia unisex name meaning "maize." It is used for children born during a good harvest or when the mother is busy harvesting maize.

Marwe (MAHR-*way*) The Nuer of southern Sudan name for their country (The Sudan), which means "land of thirst."

Masa (MAH-*sah*) Masa means "chief" in the Toma language of Guinea. The Massada River in southern Guinea derives its name from this word; MASSADA means "tributary of the chief."

Mashaka (*mah*-SHAH-*kah*) Swahili name and Kiswahili word meaning "trouble." In areas where Kiswahili is spoken, it is fairly common for children to have names that mean trouble. (See also Matata, Shida, and Taabu).

Matondo (*mah*-TOHN-*doh*) Bakongo of Zaire unisex name meaning "thanks to God."

Maulana (*mah-oo*-LAH-*nah*) Swahili name and Kiswahili title meaning "lord."

Mayanja (*mah*-YAHN-*jah*) Baganda of Uganda male name meaning "lake."

Mesfin (*mehs*-FIN) Ethiopian and Eritrean male name that means "royalty, noble."

Mfumu (*m*FOO-*moo*) Bakongo of Zaire male name meaning "hero, leader."

Mequanent (*meh*-KWAH-*nehnt*) Amharic of Ethiopia male name meaning "village headman."

Messina (*meh*-SEE-*nah*) A copper-mining town in northern Transvaal, South Africa. The name is believed to come from the Venda word *musina*, which means "the spoiler."

Michelo (*mee*-CHAY-*loh*) Tonga of Zambia unisex name that means "roots, herbs." It might be used, for example, if the parents used traditional herbs to induce pregnancy.

Mijoga (*mee*-JOH-*gah*) Giriama of Kenya name meaning "warlike." This is the name of a generation born during a time when there were wars being fought with the Oromo, a neighboring tribe.

Mikaili (*mee-kah*-EE-*lee*, *mee*-KIGH-*lee*) The Swahili version of the biblical name Michael, which means "God-like." Michael

is the prince of angels who provides sustenance to all
creatures on earth.

Mirembe (*mee-*RAYM-*bay*)   Baganda of Uganda unisex name
that means "peace."

Mlulami (*mloo-*LAHM-*ee*)   Xhosa and Zulu of South Africa male
name meaning "a kind person."

Mo (*moh*)   This prefix used in the Lingala language of Zaire
means "the substance of life."

Modu (MOH-*doo*)   This commonly heard name in Sierra Leone
means "son of." It is generally placed after the mother's
name. For example, the son of Kali might be known as Kali
Modu, the son of Jengo would be called Jengo Modu.

Mogai (*moh-*GUY)   Another name for Ngai, the Supreme God of
the Kikuyu people of Kenya. Mogai resides on Mount Kenya
and is revered as "the Divider of the Universe," "the Lord of
Nature," and "the God of All Things."

Moi (*moy*)   Kalenjin of Kenya name meaning "calves." President Daniel arap Moi became the second president of Kenya
in 1978.

Moivumba (*moy-*VOOM-*bah*)   Mende of Sierra Leone name for a
tall man. (See also Pajonga.)

Moke (*moh-*KAY)   In northern Zaire this word is quite frequently attached to male names to mean "junior, little, the
younger of the two." For instance, if a man named Molali has
a son also called Molali, the son would be referred to as
Molali Moke, meaning "little Molali."

Mokonzi (*moh-*KOHN-*zee*)   A Zairean word for "chief, headman, boss."

Momo (MOH-*moh*)   Mende of Sierra Leone variation of the
Muslim male name Mohammed, which means "the praised
one."

Mopepe (MOH-*pay-pay*)   Lingala of Zaire word for "wind." In
some dialects the word is MUPEPE (MOO-*pay-pay*).

Mona (MOH-*nah*)   A nickname from Swaziland used for a male
exhibiting jealous characteristics. It is derived from the word
umona, which means "jealousy."

Morathi (*moh-*RAH-*thee*)   Kikuyu of Kenya name for a seer or a
wise man.

Morlai (MOR-*ligh*)   Susu of Sierra Leone name for second-born males.

Motsamai (*moht-sah*-MAH-*ee*)   Basotho of Lesotho male name meaning "the traveller." The Basotho believe that some names affect a person's character. Thus, if a boy is called Motsamai, it is believed he will one day become an avid traveller.

Motu (MOH-*too*)   Lingala of Zaire word for "person, human."

Mounir (*moo*-NEER)   This Muslim male name heard in North Africa means "radiance, brilliant, luminous." Also spelled MUNIR and MUNEER, it is one of the many names of the Prophet Muhammad. Nigerian variations of this name include MUNIRU (*moo*-NEER-*oo*) and MINIRU (*mee*-NEER-*oo*). Swahili variants are MUNIIR and MUNIRI (*moo*-NEER-*ee*).

Mpula (*m*POO-*luh*)   Mpula was a local chief in northern Mozambique who is the namesake of both a town and district called Nampula. Mpula means "rain." It is also the name of Chief Mpula's people, who believe they were created from rain, in the same manner that plants are grown.

Muchese (*moo*-CHAY-*say*)   Mashona of Zimbabwe male name meaning "blade of a knife or hatchet." This name might be given to a child whose father is an excellent craftsman.

Mudashiru (*moo-dah*-SHEE-*roo*)   A Nigerian variation of the Muslim name Mudath thir, one of the names of the Prophet Muhammad that means "the cloaked one." This name could be shortened to MUDA, SHIRU or perhaps DASH.

Mudikanwi (*moo-dee*-KAHN-*wee*)   Common Shona of Zimbabwe name for males and females that means "beloved." A popular variation of this name is MUDIWA (*moo*-DEE-*wah*).

Muftau (*moof*-TOW, rhymes with "now")   A Nigerian variation of the Muslim name Miftahu-r-Rahmah, which means "key of mercy." Another Nigerian version of this name is MUFUTAU (*moo-foo*-TOW).

Mugabe (*moo*-GAH-*bay*)   The name used for kings of the Nkore Kingdom of southwestern Uganda.

Mugambi (*moo*-GAHM-*bee*)   Meru of Kenya male name that means "leader" or "headman."

Muhisani (*moo-hee*-SAH-*nee*)   The Swahili version of the name

Benedictus. It means "the one who is blessed by the Almighty with good qualities." The name is related to the Kiswahili word MUHISINI (*moo-hee*-SEE-*nee*), which means "magnanimous person, benefactor."

Muhongo (*moo*-HOHN-*goh*) A mother of the Ovimbundu of Angola may name her child Muhongo if she has an unusually long pregnancy. Traditionally, to alleviate the problem, she would consult a witch doctor and wear a cap decorated with strands of beads that fall across her face.

Mukadamu (*moo-kah*-DAH-*moo*) A Nigerian version of the Muslim name al-Muqaddam, one of the 99 names of Allah that means "the presenter, the forewarner, the advancer."

Mukama (*moo*-KAH-*mah*) The word for "king" in the Tembuzi Kingdom of southwestern Uganda.

Mulahi (*moo*-LAH-*hee*) Tonga of Zambia unisex name meaning "ants." This name would be used by a woman whose previous children had died, probably following the African tradition of selecting unattractive names for children in the hope that evil spirits will pass over them.

Coffeepot, called a Jebena, Eritrea.

Mulangira (*moo*-LAHN-*ji-rah*) Baganda of Uganda royal title and male name meaning "prince."

Mulefu (*moo*-LAY-*foo*) Swahili male name meaning "tall, lanky."

Mulele (*moo*-LAY-*lay*) Tonga of Zambia nickname for a boy or man who is lazy or tired all the time.

Murogi (*moo*-ROH-*gee*) Kikuyu of Kenya term meaning "black magic."

Muse (MOO-*say*) This Luo of Kenya male name was the name of the forefather of the

Wakula clan of Mfangano Island in Lake Victoria.

Museveni (*moo*-SEH-*veh-nee*) Lunyankole of Uganda male name meaning "veteran." Yoweri K. Museveni became president of Uganda in 1986.

Musoke (*moo*-SOH-*kay*) Baganda of Uganda male name meaning "rainbow."

Mussie (*moo-see*-AY) Eritrean and Ethiopian version of the biblical name Moses, which means "saved from the water."

Mutafa (*moo*-TAH-*fah*) A Nigerian variation of the Muslim name al-Mustafa. This is one of the many names of the Prophet Muhammad and means "the chosen one, the selected." Another Nigerian version of this name is TAFA (TAH-*fah*).

Mutia (*moo*-TEE-*uh*) The Embu and Kamba people of Kenya use this name, meaning "the honored one," as a title for those who have inherited honorary positions in society.

Mwalimu (*mwah*-LEE-*moo*) This Kiswahili word means "teacher." It is used as a title of respect in East Africa. The first president of Tanzania, Julius K. Nyerere, was referred to as Mwalimu.

Mwami (*m*WAH -*mee*) A title used in Rwanda and Burundi that is equivalent to "sultan" or "king."

Mwangi (*m*WAHN-*gee*) Very common Kikuyu of Kenya male name meaning "father of many children."

Mwani (*m*WAH-*nee*) A central African word meaning "lord" or "chief." Early Portuguese explorers (1482–83) learned of Mwani Kongo, "Lord of the Kongo people," who ruled the region south of the Zaire River.

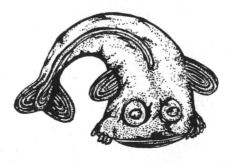

Bronze weight of the Bamun,
Ivory Coast.

N

*A hare, upon meeting a lioness one day, said reproachfully,
"I have always a great number of children while you have
only one or two now and then." The lioness replied, "That
is true, but my one child is a lion."*
an Ethiopian fable written by Lokman (c. 1100 B.C.E.)

FEMALE

Nabawanuka (*nah-bah-wahn-*OO-*kah*)   Baganda of Uganda name
that translates as "she fell in the womb when the mother
didn't know," and means that the mother became pregnant
unexpectedly.

Nabunya (*nah-*VOON-*yah*)   Baganda of Uganda female name
meaning "dimples." (Note that the "b" sounds very airy, like
a cross between "b" and "v.")

Nacala (*nuh-*KAH-*luh*)   In the Lomwe language of Mozambique
this word literally means "calm, peace, and tranquility" and
figuratively is used to mean "a place where people stay."
There are two towns in Mozambique with this name, both
located on Baia Fernão Veloso, an Indian Ocean inlet. These
towns may have been given the name Nacala in reference to
the bay's calm waters.

Nafuna (*nah-*FOO-*nah*)   Baganda of Uganda name for a girl
delivered feet first.

Nagode (NAH-*goh-day*)   Hausa of West Africa female name
meaning "I thank you," derived from the Hausa word *godiya*,
which means "thank you."

Nahimana (*nah-hee-*MAH-*nah*)   Kinyarwanda of Rwanda name
meaning "it's God's will" and "God will decide." This is also
a Kinyarwanda expression used when someone having diffi-
culties has exhausted all means to find a solution.

Najma (NAHJ-*mah*)   Swahili and Muslim female name meaning "star."

Nakafelo (*nah-kah*-FAY-*loh*)   Baganda of Uganda name used by the Enkima clan meaning "monkey."

Nakima (*nah*-KEE-*muh*)   The Swahili name for Noah's Sea (biblical).

Nakimuli (*nah-chee*-MOO-*lee*)   Baganda of Uganda female name that means "flower."

Nalo (NAH-*loh*)   Senufo of West Africa unisex name meaning "lovable."

Nalubale (*nah-loo*-VAH-*lay*)   Female name of the Baganda of Uganda that means "the Nile." (Note that the "b" is very airy, pronounced like a cross between "b" and "v.")

Nampelo (*nahm*-PAY-*loh*)   Baganda of Uganda name meaning "monkey."

Namusoke (*nahm*-SOH-*kay*)   Female name of the Baganda of Uganda that means "rainbow."

Nanteza (*nahn*-TAY-*zuh*)   Nanteza was the Queen Mother of the Buganda people of Uganda in the mid-1700s. She was the mother of kabakas (kings) Junju and Semakookiro.

Nasha (NAH-*shah*)   Maasai of Kenya and Tanzania name for females born during the rainy season.

Natorma (*nah*-TOR-*mah*)   Two females of the Susu of Sierra Leone who bear the same name can refer to each other by this nickname to mean "my namesake."

Nebyat (*neh-bee*-YAHT)   Tigrinya of Eritrea and Ethiopia name of Ge'ez origin that means "prophetess."

Nekhbet (NEHK-*beht*)   One of the earliest goddesses of ancient Egypt, Nekhbet is the guardian of the south. She is depicted as a vulture holding a ring in her claws and hovering over the king. She is also known as NEKHEBET (NEHK-*uh-beht*), NEKHEBIT (NEHK-*uh-bit*), and NEKHEBT (*neh*-KEHBT).

Netsenet (*neht-tsah*-NEHT)   Tigrinya of Eritrea and Ethiopia female name meaning "freedom."

Nieleni (*nyee-leh*-NEE)   Bambara of West Africa female name meaning "hardworking woman" and especially referring to a woman who can compete with men in food production.

Njeri (*n*-JAIR-*ee*)   Popular Kikuyu of Kenya female name meaning "belonging to a warrior, daughter of a warrior."

Nokofa (*noh*-KOH-*fah*) Fingo of South Africa female name meaning "mother of death." This name might be given to a girl born when a member of the family is dying.

Nomvula (*nohm*-VOO-*lah*) Xhosa of South Africa female name meaning "rain."

Nomzamo (*nohm*-ZAH-*moh*) Xhosa of South Africa name meaning "trial," referring to the belief that the child will face many trying times in her life. This is Winnie Mandela's Xhosa name.

Nontando (*nohn*-TAHN-*doh*) Xhosa of South Africa female name meaning "full of love."

Nontutuzelo (*nohn-too-too*-ZAY-*loh*) Xhosa of South Africa female name meaning "the comforter, the consoler."

Nosente (*noh*-SEHN-*tay*) Xhosa of South Africa female name meaning "mother of compassion."

Nsomi (*n*SOH-*mee*) A Zairean word used when referring to children who are well behaved. Such an adjective could be used as either a nickname or birth name for a child.

Nthara (*n*THAH-*rah*) Embu of Kenya female name meaning "the snatcher."

Ntirushize (*ntee-roo*-SHEE-*zay*) Kinyarwanda of Rwanda name meaning "it is not finished." This name is used if other children have died and the parents want to express that they are not sure that this newborn will live.

Ntombizodwa (*n*TOHM-*bee*-ZOHD-*wah*) Common Xhosa and Ndebele of southern Africa female name that means "daughters only." A short form of this name is ZODWA.

Ntozake (*ntoh*-ZAH-*kay*) Zulu of South Africa name that means "she comes with her own things."

Nturanyeninkiko (*ntoo-rah-nyay-neen*-KEE-*koh*) Kinyarwanda of Rwanda name meaning "I live near the courthouse (or the border)." There are various ways this name could be shortened, including TURA, YENIN, and KIKO, the latter of which is also a Kiswahili word meaning "pipe" (for smoking).

Nut (*noot*) Called the Lady of Heaven, Nut was the ancient Egyptian goddess of the sky. She is depicted as a woman with outstretched wings, or as a cow carrying the sun god Re on her back with stars on her underside.

Nyako (NYAH-*koh*) Dholuo of Kenya word for "girl."

Nyamekye (*nyah*-MAY-*chay*)   Twi of Ghana unisex name meaning "child given by God."

Nyariji (*nyah*-REE-*jee*)   Luo of Kenya female name meaning "daughter of Riji." *Nya* means "daughter of" in the Dholuo language.

Nyeki (NYEH-*kee*)   Luo of Kenya name for a second wife.

Nyeri (NYAIR-*ee*)   Embu of Kenya female name. It is also the name of a rural trading town in Kenya's central highlands. Nyeri, sometimes referred to as the "capital of Kikuyuland," is located near the foot of the Abedare Mountains.

Nyirabigega (*nyee-rah-bee*-GAY-*gah*)   This Kinyarwanda of Rwanda name is used by parents who have a granary loft. Giving a child this name expresses that the family has enough to eat and are not in need. This name could be shortened to NYIRA or RABI.

Nyoka (NYOH-*kah*)   Lingala of Zaire nickname meaning "snake." It is also the Kiswahili word with the same meaning.

Nzali (*nZAH-lee*)   Kikinubu of Tanzania female name meaning "protection."

Nzila (*nZEE-lah*)   Tonga of Zambia female name meaning "road, path, way," used for children born on the road to the hospital. A variation of this name is MAZILA.

Nzirubusa (*nzee-roo*-BOO-*sah*)   Kinyarwanda of Rwanda name that means "I am treated badly for no reason." Parents who have been punished for something they didn't do might give a child this name.

MALE

Nafasi (*nah*-FAH-*see*)   Swahili name meaning "to love good times" and a Kiswahili word meaning "spare time, opportunity."

Naiser (*nigh*-SAIR)   This Maasai male name refers to the founder of one of the five original Maasai clans.

Namaqua (NUH-*mah-kwuh*)   The plural form of the name of the Nama, a Hottentot people of Namibia. Namaqua means "men of men."

Narigisi (*nahr-ee*-GEE-*see*)   This is the Kiswahili version of the name Narcissus. According to Greek mythology, Narcissus was a handsome youth who fell in love with his own reflection in a pool of water until he was transformed into a flamboyant flower of the same name. The Narcissus flower is frequently recalled by Swahili poets as a symbol of a beautiful woman's eyes.

Nasiru (*nah-*SEER*-oo*)   A Nigerian variation of the Muslim name Nasir, which means "helper, assistant."

Navo (NAH-*voh*)   Uncommon male name from Sierra Leone meaning "money."

Ndoki (*n*DOH-*kee*)   Ndoki is a virgin rain forest in the Congo that is home to lowland gorillas. The name means "dark magic, sorcerer."

Nfatorma (N*fat-*OR*-mah*)   Two males of the Susu of Sierra Leone who bear the same name can refer to each other by this nickname which means "my namesake."

Skull guardian figure. Kota, Gabon.

Ngayabarambirwa (*ngah-yah-bah-rah-m*BEER*-wah*) Kinyarwanda of Rwanda name meaning "I hate people who aren't patient." This name could be shortened in various ways, including NGAYA and MBIRWA.

Ngonga (*n*GOHN-*gah*)   Ovimbundu of Angola male name meaning "eagle."

Niko (NEE-*koh*)   Kiswahili for "I am here."

Niyibizi (*nee-yee-*BEE*-zee*)   Kinyarwanda of Rwanda name that means "God knows." Parents who are having problems at the time of their child's birth might use this name to express their confidence that God will help them.

Nkejuwimye (*nkay-joo-*WEEM*-yay*)   Kinyarwanda of Rwanda name meaning "anyone can be my leader, I respect the one who wins."

Noma (NOH-*mah*)   Hausa of West Africa male name meaning "farming." SARKIN NOMA is a title meaning "chief of the farmers" and is used for the presidents of farmers organizations.

Ntampuhwe (*ntahm-*POO*-way*)   Kinyarwanda of Rwanda name meaning "no pity." This name may be chosen by parents who are having problems and no one seems to want to help them. The parents are feeling sorry for themselves and in turn are expressing that they don't pity anyone else either. Ntampuhwe might also be used if someone who had been very helpful to the parents has died, in which case the name refers to death having no pity.

Ntimbanjayo (*nteem-bahn-*JAH*-yoh*)   Wagoni of Tanzania male name meaning "one who takes big strides." Possible short forms of this name could be BANJA, JAYO, or TIM.

Nyabera (*nyah-*BAIR*-ah*)   Luo of Kenya male name that means "the good one."

Nyakallo (*nyah-*KAH*-loh*)   Unisex name of the Basotho of Lesotho meaning "merriment."

Nyiragerero (*nyee-rah-gay-*RAY*-roh*)   Kinyarwanda of Rwanda name for a child born at the market or when the mother has just returned from the market. This name might be shortened to GERE or RAY.

Nzitunga (*nzee-*TOON*-gah*)   Kinyarwanda of Rwanda name that means "I depend only upon myself."

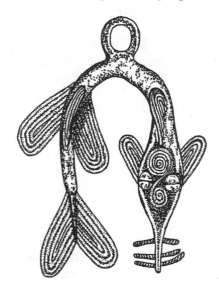

Catfish pendant of the Akan people of Ghana. The catfish represents danger from the Asante proverb "The river fish's game is no safe game."

O

*A man's deeds are of greater importance than the facts
of his birth.*
Maasai of East Africa proverb

FEMALE

Oafe (*oh*-FAY)   Ishan of Nigeria name meaning "your descent matters."

Oafetalo (*oh-fay*-TAH-*loh*)   Ishan of Nigeria name meaning "you must have support to be bold."

Okahandja (*oh-kuh*-HAHN-*juh*)   A town and river in central Namibia. Okahandja means "the small wide one."

Oke (*oh*-KAY)   Yoruba of Nigeria name meaning "a bag," used for a child born when the membrane has not ruptured.

Oku (*oh*-KOO)   Yoruba of Nigeria name that means "the dead" and is used by a mother who has had other children die. (See Akuji.)

Olabisi (*oh-lah*-BEE-*see*)   Unisex name of the Yoruba of Nigeria meaning "increased honors." It is also used as a surname.

Olajumoke (*oh-lah-joo*-MOH-*kay*)   Yoruba of Nigeria name meaning "everybody is raising me." Short forms could be OLA, MOKE, or JUMOKE. (See entry for Jumoke.)

Olufemi (*oh-loo*-FEH-*mee*)   Yoruba of Nigeria name meaning "God loves me." Although traditionally this was primarily a boy's name it is now being used by both males and females. This name could be shortened to FEMI.

Oluina (*oh-loo*-EE-*nah*)   Ovimbundu of Angola term meaning "the family of my mother."

Olusola (*oh-loo*-SHOH-*lah*)   Unisex Yoruba of Nigeria name meaning "God does me honor." A short form is SOLA.

Olutobi (*oh-loo*-TOH-*bee*)   A Yoruba of Nigeria unisex name meaning "God is mighty." A short form of this name is TOBI.

110

Oluwatoyin (*oh-loo-wah*-TOHN-*yee*) Yoruba of Nigeria female name meaning "The Lord to be praised, God is worthy of worship." Popular short forms of this name are OLUTOYIN and TOYIN. (This name is fairly difficult to pronounce; check with a native Yoruba speaker to hear the name said precisely.)

Omodara (OH-*moh*-DAH-*rah*) Yoruba of Nigeria female name meaning "the child is good."

Omolewa (OH-*moh*-LAY-*wah*) Yoruba of Nigeria female name meaning "the child is beautiful."

Opelenge (*oh-pay*-LAYN-*gay*) Yoruba of Nigeria female oriki name for a slender person. (See Aduke.)

Opeyemi (OHK-*pay*-YEH-*mee*) Yoruba of Nigeria unisex name meaning "glory be to me."

Orilonise (*oh-ree-loh*-NEESH-*ay*) An obscure Yoruba of Nigeria name derived from the sentence "it is my good fortune or destiny that makes me what I am, so please do not begrudge me." This is more often used as a proverb than as a name. It could be shortened to NISE.

Orma (OR-*muh*) This is the name that one branch of the Oromo people living in Kenya use for themselves. It signifies "free men."

Otiti (*oh*-TEE-TEE) An Ishan of Nigeria generic name for baby girls. This name is given to all baby girls for their first three months until a permanent name is selected. This is similar to the Edo name for baby girls, Atiti. (Ishan is a dialect of the Edo language.)

MALE

Oburu (*oh*-BOOR-*oo*) Luo of Kenya male name for a child born during a traditional funeral rite in which cows are chased, representing the chasing away of evil spirits, which allows the dead to pass to the otherworld in peace. The name is derived from the Dholuo word *buru*, which means "ash."

Ochola (*oh*-CHOH-*lah*) Luo of Kenya male name used when the father died while the mother was pregnant.

Odheru (*oh*-THAIR-*oo*, "th" as in "the") Luo of Kenya traditional basket name (see Adita) referring to a flat, tray-like basket.

Ogbe (OHG-*bay*) Tigrinya of Eritrea and Ethiopia male name meaning "shelter."

Oginga (*oh*-GIN-*guh*)   Luo of Kenya male name meaning "one who drums, the drummer." Jaramogi Oginga Odinga (c. 1912–1994), a leader of Kenya's independence struggle, served as the country's first vice president in Jomo Kenyatta's administration. After leaving government service, Odinga was a long-time opposition figure in the country and was the political leader of Kenya's Luo people, the second largest ethnic group in the country.

Ogundipe (*oh-goon*-DEE-*pay*)   Yoruba of Nigeria name meaning "Ogun (the god of war) consoles me with this." A popular short form of this name is DIPE.

Ogwel (*oh*-GWEHL)   Luo of Kenya male name meaning "bowlegged."

Okal (*oh*-KAHL)   Luo of Kenya male name meaning "to cross, to go beyond."

Okumu (*oh*-KOO-*moo*)   Luo of Kenya male name used when a woman gets pregnant before menstruating.

Okuthe (*oh*-KOOTH-*ay*)   Luo of Kenya male name meaning "the thorny one."

Olaniyonu (OH-*lah-nee*-YOH-*noo*)   Yoruba male name meaning "riches entail problems." A Yoruba proverb says, *The man who stumbles on riches names his son Olaniyonu.* This proverb is used to comment on a person who attempts to play down newly acquired wealth as a roundabout way of boasting.

Olatunde (*oh-lah*-TOON-*day*)   Edo of Nigeria name meaning "wealth comes again."

Olen Kijabe (OH-*lehn-kee*-JAH-*bay*)   In the Maasai language of Kenya and Tanzania this means "the cold place." Kijabe is a small town in central Kenya that sits 7,000 feet (2,135 meter) high. It is the site of an important missionary station in East Africa that includes a hospital and boarding high school.

Oliech (*oh-lee*-AYCH)   Luo of Kenya male name derived from the Dholuo word *liech*, which means "elephants."

Olujimi (*oh-loo*-JEE-*mee*)   Yoruba of Nigeria male name meaning "God gave me this."

Olumoroti (*oh-loo-moh*-ROH-*tee*)   Uncommon unisex name of the Yoruba of Nigeria that means "it is only with God that I stand." A short form could be MOROTI.

Omel (*oh*-MEHL)   Luo of Kenya male name. According to tradition, Omel was grandson of Okal, founder of the Luo people. Omel led the Luo from their original home in southern Sudan into western Kenya where they now reside.

Omope (*oh*-MOH-*pay*)   Yoruba of Nigeria name meaning "the child is late." It is used for those children born after the normal nine-month gestation period.

Ooko (*oh*-OH-*koh*)   Luo of Kenya male name used when the mother doesn't arrive at the hospital in time for the baby's delivery. It is derived from the Dholuo word *oko*, which means "outside."

Oringo (*oh*-REEN-*goh*)   Luo of Kenya male name for someone who likes to hunt and to eat meat. The Dholuo word *ringo* means "meat."

Orwa (*or*-WAH)   Luo of Kenya male name used if the baby gave the mother trouble during pregnancy. (Pronounced properly, the "r" is rolled.)

Otuho (*oh*-TOO-*oh*)   The Otuho are an ethnic group living in the Equatoria Province of southern Sudan. Their name means "finishing" or "diminishing" in reference to the group's tendency to fight others as a test of bravery and power and their subsequent loss of men due to this trait.

Owino (*oh*-WEEN-*oh*)   Luo of Kenya name for a boy born with the umbilical cord wrapped around his neck. This name is derived from the Dholuo word *wino*, which means "umbilical cord."

Small bronze masks represent the faces of enemies killed in battle. Baole of Ivory Coast.

Owiti (*oh*-WEE-*tee*)   Luo of Kenya male name that means "sent away" and refers to the ritual of symbolically sending newborns away in a basket. (See Adita.)

Oyewole (OH-*yay*-WOH-*lay*)   Yoruba of Nigeria name meaning "title enters the house." Traditionally this name was used for children born into high-class or royal families. A popular short form of this name is WOLE.

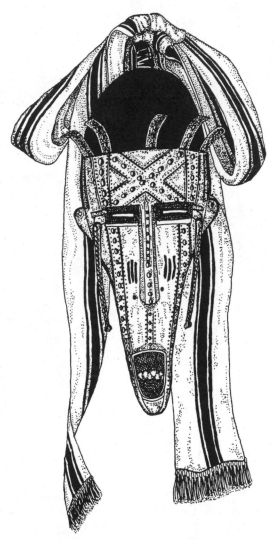

Marka mask, Mali

P

Quiet, my brother
Don't cry, baby
So mother may come back
From the farm with some grain
The grains of millet
Sleep now, our child
Our mother is on the way
Quiet my brother.

> traditional lullaby of the
> Kalenjin of Kenya

FEMALE

Paingoni (*pah-een-*GOH-*nee*) Massai of Kenya and Tanzania name adopted by females or males who have exchanged a large bull.

Paleley (*puh-*LAY-*lay*) The word for "sweet" in the Kuku language of southern Sudan.

Palesa (*pah-*LAY-*sah*) Basotho of Lesotho female name meaning "flower."

Pandasala (*pahn-dah-*SAH-*lah*) Ovimbundu of Angola female name derived from the proverbial saying *O pandasala utima wove; kutima wukuene ombala yikuavo*. Literally this translates as "you search your own heart; at the heart of another village another" and means "the heart knows its own bitterness but it cannot know that of another."

Pasua (*pah-*SOO-*ah*) Swahili name for a child born by Caesarean operation. It is derived from the Kiswahili word of the same spelling, which means "to tear, to split."

Patanisha (*pah-tah-*NEE-*shah*) Swahili name meaning "reconciliation" derived from the Kiswahili verb of the same spelling, which means "to reconcile."

MALE

Pandare (*pahn-dahr-*AY)   A Massai of Kenya and Tanzania name adopted by males or females who have exchanged several goats.

Pajonga (*pah-*JOHN-*guh*)   Mende of Sierra Leone name for a tall man. (See also Moivumba.)

Paulo (*pah-*OO-*loh*)   A Bantu form of the biblical name Paul, used by the Banyoro of western Uganda as a christening name. Paul means "a place of rest."

Piipi (PEE-*pee*)   This unisex nickname of the Tonga of Zambia represents the sound of a horn. It is given to children who like to make honking noises when playing with toy cars.

Polo (POH-*loh*)   Basotho of Lesotho male name derived from the word *polomahwashe*, meaning "alligator."

Polongoma (*poh-loh-n*GOH-*muh*)   Male name of the Luo-Abasuba people of Kenya. Polongoma was a leader of the Wasaki clan who lived on Mfangano Island in Lake Victoria during the 1800s.

Popota (*poh-*POH-*tah*)   Tonga of Zambia male name that means "talkative, shouter." It is used for persons who tend to dominate conversations, sometimes even by shouting.

Maiden spirit mask, Nigeria

R

Instruction in youth is like engraving in stones.
Berber of North Africa proverb

FEMALE

Rabi (RAH-*bee*) A Nigerian variation of the Muslim name Rabiatul-Adawiyyah, a Muslim mystic known for her selfless service to and love of God.

Rabia (*rah*-BEE-*ah*) Swahili version of the Muslim name Rabiyah, which means "spring" and is probably related to the name above.

Rahab (RAY-*hab*) A biblical female name meaning "large," which was used as a symbolic term for the country of Egypt, then considered an insolent and violent place.

Rahwa (*rah-huh*-WAH) Tigrinya of Eritrea and Ethiopia female name meaning "coming out of misery," especially referring to people whose economic status has improved.

Rakaya (*ruh*-KIGH-*yuh*) An unusual Tunisian female name derived from the Arabic word meaning "soft."

Ramona (*rah*-MOH-*nah*) Basotho of Lesotho female name that means "selfishness."

Ramota (*rah*-MOH-*tah*) A Nigerian variation of the Muslim name Rahmah, which means "mercy." Rahmah was wife of the Prophet Ayyub (Job). Another Nigerian version of this name is RAMAT (*rah*-MAHT).

Remi (REH-*mee*) A Nigerian variation of the Muslim and Swahili name Ramlah. (See Laoratu.)

Rig'at (*rig*-AHT) Tigrinya of Eritrea and Ethiopia female name meaning "calm, settled." Traditionally this name was given to girls born during times of peace in a community.

Rimka (RIM-*kah*) Eritrean version of the biblical name Re-

117

becca, which means "she who ensnares with the tender bonds (as in marriage)."

Rishan (*ri*-SHAHN) Tigrinya of Eritrea and Ethiopia female name that means "palace, big building."

Rita (REE-*tah*) Hausa of West Africa female name meaning "engagement ring, betrothal."

Riziki (*ree*-ZEE-*kee*) Swahili female name and Kiswahili word meaning "sustenance."

Rogo (ROH-*goh*) Hausa of West Africa female name meaning "cassava" and signifying "fertile." Also, a Luo of Kenya surname.

Rozi (ROH-*zee*) East African female name derived from the English word and name "rose."

Ruakari (*roo*-KAH-*ree*) A Banyankole of southwest Uganda clan name. It is also used as a personal name by descendants of the clan.

Rukia (*roo*-KEE-*uh*) This popular female name in Somalia is a variation of the Muslim female name Ruqiyyah. Ruqiyyah means "superior" and refers to one of the Prophet Muhammad's daughters. Nigerian variants include RUKA (ROO-*kah*), REKHIA (RAY-*kee-ah*), and RAKIATU (*rah-kee*-AH-*too*).

MALE

Rabana (*rah*-BAH-*nah*) This Swahili term means "Our Lord God." It can also be spelled RABUNA (*rah*-BOO-*nah*).

Rabo (RAH-*boh*) Hausa of West Africa name meaning "luck." Although this is a unisex name it is used most often for males.

Rach (*rahch*) Oromo of Ethiopia and Kenya male name meaning "frog." Parents whose previous children had died might select this negative name in an attempt to ward off evil.

Raffet (RA-*feht*) Arabic male name commonly heard in Egypt meaning "high rank, dignity."

Raimi (*rah*-EE-*mee*) A Nigerian variation of the Muslim name ar-Raheem or ar-Rahim, which means "the most compassionate" and is one of the 99 names of Allah.

Ramadhani (*rah-mah*-THAH-*nee*) A Swahili name for those born during Ramadan, the ninth month of the Muslim year, marked by fasting each day from sunrise to sunset. A Muslim version of this name is RAMADAN (*rah-mah-DAHN*).

Ramosa (*rah-MOH-sah*) Basotho of Lesotho name meaning "the friendly one, the merciful one."

Ramses (*RAM-seez*) This name of twelve kings of Egypt means "sun born."

Re (*ray*) Also known as RA (*rah*), he is a mythological sun god of ancient Egypt. Also known as the father of the gods and the god of kings, Re is usually represented by a hawk's head crowned by a golden disk.

Reth (*rehth*) The title used by royal families of the Shilluk people of southern Sudan equivalent to "king."

Rezene (*reh-ZEHN-ay*) Tigrinya of Eritrea and Ethiopia male name meaning "with heavy pride."

Risku (*REES-koo*) Hausa of West Africa male name meaning "prosperity."

Russom (*roo-SOHM*) Tigrinya of Eritrea and Ethiopia male name meaning "their head, their boss."

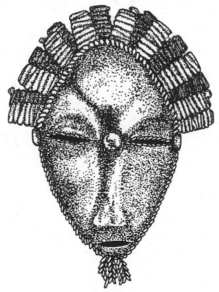

Baule people of Cote D'Ivoire i small bronze mask, representing the face of enemy killed in battle.

S

There is no wealth where there are not children.
Liberian proverb

FEMALE

Sadatina (*sah-dah-*TEE-*nah*)   This Swahili term means "our lady, my lady." It is also spelled SAIDATINA (*sah-ee-dah-*TEE-*nah*) and could be shortened to SADA or TINA.

Safara (*sah-fah-*RAH)   Ethiopian and Eritrean female name of Ge'ez origin meaning "her place," referring to the Virgin Mary.

Safina (*sah-*FEE-*nah*)   The Kiswahili word meaning "Noah's Ark."

Sakegamada (SAH-*kay-guh-*MAH-*duh*)   This name of a village in Takaba Division of northeastern Kenya means "happy hill" in the Oromo language.

Sarama (*sah-rah-*MAH)   Bambara of West Africa word meaning "nice girl, beautiful girl."

Sarda (SAHR-*dah*)   Oromo of Ethiopia and Kenya name meaning "hastily, hurried." This name might be used if the birth was rushed or perhaps as a nickname for a child that rushes around all the time.

Sayidana (*sah-yee-*DAH-*nah*)   A Swahili term of endearment meaning "our princess."

Sefiyetu (*say-fee-*EH-*too*)   A Nigerian variation of the Muslim name Safiyyah, which means "pure" and refers to a wife of the Prophet Muhammad.

Seghen (SEH-*gehn*)   Tigrinya of Eritrea and Ethiopia female name meaning "ostrich."

Sekhmet (SEHK-*meht*)   Meaning "powerful," this was the name of an ancient Egyptian goddess. Sekhmet was depicted as having a woman's body and a lionness's head accompanied by a solar disk and a cobra. She represented the sun's destructive powers.

Selas (*seh*-LAHS)   An Eritrean and Ethiopian female name of Ge'ez origin meaning "Trinity."

Luba-Shankadi neck rest. Zaire

Semainesh (*seh*-MIGH-*nehsh*)   An Eritrean name of Amharic origin that means "you are the sky."

Semira (*seh*-MEER-*ah*)   Tigrinya of Eritrea and Ethiopia female name meaning "fulfilled."

Serwa (SAIR-*wah*)   Ghanaian female name meaning "jewel."

Shahrazad (SHAH-RUH-ZAHD)   Swahili female name meaning "princess." It is a version of the name Scheherazade, one of the protagonists of the fable the *Arabian Nights*. According to the story, this Persian beauty married a king who intended to behead her, but for 1,001 nights she wove such fascinating tales about characters such as Aladdin, Ali Baba, and Sinbad that the king fell in love with her and rescinded his plan.

Shamsa (SHAHM-*sah*)   Also SHAMSIYA (*shahm*-SEE-*yah*)and SHEMSA (SHEHM-*sah*), this Swahili female name means "sun, sunshine." An Egyptian form is SHAMS (*shahms*).

Shangazi (*shahn*-GAH-*zee*)   The Kiswahili word for "aunt," although in urban areas "aunti" is more commonly used.

Shangwa (SHAHN-*gwah*)   Mashona of Zimbabwe female name derived from the word of the same spelling, which means "famine." A child born during a period of hunger might be given this name.

Shangwe (SHAHN-*gway*)   Swahili female name and Kiswahili word that means "rejoicings, celebration."

Shasa (SHAH-*sah*)   Bushman of the Kalahari (southern Africa) name that means "good or precious water."

Sherehe (*shair*-AY-*hay*)   Kiswahili word meaning "triumphant rejoicing."

Sheshe (SHAY-*shay*)   A Kiswahili word for "beauty."

Shiba (SHEE-*buh*)   Swahili female name and Kiswahili word meaning "full, satiated, satisfied."

Shida (SHEE-*duh*)   Swahili name and Kiswahili word meaning "trouble, hardship."

Shori (SHOH-*ree*)   A Swahili name for the crested nightingale, a songbird heard before sunrise on the East African coast.

Shumpa (SHOOM-*pah*)   Tonga of Zambia name used for female children who are troublesome.

Sibajene (*see-bah*-JAY-*nay*)   Unisex name of the Tonga of Zambia that means "did not find." It might be chosen, for example, if the mother gave birth in another village before she could find the headman of that village. This name could also be used if the father dies soon after the child's birth.

Sika (SEE-*kah*)   Twi of Ghana female name meaning "money."

Sikujwa (*see*-KOOJ-*wah*)   Swahili name for a child born unexpectedly.

Simini (*si-mi*-NEE)   Susu of Sierra Leone name for a baby girl who has some features like her grandmother. The name means "looks like grandmother."

Simwatalana (*see-mwah-tah*-LAH-*nah*)   Tonga of Zambia unisex name meaning "talkative." Short forms could be TALANA or LANA (Lana itself is a female name of Latin origin meaning "the woolly one, the soft and cuddly one").

Sondo (SOHN-*doh*)   Tonga of Zambia name for children born on Sunday.

Sudetu (*soo*-DAY-*too*)   A Nigerian variation of the Muslim female name Shuhdah, who was a prominent twelfth-century intellectual from Baghdad.

Suubi (SOO-*vee*)   Baganda of Uganda unisex name meaning "hope." (Note that the "b" is very airy, pronounced like a cross between "b" and "v.")

MALE

Sadiki (*sah*-DEE-*kee*) A Swahili variation of the Muslim name as-Sadiq, which means "the truthful" and is one of the names of the Prophet Muhammad. Sadiki is also a Kiswahili verb meaning "to believe." Nigerian versions of this name include SADIKU (*sah*-DEE-*koo*)and SEDI (SEH-*dee*).

Saidi (*sah*-EE-*dee*) Swahili male name meaning "helper." SAID is an Arabic variant of the same name.

Saitoti (*sigh*-TOH-*tee*) Maasai of Kenya and Tanzania male name meaning "the one who is generous."

Salako (*sah-lah*-KOH) Yoruba of Nigeria name for a male born with his head and body covered with the ruptured membrane.

Salimu (*sah*-LEE-*moo*) Swahili male name and Kiswahili verb meaning "to greet."

Samawati (*sah-mah*-WAH-*tee*) Kiswahili word and place name meaning "sky blue" and "a heavenly place."

Sarki (SAHR-*kee*) A Hausa of West Africa title for a chief.

Satima (*sah*-TEE-*muh*) Maasai word meaning "young bull calf," this is the name of the highest peak of the Aberdare Mountains in Kenya. Satima is 13,120 feet (4,002 meters) high. The full Maasai name for this mountain is Ol Doinyo Lesatima.

Sautu (*sah*-OO-*too*) Tonga of Zambia male name that means "salt." It might be given, for example, to a child whose deceased relatives ate a lot of salt.

Sem'on (*sehm*-OHN) Eritrean and Ethiopian version of the biblical name Simon, which means "(The Lord) hath heard."

Sendibada (*sehn-dee*-BAH-*dah*) This Swahili male name comes from the Kiswahili expression *siendi baada*, which means "I'm not coming after" or "I am always there before everybody else." It is also believed to be a version of the name Sinbad, the famed Persian traveller who made seven wonderful sea voyages as one of the protagonists in the story the *Arabian Nights*.

Sengendo (*sayn*-GEHN-*doh*) Baganda of Uganda male name meaning "journeys."

Senwe (SAYN-*way*) An uncommon Mashona of Zimbabwe male name derived from a word meaning "a dry stalk of grain," indicating that the child was thin and feeble at birth.

Shaihi (SHAY-*hee*) Hausa of West Africa term of respect meaning "the knowledgeable one." SHAIHUN MALLAMI (SHAY-*hoon*-MAH-*lahm-ee*) is the title used for a professor. It is derived from *shaihi* plus *mallam*, a Hausa word meaning "teacher," which is equivalent to the Kiswahili word *mwalimu*. (See entry under M.)

Shamafuta (*shah-mah*-FOO-*tah*) Nickname for males of the Tonga of Zambia meaning "fat." It would be used for someone who likes eating the fat from meat. (See Mafuta.)

Shamshuni (*shahm*-SHOO-*nee*) Swahili version of the biblical name Samson which means "the man from the east, sunlike." Samson, was a judge of Israel for twenty years and was noted for his great strength.

Shange (SHAHN-*gay*) Zulu of South Africa name that means "who walks like a lion."

Shekarau (*shay-kahr*-OW) This popular Hausa of West Africa male name means "longer than a year" and is applied to children that stay in the womb longer than nine months. It may also be used as a nickname for someone who stays away from home for a long period.

Shopo (SHOH-*poh*) This old-fashioned male name of the Mashona of Zimbabwe refers to a type of spear that is no longer used.

Shuka (SHOO-*kah*) Hausa of West Africa male name meaning "to sow (as in farming)."

Siaju (*see*-AH-*joo*) Tonga of Zambia male name meaning "hunter."

Siapole (*see-ah*-POH-*lay*) Nickname for males of the Tonga of Zambia that means "no problem."

Sibbilishokwe (*see-bee-lee*-SHOH-*kway*) Tonga of Zambia male name meaning "traveller." This might be used if the baby's father travels or goes hunting often. Short forms of this name could be BILI or SHOKWE.

Sid (*seed*) A term of respect attached to Muslim male names that is very commonly used in Mauritania and other parts of North Africa. Also spelled SIDI, the term can be translated as "lord," "chief," or "prince." Examples of this type of compound name are SID-MUKHTAR (*seed*-MOOK-*tahr*) and SID-RAH-MAN (seed-RAH-mahn). (Mukhtar means "the chosen one" and Rahman means "the merciful.")

Sikoliwe (*see-koh*-LEE-*way*) Sindebele of Zimbabwe name meaning "we have enjoyed ourselves, we are satisfied."

Siluwe (*see*-LOO-*way*) Nickname for males of the Tonga of Zambia that means "leopard."

Sinumvayabo (*see-noom-vah*-YAH-*boh*) Kinyarwanda of Rwanda name that means "I don't listen to their words." This name is used when someone, such as a neighbor, has given the parents bad advice or has gossiped about them. The parents use this name to show that the other person is mistaken. SINU, VAYABO, or YABO might be short versions of this name.

Sinzabakwira (*seen-zah-bahk*-WEE-*rah*) Kinyarwanda of Rwanda name meaning "I am not enough to be shared between them." This name is used when the parents have many enemies. The parents are telling the enemies that they should cease because there is no reason to betray people like them. This name could be shortened to SINZA, BAKWIRA, or ZABAK.

Sishokwe (*see*-SHOHK-*way*) Tonga of Zambia male name meaning "hunter."

Sulemani (*soo-lay*-MAHN-*ee*) This is the Swahili version of the biblical Solomon, the last of King David's sons by Bathsheba. The name means "peaceful."

Sumana (*soo*-MAH-*nah*) A Mende of Sierra Leone variation of the Muslim name Othman, which means "wealthy" and refers to the third Khalifa (secular and religious head of Islam).

Suntwe (SOON-*tway*) A nickname for males of the Tonga of Zambia that means "hyena." This might be used for a person who is very mobile like a hyena.

T

I go out to dribble my name
over your footmarks in the dirt: Tafataona;
Before we die yet, we shall have seen . . .
Before we die yet, we shall have realized
Why should you name a child so?

Tafataona Mahoso

FEMALE

Tadelesh (*tah-deh-*LEHSH) Tigrinya of Eritrea and Ethiopia female name meaning "lucky."

Tadj (*tahdj*) Swahili female name meaning "crown." It is related to the Kiswahili word for crown, TAJI (TAH-*jee*).

Taifa (TIGH-*fuh*, *tah-*EEF-*ah*) This Kiswahili word means "nation" or "tribe."

Takaba (*tah-*KAH-*bah*) The main town of the Takaba Division of northeastern Kenya. Its name means "short cut" or "stride" because it is considered the center of everything in the area.

Talabi (*tah-lah-*BEE) Yoruba of Nigeria name for female children born with the head and body covered with the ruptured membrane.

Tala-Tala (TAH-*lah-*TAH-*lah*) Kikongo and Lingala of central Africa word meaning "mirror" and described as "something full of light, like water, that you can see through to the other world." Also spelled Talatala, it has been used as a nickname.

Tamanisha (*tah-mah-*NEE-*shah*) Kiswahili verb meaning "to allure."

Tamasha (*tah-*MAH-*shah*) Swahili name meaning "happy occasion" and Kiswahili word for "pageant, a show."

Tarakwet (TAHR-*ah-kweht*) Pokot of Kenya name meaning "cedar trees." Tarakwet is a mountain in the Turkana region that rises 8,259 feet (2,519 meters) high.

Tarana (*tah*-RAH-*nah*) Hausa of West Africa name for females born in daytime, derived from the word *rana*, meaning "day."

Tazara (*tah*-ZAHR-*ah*) The nickname for a railway line constructed in 1975 running between Tanzania on the East African coast and the inland country of Zambia. The Tazara line was built to bypass South African ports—at the time being boycotted because of the country's apartheid system—to deliver goods to landlocked southern African nations.

Tenen (*teh*-NAY) Bambara of West Africa name for females born on Monday.

Teshi (TAY-*shee*) Kiswahili word meaning "cheerful, prone to laughter."

Thanayi (*tan*-AH-*yee*) Xhosa of South Africa name meaning "child of happiness."

Thandeka (*tan*-DAY-*kuh*) Zulu of South Africa female name meaning "the loved one."

Thandiwe (TAN-*dee-way*, *tahn*-DEE-*weh*) Common Zulu, Xhosa, and Ndebele of southern Africa female name meaning "beloved." The short form of this name is THANDI (TAN-*dee*).

Thema (TAY-*mah*) Akan of Ghana name meaning "queen."

Themba (TEHM-*bah*) Zulu of South Africa female name meaning "trusted."

Thembeka (*tehm*-BAY-*kuh*) Zulu and Xhosa of South Africa female name meaning "trustworthy."

Tiaret (*tyahr*-EHT) A town in northern Algeria. The name is believed to mean "lioness."

Tiassale (*tyah*-SAH-*lay*) A village in southern Cote d'Ivoire. There are several beliefs on how this location earned its named. Some believe that a former queen remarked, *tiassale*, meaning "it is forgotten," upon departing the village.

Dogon ring. Mali.

Others say that the name is derived from the Baule word *gyassale*, which means "the rocks are there." It may also come from the name of the river spirit Tiassa. (This name could be shortened to TIASSA.)

Tibletz (*tib*-LEHTZ) Tigrinya of Eritrea and Ethiopia female name that means "may she outshine, may she outsmart."

Timneet (*tim*-NEET) Tigrinya of Eritrea and Ethiopia female name meaning "wish."

Tolulope (TOH-*loo*-LOH-*pay*) Yoruba of Nigeria female name meaning "praise be to the Lord." This name is derived from *olu*, meaning "Lord," and *ope*, meaning "praise." TOLU is a common short form of this name.

Trhaas (*tur*-HAHS) Tigrinya of Eritrea and Ethiopia female name meaning "may she bring blessings."

Tsabo (*tSAY-boh*) Female name of the Basotho of Lesotho meaning "knowledge." (Note that the initial sound is similar to the "ts" sound one makes when calling someone's attention.)

Tsitsi (SEET-*see*) A popular female name in Zimbabwe meaning "mercy."

Tumaini (*too-mah*-EE-*nee*) Swahili female name and Kiswahili word meaning "hope."

Twamvula (*twahm*-VOO-*lah*) Tonga of Zambia unisex name for the last born of many children. It means "numerous, too much."

MALE

Taabu (TAH-*boo*) Swahili unisex name and Kiswahili word meaning "trouble, difficulty."

Tafataona (*tah-fah-tah*-OH-*nah*) Zimbabwean name that means "before we die, we shall have seen."

Tai (*tigh*) A Kiswahili word for "eagle." Another Kiswahili word for eagle is KOHO (KOH-*hoh*).

Taka (TAH-*kah*) Luo of Kenya male name and the name of a forefather of the Wakinga clan living on Mfangano Island. *Taka* is also a Kiswahili verb meaning "to want."

Tanko (TAHN-*koh*) Very popular Hausa of West Africa name for the first son born after several daughters.

Tata (TAH-*tah*) Both the Bakongo and Xhosa word for father. Tata is also a Kiswahili word meaning "to tangle, perplex."

Tatau (*tah*-TAH-*oo*)   Hausa of West Africa male name meaning "aristocrat."

Tayari (*tah*-YAH-*ree*)   Swahili name and Kiswahili word meaning "ready."

Tayibu (*tah*-YEE-*boo*)   A Nigerian form of the Muslim name Tayyib, one of the names of the Prophet Muhammad that means "the good one, the chaste one."

Tefo (TEHF-*oh*)   Basotho of Lesotho male name meaning "payment."

Tekie (*tehk-ee*-AY)   Tigrinya of Eritrea and Ethiopia male name meaning "I have replaced, I have substituted." This would be used, for example, if the child was born after a brother or sister had died, or after the parents had fulfilled a difficult mission. An Amharic version of the name is TEKKU (TUH-*koo*).

Tesfazghi (*tehs*-FAHZ-*gee*)   Also spelled TASFAZGI, this Eritrean and Ethiopian male name of Ge'ez origin means "God's hope, promise of the Lord."

Tesfu (*tehs*-FOO)   Tigrinya of Eritrea and Ethiopia male name meaning "his hope."

Teshome (*tay*-SHOH-*may*)   Tigrinya of Eritrea and Ethiopia male name meaning "give a title," signifying that the family expects the child to become a leader, to bear a title.

Tewelde (*tuh*-WEHL-*day*)   Eritrean and Ethiopian male name of Ge'ez origin meaning "he was born." This can be used in compound names such as TEWELDE BERHAN (the Light was born) and TEWELDE MEDHIN (the Savior was born).

Thothmes (TOHT-*mehs*, THOTH-*mehz*)   A black Egyptian general and ruler of Egypt during the second millennium. A former priest, Thothmes expanded the Egyptian kingdom.

Tiju-Iku (*tee-joo*-EE-*koo*)   Yoruba of Nigeria name meaning "be ashamed to die," used for a child born after a mother has had previous children die. (See Akuji.)

Tirfe (TEER-*fay*)   Tigrinya of Eritrea and Ethiopia male name meaning "spared."

Tochukwu (*toh*-CHOO-*koo*)   Igbo of Nigeria male name that means "praise God."

Topwe (TOH-*pway*)   Mashona of Zimbabwe name referring to a type of vegetable.

Toubou (TOO-*boo*)   The name of a people living in the Tibesti mountain region of northern Chad. These indigenous residents of the Sahara Desert are nomadic herders and number only about 150,000. The name Toubou is believed to mean "man from Tibesti."

Tumbui (*toom*-BOO-*ee*) Mende of Sierra Leone name for a short man. (See also Gendeme.)

Tumo (TOO-*moh*) Basotho of Lesotho male name meaning "fame."

Turkana (*tur*-KAH-*nah*) The Turkana people live in the semi-arid plains of northwestern Kenya around Lake Turkana. Turkana means "people of the caves" because these people originally lived in caves on mountainsides for protection.

Tutankhamun (TOOT-*ahngk*-AH-*muhn*) Meaning "living image of Amun (the air and wind god)," this was the name of an Egyptian king of the eighteenth dynasty. Also spelled TU-TANKHAMON and TUTANKHAMEN, King Tut's treasure-filled tomb was discovered by archaeologists in 1922.

Tuyeni (*too*-YEH-*nee*) Popular unisex name of the Ovambo of northern Namibia that means "let us go." An example has been cited of this name being given to a baby boy whose mother had lived for many years in exile during Namibia's struggle for independence from South Africa.

Twaambo (TWAHM-*boh*) Unisex name of the Tonga of Zambia that means "talkative, quarrelsome." This name might be given if there is a dispute over who is really the father of the child.

Twon (*twown*) Acholi of northern Uganda word for a "strong, important person, a bull."

U, V

Va undila ohumba longalo; ocipala kundila.

You can borrow a basket and a sieve;
you cannot borrow a face.

Ovimbundu of Angola proverb on individuality,
used by women who have lost a child

FEMALE

Ufwenuka (*oo-fway-*NOO-*kah*) This Tonga of Zambia name is said to mean "to lift up one's head when feeling hungry or cold."

Uhuti (*oo-*HOO-*tee*) Swahili term meaning "my sister."

Ujana (*oo-*JAH-*nah*) A Kiswahili word meaning "youth."

Ummi (OO-*mee*) This Swahili female name and term means "my mother." It is related to the Muslim name Umm, which means "mother" and refers to Umm Kulthum, one of the daughters of the Prophet Muhammad. Nigerian variations of this name include UMU (OO-*moo*), KULUSUMI (*koo-loo-*SOO-*mee*), KATIMU (*kah-*TEE-*moo*), and KATUMI (*kah-too-mee*).

Upendo (*oo-*PEHN-*doh*) Swahili unisex name and Kiswahili word meaning "love."

Vatukemba (*vah-too-*KAYM-*bah*) Ovimbundu of Angola female name derived from the proverbial saying *va tu kemba; Suku wa tu kemba omuenyo*, which means "they lie to us; God lied to us about life."

Vatusia (*vah-too-*SEE-*ah*) A woman of the Ovimbundu of Angola might adopt this name of despair after loved ones have died. It is derived from the proverbial saying *va tu sia*, which means "they leave us behind."

Visolela (*vee-soh-*LAY-*lah*) Ovimbundu of Angola female name derived from the proverb *ovisolela violomupa; vi pungula vio-*

Ikhoko pendant, worn by the Bapend. Zaire.

pongala. This literally translates as "longings are waterfalls; those you pick over are of the drying trays" and means that one can use good judgment about ordinary things in life, like sorting beans and maize on drying trays, but affairs of the heart are uncontrollable like waterfalls.

Vondila (*vohn*-DEE-*lah*) A woman of the Ovimbundu of Angola might give herself this name of despair after she has lost a child. It is derived from the proverb *va undila ohumba longalo; ocipala kundila*, which means "one may borrow a basket and a sieve; a face you cannot borrow."

Vumba (VOOM-*bah*) Mashona of Zimbabwe female name derived from the verb *ku fumba*, which means "cause to die." This name is used especially by mothers who have lost many children.

MALE

Uba (OO-*bah*) Hausa of West Africa male name meaning "father, Lord." Uba is frequently heard as a nickname for eldest sons because the firstborn male child in a family is often named after his father or grandfather, thus others refer to this child as Uba as a sign of respect for his namesake.

Umi (OO-*mee*) Luo of Kenya male name meaning "servant."

Urowo (*oo*-ROH-*woh*) Luo of Kenya male name that means "tall."

Usenge (*oo*-SAYN-*gay*) Ovimbundu of Angola name for a male child born in a field or in the woods. It is derived from the words *ka usenge* which mean "the bush."

Uwamahoro (*oo-wah-mah*-HOH-*roh*) Kinyarwanda of Rwanda name meaning "peacemaker."

Uwamurengeye (*oo-wah-moo-rayn*-GAY-*yay*) Kinyarwanda of Rwanda name used when a parent has been betrayed by someone who should have supported them, such as a family member or a friend. It could be shortened to MURENGE or RENGE.

Uwimana (*oo-wee*-MAH-*nah*) Kinyarwanda of Rwanda name meaning "belongs to God."

Uwitonze (*oo-wee*-TOHN-*zay*) Kinyarwanda of Rwanda name used as a way to advise someone to go slowly with things.

Uwizeye (*oo-wee*-ZAY-*yay*) Kinyarwanda of Rwanda name meaning "trust in God, he will give you everything."

Uzabakiliho (*oo-zah-bah-kee*-LEE-*hoh*) Kinyarwanda of Rwanda name meaning "one who lives in the future understands the present."

Vembo (VAYM-*boh*) Mashona of Zimbabwe male name meaning "mushuku juice." (Mushuku is the fruit of the loquat tree.)

Vumilia (*voo-mee*-LEE-*ah*) Swahili male name and Kiswahili word meaning "have courage, bear patiently."

Mythological God of ancient Egypt. Best protector of women in childbirth. Egypt.

W

The fruit must have a stem before it grows.
Jabo of West Africa proverb

FEMALE

Wahu (WAH-*hoo*)   Kikuyu of Kenya female name that means "the pregnant one."

Walta (WAHL-*tah*)   Tigrinya of Eritrea and Ethiopia female name meaning "shield."

Wamuhu (*wah*-MOO-*hoo*)   Kikuyu of Kenya female name meaning "from the ash."

Waraka (*wah*-RAH-*kah*)   Swahili female name and Kiswahili word that means "letter, document." According to Swahili legend, Waraka was a fortune-teller during the time of Mohammed.

Weynee (WAY-*nee*)   Also spelled WEINI, this Tigrinya of Eritrea and Ethiopia female name means "grape." A compound variation of this name is TSEGEWEINI (*tseh-geh*-WAY-*nee*), meaning "pollen of the grape plant."

Winta (WEEN-*tah*)   Tigrinya of Eritrea and Ethiopia female name meaning "desire."

Wonye (WOHN-*yuh*)   Vai of Liberia and Sierra Leone name for a large ant. Ugly names such as this are used to ward off death and evil, especially by a mother who has had other children die.

Wubet (*wuh*-BEHT)   Tigrinya of Eritrea and Ethiopia female name meaning "beauty." An Amharic variation of this name is WUB (*wuhb*).

Wudasse (*woo*-DAH-*say*)   Tigrinya of Eritrea and Ethiopia female name meaning "praise."

134

MALE

Wagulo (*wah*-GOO-*loh*)   The name of an ethnic group living on Rusinga Island in Lake Victoria, Kenya. Wagulo means "grandfathers."

Wahran (*wah-huh*-RAHN)   The name of a medieval Berber chief. It is derived from the Berber word *iren*, which means "lions." Wahran is the Arabic version of the name Oran, a city and province in northwestern Algeria.

Waiyaki (*wigh*-YAH-*kee*)   Swahili male name meaning "unto you."

Wal (*wahl*, pronounced staccato)   A common male name of the Dinka of southern Sudan. Wal was a religious prophet of the early 1900s. The word wal means "medicine" in Dinka language. When it is used as a name it can mean "luck" or "magic."

Waluwi (*wah*-LOO-*wee*)   The name of this clan of people living in western Kenya means "fishermen."

Wasaki (*wah*-SAH-*kee*)   The name of this ethnic group found in western Kenya means "the enemy."

Wigasi (*wee*-GAH-*see*)   Luo-Abasuba of Kenya word meaning "restless." Wigasi Hill is found in the Homa Bay area of western Kenya. It got its name from an eighteenth-century ruler and the founder of the Wagasi clan, Koboye, who loved to wander and hunt.

Wolde'ab (wehl-deh-AHB)   Eritrean and Ethiopian male name of Ge'ez origin meaning "son of God." Wolde, which means "son of," is a prefix used in combination with other names; a variant spelling of this prefix is WALDA. Examples include WOLDE MARIAM (son of Mariam), WOLDE DAWIT (son of David), and WALDA BERHAN (son of the Light).

Worede (*wuh-ruh*-DAY)   Eritrean and Ethiopian male name meaning "came from above, he descended." Variations of this name are WARRADA and WEREDE.

X, Y

Ancient things remain in the ears.
Ashanti of Ghana proverb

FEMALE

Xinavane (*shee-nah-*VAH-*nay*)   A village in southern Mozambique. The name is derived from the Changana word *nava*, which means "to spread, to propagate," in reference to the fertile land of the area on which anything will grow.

'Yar Arziki (*air-*AHR-*zee-kee*)   Hausa of West Africa name meaning "daughter of fortune." It is most often used as a term of endearment and encouragement for well-behaved children. *Yar* is a Hausa term for "daughter" and *arziki* means "prosperity, wealth, riches."

Yasumini (*yah-soo-*MEE-*nee*)   A Swahili version of the name Jasmine, which is a shrub bearing fragrant flowers found on the coast of East Africa as well as in other locales around the world. Also spelled YASMIN (YAHS-*meen*), the name symbolizes "friendliness" and "sweetness."

Yehdega (YEH-*deh-gah*)   Tigrinya of Eritrea and Ethiopia female name meaning "let her life be spared."

Yejide (*yeh-jee-*DEH)   Yoruba of Nigeria name meaning "the image of her mother."

Yendelela (*yayn-day-*LAY-*lah*)   Ovimbundu of Angola female name derived from the proverb *ya endelela ka lelalela pekonjo*. This translates literally as "the animal that keeps going does not stay fat on the hoof" and means that a person who is prestigious at home is ignored when among strangers. This could be shortened to YENDE or LELA.

Yenge (YEHN-*gay*)   Mende of Sierra Leone female name meaning "work."

Yetunde (*yeh-*TOON-*day*)   Yoruba of Nigeria name meaning

136

"mother comes back," used for the first female child born after the death of her paternal grandmother. A popular short form of this name is TUNDE.

Yirga-Alem (*yir-gah-ah*-LEHM) Tigrinya of Eritrea and Ethiopia female name meaning "let the world settle, let the world calm down."

MALE

Xolani (*!koh*-LAH-*nee*) Xhosa of South Africa male name meaning "please forgive." (Note that the initial "k" should be said with a clicking sound.)

Yaka Laman (YAH-*kah lah*-MAHN) This Oromo of Ethiopia and Kenya name means "the two baobabs" and is the name of a historical site in eastern Kenya.

Yakubu (*yah*-KOO-*boo*) Also spelled YA'QUUB, this Swahili name is a version of the biblical Jacob, the son of Isaac. The name means "supplanter."

Yalwa (*yahl*-WAH) This popular Hausa of West Africa unisex name means "abundance, plenty." It may be used to infer that the child will bring good fortune, or that the child was born in times of prosperity.

Yaro (YAH-*roh*) Hausa of West Africa name meaning "son."

Yassoungo (*yah*-SOON-*goo*) Senufo of West Africa unisex name meaning "something you adore."

Yeremiya (*yair-ay*-MIGH-*uh*) A Bantu form of the biblical name Jeremiah, used by the Banyoro of western Uganda as a christening name. Jeremiah means "exalted."

Yeshak (*yuh*-SHAHK) Ethiopian version of the Hebrew name Isaac which means "laughter."

Yifter (YIF-*tur*) Tigrinya of Eritrea and Ethiopia male name meaning "let him create."

Yigo (YEE-*goh*) Soninke of West Africa term for a young man.

Yikealo (*yi*-KAH-*loh*) Tigrinya of Eritrea and Ethiopia male name meaning "He is able" (referring to God). This name is usually used after a period of infertility.

Yilma (YIL-*mah*) Also spelled YELMA, this Amharic of Ethiopia male name means "may he prosper."

Yohana (*yoh*-HAH-*nah*) This Eritrean male name has just come into vogue in the last few years. Yohana is a term that was coined during Eritrea's recent independence from Ethiopia to mean "congratulations."

Yomi (YOH-*mee*)   Nigerian name meaning "save me."

Yosefu (*yoh*-SAY-*foo*)   A Bantu form of the biblical name Joseph, used by the Banyoro of western Uganda as a christening name. Joseph means "increase." A Swahili version of this name is YUSUFU (*yoo*-SOO-*foo*).

This cross, called a Barchekeia, is a popular design among the Hausa women.

Z

Zaila from a distant town,
Zaila from a distant town,
Whoever sees Zaila gives a thousand (cowries),
Even if it breaks a poor man,
Or he gives her five hundred.

Song for Zaila, from the book *Baba of Karo: A Woman of the Muslim Hausa* (1954)

FEMALE

Zaafarani (*zahah-fah-*RAH-*nee*)   Swahili female name meaning "saffron."

Zaila (*zah-*EE-*lah,* ZIGH-*luh*)   Hausa of Nigeria female name.

Zaire (ZIGH-*ear,* *zah-ear*)   The name of this country in central Africa is a Portuguese corruption of the local word for river, *nzari* (*n*ZAIR-*ee*). Zaire straddles the equator and is four times the size of France.

Zamangirra (*zah-mahn-*GEER-*ah*)   This unusual Hausa of West Africa female name literally means "the permanence of the eyebrow." One story tells of a second wife who decided to give her new female slave this name as a way of warning her husband's first wife that just as the eye (the second wife) cannot be separated from the eyebrow (the first wife)—no matter how much they dislike each other—this slave girl could not be separated from the second wife, no matter how much the first wife dislikes the fact that the second wife acquired such a valuable possession.

Zara Maryam (ZAHR-*ah* MAHR-*ee-ahm*)   Ethiopian name of Ge'ez origin meaning "seed of Mary."

Zarina (*zah-*REE-*nah*)   Swahili female name meaning "golden." It could be shortened to ZARI, itself a Kiswahili word meaning "golden thread, brocade."

Zebib (*zeh*-BEEB)   Tigrinya of Eritrea and Ethiopia female name meaning "raisin." This is also the name of a popular alcoholic beverage produced in Asmara, the capital of Eritrea, which is reminiscent of the aniseed-flavored Greek liqueur ouzo.

Zene (ZAY-*nay*)   A Nigerian variation of the Muslim name Zaynab, which means "beautiful" and refers to a wife of the Prophet Muhammad as well as his eldest daughter. Another Nigerian variant of this name is ZAINABU (*zay*-NAH-*boo*).

Zenaga (ZI-*nah-guh*)   These Berber people of West Africa were traditionally warlike nomads living along the banks of the Senegal River in northern Senegambia. Their name is one possible origin of the country name Senegal.

Zewdi (*zoh*-DEE)   Unisex name from Eritrea that means "crown."

Zindzi (ZIND-*zee*)   Common Xhosa and Zulu of South Africa female name meaning "to be anchored, to be stable." This is the name of one of the daughters of Nelson and Winnie Mandela.

Zufan (*zoo*-FAHN)   Tigrinya of Eritrea and Ethiopia female name meaning "throne."

Zuli (ZOO-*lee*)   A Nigerian variation of the Muslim name Zalikha or Zulaykha, which means "brilliant, ahead" and refers to a wife of the Prophet Yusuf (Joseph). Other versions of this name include ZENIATU (*zeh-nee*-AH-*too*) and SULI (SOO-*lee*).

Zwelitsha (*zweh*-LEET-*shuh*)   A township in the eastern Cape Province of South Africa. Zwelitsha is a Xhosa name meaning "new world."

MALE

Zaci (ZAH-*see*)   According to the Bavili people of central-west Africa, Zaci is the god of fatherhood. He is represented by thunder, lightning, and tornadoes.

Zaki (ZIGH-*kee*)   Hausa of West Africa male name meaning "lion" and signifying "prowess."

Zakwani (*zah*-KWAH-*nee*) Swahili male name meaning "thriving." A nickname could be ZAK.

Zamoyoni (*zah-moh*-YOH-*nee*) A Swahili male name meaning "of the heart." This could be shortened to MOYO, itself a name and word meaning "heart," as well as ZAMO or YONI.

Zenawi (*zehn-ah*-WEE) Tigrinya of Eritrea and Ethiopia male name that means "good news." A short form could be ZENA, itself an Amharic name meaning "news, fame."

Zeru (*zeh*-ROO) Tigrinya of Eritrea and Ethiopia male name meaning "his seeds, descendent of." This name is often used in combination with other names, such as ZERU DANIEL (*zeh*-ROO *dahn-ee*-EHL), which mean "descendant of Daniel."

Zimanakwangwa (*zee-mah-nah*-KWAHN-*gwah*) Tonga of Zambia male name that means "a person who travels a great deal." This name could be shortened in various ways, such as ZIMA, MANA, or ZIMANA.

Ziraili (*zee-rah*-EE-*lee*) The Swahili version of the biblical name Azriel, which means "help of God."

Zo (*zoh*) Vai of Sierra Leone and Liberia term for a spiritual leader.

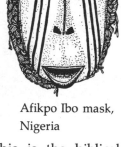

Afikpo Ibo mask, Nigeria

Zoan (ZOH-*ahn*) Meaning "departure," this is the biblical name for an ancient city located along the Nile River in Lower Egypt. The city was called Tanis by the Greeks and is known as San in modern times.

Zoob (*zoob*) A Nigerian variation of the Muslim name Zubayr ibn Awwam, who was a companion of the Prophet Muhammad. Other Nigerian forms of this name, which means "strong, brave," include ZEBERU (*zeh*-BAIR-*oo*) and ZUBERU (*zoo*-BAIR-*oo*).

Zwelithini (*zwehl-eh-*TEE-*nee*)   Zulu of South Africa male name meaning "what is the nation saying?" This is the name of the current Zulu king. Translated literally it means "what is the world saying?" but in the context of the king's name, "the world" refers to the Zulu nation.

Hornbill mask, Ivory Coast

PART III
APPENDICES

Bronze pendant. Senufu, Ivory Coast.

APPENDIX A

NAME CHARTS

Charts of Names by Day of Week Born, Time of Day Born, Season of Birth, Order of Birth, and Twin Names

DAY OF THE WEEK NAMES

Baule of Cote d'Ivoire and Ghana[1]

	MALE	FEMALE
Monday	Kwasi (KWAH-*see*)	Akissi (*ah*-KEE-*see*)
Tuesday	Kwajo (KWAH-*joh*)	Adjoua (*ah*-JOO-*ah*)
Wednesday	Konan (KOH-*nan*), Konenan (KOH-*nay-nan*)	Amenan (*ah*-MAY-*nahn*)
Thursday	Kouakou (KWAH-*koo*, KOO-*ah-koo*), Kacou (KAH-*koo*)	Ahou (AH-*oo*)
Friday	Yao (YAH-*oh*)	Aya (AH-*yah*)
Saturday	Kossi (KOH-*see*)	Affoue (AH-*foo-way*)
Sunday	Kouame (KWAH-*may*, KOO-*ah-may*)	Amoin (AH-*moh-eh*), Amoue (AHM-*way*)

Agni of Cote d'Ivoire[2]

	MALE	FEMALE
Monday	Kadia	Adijoba
Tuesday	Kablan	Ablan
Wednesday	Kakou	Akomba
Thursday	Koao	Yaba
Friday	Kofí	Afibá
Saturday	Kouamé	Aama
Sunday	Kouassi	Akassi

Gen of Togo[3]

	MALE	FEMALE
Monday	Kodzo	Kodzoa
Tuesday	Komla	Ablavi

	MALE	FEMALE
Wednesday	Kwaku	Akuavi
Thursday	Yawo	Ayaba
Friday	Kofi	Kofiwa
Saturday	Akpa	Ambavi
Sunday	Kwasi	Kwasiele

Efe of Benin and Togo[4]

	MALE	FEMALE
Monday *Dzoda*	Kodzo	Adzoa
Tuesday *Brada*	Komla	Abra
Wednesday *Kuda*	Aku, Anku, Koku, Kowu	Akuwa
Thursday *Yawoda*	Yawo	Yawa
Friday *Fida*	Kofi	Afiba
Saturday *Memleda*	Komla	Ama
Sunday *Kwasida*	Kosi	Akosiba

Fanti of Ghana[5]

	MALE	FEMALE
Monday	Kudjo	Ajua
Tuesday	Kobina, also spelled Cobina (*koh*-BEE-*nah*)	Abraba
Wednesday	Kweku	Ekua
Thursday	Kwo, Kwaw	Aba
Friday	Kofi	Efoa
Saturday	Kwamina	Amma
Sunday	Kwesi	Akosua

Twi of Ghana[6, 7]

	MALE	FEMALE
Monday *Dwoda*	Kwadwo, Kojo (KOH-*joh*)	Adwowa, Ajua

	MALE	FEMALE
Tuesday *Benada*	Kwabena (*kwah*-BAY- *nah*), Kobla (KOH-*blah*), Kwabina (*kwah*-BEE- *nah*), Kobina (*koh*-BEE- *nah*)	Abena, Abla
Wednesday *Wukuda*	Kwaku (KWAH-*koo*), Kweku (KWAY-*koo*)	Akua, Aku
Thursday *Yaw'da*	Yaw, Yao (YAH-*oh*), Kwao	Ya, Yawa, Aba
Friday *Fida*	Kofi (KOH-*fee*)	Afua, Afia
Saturday *Memeneda*	Kwame (KWAH-*may*), Kwarmine	Amma, Ama
Sunday *Kwasida*	Kwasi (KWAH-*see*), Kwashi (KWAH-*shee*), Kwesi (KWAY-*see*)	Akosua, Akwasiba, Akosia

Twi of Ghana
Kra Names[8]

	MALE	FEMALE
Monday	Ajo, Kojo	Ajo, Ajua
Tuesday	Abla	Abla
Wednesday	Aku	Aku
Thursday	Awo, Aho	Awo, Aho
Friday	Afi	Afi
Saturday	Ameng	Ameng
Sunday	Awushi	Awushi

Igbo of Nigeria
(Market Days)[9]

	MALE	FEMALE
Eke	Okeke, Nweke	Mgbeke
Orie	Okeli, Nwoye	Mgboli
Afo	Okafo, Nwafo	Mgbafo
Nkwo	Okonkwo, Nwankwo	Mgbonkwo

Hausa of West Africa[10]

	MALE	FEMALE
Monday *Litinnin*	Tanimu (*tah*-NEE-*moo*)	Tani (TAH-*nee*), Altine (*ahl*-TEE-*nay*)

	MALE	FEMALE
Tuesday *Talata*	Dantala (*dahn*-TAH-*lah*) means "son of Tuesday," Tatu (TAH-*too*), Talatu (*tah*-LAH-*too*)	Talatu (*tah*-LAH-*too*), Lanti (LAHN-*tee*), Lantana (LAHN-*tah-nah*)
Wednesday *Laraba*	Balarabe (*bah*-LAH-*rah-bay*) literally means "an Arab" and signifies someone who comes on Wednesday	Balaraba (*bah*-LAH-*rah-bah*), Laraba (LAH-*rah-bah*), Larai (LAH-*ray*), Lauretu (*low*-REH-*too*, *low-reht*)
Thursday *Alhamis*	Danlami (*dahn*-LAH-*mee*) means "son of Thursday"	Lami (LAH-*mee*), Laminde (*lah*-MEEN-*day*)
Friday *Jumaah*	Danjuma (*dahn*-JOO-*mah*) meaning "son of Friday"	Jummai (*joo*-MIGH)
Saturday *Asabar*	Danasabe (*dahn*-AH-*sah-bay*) means "son of Saturday," Sati (SAH-*tee*) means "weekend"	Assibi (*ah*-SEE-*bee*), Asabe (*ah*-SAH-*bay*), Gude (GOO-*day*)
Sunday *Lahadi*	Danladi (*dahn*-LAH-*dee*) means "son of Sunday"	Ladi (LAH-*dee*)

Bambara of Mali [11]

	MALE
Thursday	Lamissa (*lah*-MEES-*ah*)
Friday	Guediouma (*gay*-DJOO-*mah*), a common short form of this name is Diouma—the French spelling of Juma
Saturday	Sibiri (*see-bi*-REE)
Sunday	Kary (KAH-*ree*)

TIME OF DAY AND SEASON NAMES

Luo of Kenya [1]

	MALE	FEMALE
Very early in the morning (just before dawn)	Omondi (*oh*-MOHN-*dee*), derived from the Dholuo word *imondo* meaning "very early in the morning"	Amondi (*ah*-MOHN-*dee*)

	MALE	FEMALE
At daybreak (around five or six A.M.)	Ogweno (*oh-*GWAY-*noh*), derived from the Dholuo word for "chicken" referring to the time the roosters crow	
In the morning	Okinyi (*oh-*KEEN-*yee*), from the Dholuo word *gokinyi*, which means "morning"	Akinyi (*ah-*KEEN-*yee*)
Late in the morning on a sunny day	Onyango (*ohn-*YAHN-*goh*), from the word meaning "around nine or ten A.M."	Anyango (*ahn-*YAHN-*goh*)
Late in the morning on a hazy or foggy day	Oluoch (*oh-loo-*WAHCH)	Aluoch (*ah-loo-*WAHCH)
Near noon	Ochieng (*oh-chee-*EHNG), from the Dholuo word *chieng*, which means "sunny"	Achieng (*ah-chee-*EHNG)
In the afternoon/ early evening (before dark)	Odhiambo (*oh-thee-*AHM-*boh*, "th" as in the), means "in the evening"	Adhiambo (*ah-thee-*AHM-*boh*)
At night	Otieno (*oh-tee-*EH-*noh*), from the Dholuo word *gotieno*, which means "night"	Atieno (*ah-tee-*EH-*noh*)
Around midnight	Oduor (*oh-*DOO-*or*), means "midnight"	

Tonga of southern Zambia[2]

	MALE/FEMALE
Born at dawn	Buchedo (*boo-*CHAY-*doh*) means "dawn" Junza (JOON-*zah*) means "tomorrow"
Born in late afternoon or before sunset	Mazuba (*mah-*ZOO-*bah*) means "days"
Born at sunset	Libbila (*lee-*BEE-*lah*) means "setting sun"
Born after supper/before bedtime	Jolezya (*joh-*LAYZ-*yah*) means "evening"

MALE/FEMALE	
Born during the night	Busiku (*boo*-SEE-*koo*) means "night" Muzwenge (*moo*-ZWAYN-*gay*) means "light" and refers to making a fire from reeds during the delivery
Born during a full moon	Chizyuka (*chee*-ZYOO-*kah*)

Oromo of Ethiopia and Kenya[3]

	MALE	FEMALE
Born at sunrise	Boro (BOHR-*oh*), Boru (BOHR-*oo*)	Diram (DEER-*ahm*), Diramu (DEER-*ah-moo*), Hadiramu (HAH-*deer-ahm*), means "dawn"
Born at noon	Gwiyo, Guyo (GOO-*yoh*)	Gwiyato (*gwee*-YAH-*toh*), Guyato (*goo*-YAH-*toh*)
Born in the late afternoon		Safo (SAH-*foh*)
Born at sunset	Galgalo (*gahl*-GAHL-*oh*), derived from *galgala*, the Oromo word for "evening"	Galgalo, Galgalle (*gahl*-GAHL-*ay*)
Born at night	Dukana (*doo*-KAH-*nah*), *dukan* means "darkness"	Hadukana (HAH-*doo-kah-nah*)
Born during the rainy season	Roba (ROH-*bah*), means "rain"	Haroba (HAH-*roh-bah*)

Luo of Kenya[4]

	MALE	FEMALE
Born during the planting season	Okomo (*oh*-KOH-*moh*), derived from the Dholuo word *komo*, which means "to plant"	Akomo (*ah*-KOH-*moh*)
Born during weeding season	Odoyo (*oh*-DOH-*yoh*), from the word *doyo*, which means "to weed"	Adoyo (*ah*-DOH-*yoh*)
Born during harvest season	Okeyo (*oh*-KAY-*yoh*), from the word *keyo*, which means "to harvest"	Akeyo (*ah*-KAY-*yoh*)

	MALE	FEMALE
Born during rainy season	Okoth (*oh*-KOHTH), from the word *koth*, which means "rain"	Akoth (*ah*-KOHTH)
Born during the muddy season	Ochuodho (*oh-choo*-OH-*thoh*, "th" as in the), means "muddy"	Achuodho (*ah-choo*-OH-*thoh*)
Born during a famine	Okech (OH-*kaych*), from the word *kech*, which means "hunger"	Akech (AH-*kaych*)

Tonga of southern Zambia[5]

	MALE/FEMALE
Born during the period of hunger preceding the harvest season	Mwajananzala (*mwah-jahn-ah-nZAH-lah*) means "you have found hunger" Nzala (*nZAH-lah*) means "hunger"
Born in autumn	Mwaka (MWAH-*kah*) means "year"
Born during the cold season	Mapeyo (*mah*-PAY-*yoh*), Siampeyo (*see-ahm*-PAY-*yoh*) both mean "cold season"
Born during August	Malambwa (*mah*-LAHM-*bwah*) means "small holes in which maize seeds are planted"
Born during the rainy season	Mainza (*mah*-EEN-*zah*) means "rainy season," Hamvula (*hahm*-VOO-*lah*) means "rain," Shavula* (*shah*-VOO-*lah*), means "rain"
Born during a period of continuous rains	Miyoba (*mee*-YOH-*bah*)

* An example has been cited of this name being chosen because the child's father was always getting soaked when hunting or visiting during the rainy season.

Abaluyia of Kenya[6]

	MALE	FEMALE
Born during the harvest season	Wekesa (*way*-KAY-*sah*)	Nekesa (*nay*-KAY-*sah*)
Born during the rainy season	Wafula (*wah*-FOO-*lah*)	Nafula (*nah*-FOO-*lah*)
Born during a drought	Simiyu	Nasimiyu
Born during the planting season	Maraka	Nakhumicha
Born during a locust invasion	Wasike (*wah*-SEE-*kay*)	Nasike (*nah*-SEE-*kay*)

Basotho of Lesotho[7]

	MALE	FEMALE
Born during the rainy season	Pule (POO-*lay*), means "rain"	Pulane (*poo*-LAH-*nee*), means "little rain" Puleng (POO-*layng*), means "rain"

ORDER OF BIRTH NAMES

Bari of southern Sudan[1]

	MALE	FEMALE
First	Jada, Yuggusuk, Loro, Lengsuk (firstborn son following a daughter)	Kapuki, Sukoji (firstborn daughter following a son)
Second	Lado (sometimes Swaka)	Poni
Third	Wani, Wanike	Jwan
Fourth	Pitia	Pita
Born after three or more siblings of the opposite sex	Konyi	Kiden (means "middle")

Anuak of southern Sudan[2]

	MALE	FEMALE
First	Umot	Amot
Second	Ujulo	Ajulo
Third	Ubonga	Abonga

Bassari of Togo—Koli Clan[3]

	MALE	FEMALE
First	Kpanté	Gnamba
Second	Nadjombé	Dapo
Third	Gno	Djai
Fourth	Nabin	Mawaté
Fifth	Djawé	Kpindi

Bassari of Togo—Nataka Clan[4]

	MALE	FEMALE
First	Gbati	Numfom

	MALE	FEMALE
Second	Napo	Ikpini
Third	Gbandi	Adja
Fourth	Lantam	Mumfaé
Fifth	Kissao	Kidjui

Bassari of Togo—Nawale Clan[5]

	MALE	FEMALE
First	Kondi	Mutoni
Second	Nikabou	Nikpibe
Third	Gnandi	Pombo
Fourth	Dare	Djabi
Fifth	Unon	Kpinde

Bassari of Togo—Nayur Clan[6]

	MALE	FEMALE
First	Tchapo	Kungbon
Second	Waké	Wapondi
Third	Uyi	Gnankan
Fourth	Gbaré	Obo
Fifth	Ido	Marib

Twi of Ghana[7]

	MALE	FEMALE
Third	Mensa	Mansa
Fourth	Anang	Manang
Seventh	Asong	Asong
Eighth	Botwe	Botwe
Ninth	Akrong	Nkromma
Tenth	Badu	Baduwa

Akan of Ghana[8]

	MALE/FEMALE
First	Baako
Second	Manu
Third	Mensa, Mansa
Fourth	Anan, Anani
Fifth	Enu
Sixth	Nsia
Seventh	Asong, Nsonowa
Eighth	Awotwi

	MALE/FEMALE
Ninth	Nkruma
Tenth	Badu (female—Baduwa, Baidoo)
Eleventh	Dubaku

Makono of Sierra Leone[9]

	MALE	FEMALE
First	Sahr (*sah*)	Sia (SEE-*ah*)
Second	Komba (KOHM-*bah*)	Kumba (KOOM-*bah*)
Third	Fa (*fah*)	Finda (FEEN-*dah*)

Efik and Ibibio of Nigeria

	MALE
First	Akpan
Second	Udoh, Udoudo
Third	Ita

Swahili of East Africa

	MALE/FEMALE
First	Mosi (*moh-see*)
Second	Pili (PEE-*lee*)
Third	Tatu (TAH-*too*)

NAMES FOR TWINS, CHILDREN BORN NEAR TWINS AND THE PARENTS OF TWINS

Yoruba of Nigeria[1]

	MALE	FEMALE
Firstborn of twins	Taiwo (TIGH-*woh*, *tah*-EE-*woh*), from *to-aiye-wo*, which means "have the first taste of the world," Taiye (TIGH-*ay*)	Taiwo, Taiye
Second born of twins	Kehinde (*keh*-IN-*day*), which means "the one who lags behind"	Kehinde
First child born after twins	Idowu (*ee*-DOH-*woo*)	Idowu

	MALE	FEMALE
Second child born after twins	Idogbe	Alaba (AH-*lah-bah*)

Hausa of West Africa [2]

	MALE	FEMALE
Firstborn of twins	Hassan (HAH-*sahn*), means "handsome"	Hasana (*hah*-SAH-*nah*), means "beautiful"
Second born of twins	Husseini (*hoo*-SAYN-*ee*), Husayn (*hoo*-SAYN), means "handsome"	Huseina (*hoo*-SAYN-*ah*), means "beautiful"
First child born after twins	Gaddo (GAH-*doh*), also spelled Gado, means "inheritor"	Gaddo
Child born before twins	Gambo (GAHM-*boh*)	Gambo

Nuer of southern Sudan [3]

	MALE	FEMALE
Firstborn after twins	Bol	Nyabol
Second born after twins	Geng, Kaat	Nyageng, Nyacwiil
Third born after twins	Tot	Nyatoot

Bari of southern Sudan [4]

	MALE	FEMALE
Firstborn twin	Ulang, the name of a bird	Bojo, means "despiser of her twin"
Second born twin	Lado, second born male name	Jore, means "full"
Firstborn after twins	Mogga, means "he is held by twins"	Gune, means "big-headed"

Dinka of southern Sudan [5]

	MALE	FEMALE
First set of twins	Ngor and Chan	Anger and Achan

	MALE	FEMALE
Second set of twins	Achwil and Madit; also spelled Acuil (*ah*-CHWEEL), which means "kite" as in the bird	Achwil and Adit
First child born after twins	Bol (*bohl*)	Nyanbol, Nyibol, Nibol (NI-*bohl*)

Ovimbundu of Angola[6]

	MALE/FEMALE
Firstborn twin	Njamba (*n*JAHM-*bah*), derived from the word *onjamba*, which means "elephant"
Second born twin	Hosi (HOH-*see*), derived from the word *ohosi*, which means "lion"
Third born (of triplets)	Ngeve (*n*GAY-*vay*), derived from the word *ongeve*, which means "hippopotamus"
First child born after twins	Kasinda (*kah*-SEEN-*dah*), derived from the word *osinda*, which refers to the dirt that blocks the passageway behind a burrowing animal
Mother of twins	Nanjamba (*nahn*-JAHM-*bah*), from *na*, meaning "mother" + *olonjamba* meaning "twins"
Mother of triplets	Nelongo (*nay*-LOHN-*goh*), from *na* + *elongo* meaning "triplets"

Goun of Benin[7]

	MALE	FEMALE
Twin names	Zinsou	Zinsa
First child born after twins	Dossou	Dossi
Second born after twins	Dosa	Dohwe
Third born after twins	Donyo	Dohwevi

Ga of Ghana[8]

	MALE	FEMALE
Elder twin	Ako	Akwele
Younger twin	Akwuete	Akuoko
First child born after twins	Tawia	Tawia
Second born after twins	Ago	Ago

	MALE	FEMALE
Third born after twins	Abang	Abang

Luo of Kenya[9]

	MALE	FEMALE
Firstborn twin	Opiyo (*oh*-PEE-*yoh*)	Apiyo (*ah*-PEE-*yoh*)
Second born twin	Odongo (*oh*-DOHN-*goh*)	Adongo (*ah*-DOHN-*goh*)

Bakongo of central-west Africa[10]

	MALE/FEMALE
A twin	Mapasa (*mah*-PAH-*sah*)
Firstborn twin	Nzuzi (*n*ZOO-*zee*)
Second born twin	Nsimba (*n*SIM-*bah*)
Second child born after twins	Lukombo (*loo*-KOHM-*boh*)

SOME POPULAR TWIN NAMES OF THE SOTHO OF SOUTHERN AFRICA[11]

	FIRST BORN OF IDENTICAL TWINS	SECOND BORN OF IDENTICAL TWINS
Male (these names are used in pairs, as shown; the second born names are diminutive forms)	Masilo (*mah*-SEE-*loh*), a legendary name	Masilonyane
	Molefi (*moh*-LAY-*fee*), means "payer"	Molefinyane, means "little payer"
	Ntai, a legendary name	Ntainyane
Female	Mosemodi, a legendary name	Mosemotsane
	Mesi, means "smoke"	Mesinyane, means "little smoke"
	Masimong, means "at the fields"	Masingwaneng, means "at the small fields"
	Dipuo, means "talks, rumors"	Dipuonyane, means "small talks, rumors"

	FIRST OF FRATERNAL TWINS	SECOND OF FRATERNAL TWINS
If first twin is male and second twin is female	Thabo (TAH-*boh*), means "joy"	Thabang, means "be happy"
	Thabiso, means "that which gratifies"	Nthabiseng, means "make me happy"
	Tshepo, means "trust, hope"	Tshepiso, means "promise"
	Moromodi, a legendary name	Moromotsane
If first twin is female and second twin is male	Mpho, means "gift"	Neo, means "present"
	Ntshiuwa, means "forsaken one"	Mosiuwa, means "forsaken one"

Baganda of Uganda[12]

	MALE	FEMALE
Firstborn twin	Wasswa (WAHS-*wah*)	Babirye (*bah*-BEER-*ee-eh*)
Second born twin	Kato (KAH-*toh*)	Nakato (NAH-*kah-toh*)
Child born before twins	Kigongo (CHEE-*gohn-goh*)	Kogongo
First child born after twins	Kizza (CHEE-*zah*)	Kizza
Second child born after twins	Kagwa (KAH-*gwah*)	Nakagwa (NAH-*kah-gwah*)
Third child born after twins	Kamya (KAHM-*ee-ah*)	Nakamya (NAH-*kahm-ee-ah*)
Fourth child born after twins	Kityo (CHEET-*ee-oh*)	Nakityo (NAH-*cheet-ee-oh*)

	FATHER	MOTHER
Parents of first set of twins	Ssallongo (*sah*-LOHN-*goh*)	Nalongo (*nah*-LOHN-*goh*)
Parents of second set of twins	Ssabalongo (*sah-bah*-LOHN-*goh*)	Nabalongo (*nah-bah*-LOHN-*goh*)

APPENDIX B

AFRICAN SURNAMES

Surnames, as we know them, are not indigenous to most African cultures. Traditionally Africans have had one or more personal names, but rarely did there exist a common name handed down to all family members from generation to generation.

In many societies the father's first name became the child's second name and in this way a person's heritage was traced. An Igbo boy named NWANDU OJI was the son of Oji. His father, called OJI CHINUA, was the son of CHINUA. The Dinka of southern Sudan name DENG D'AROB DE BIONG signifies Deng, son of Arob, son of Biong. Several tribes of southern Africa imparted one name on children at birth and another name—called a praise name, or *isibongo* in the Zulu language—at the age of maturity, which was signalled primarily by circumcision or marriage. Praise names usually indicated the clan, blood set, or other group to which the person belonged.

Individuals were also distinguished by adopting names related to their social standing or to events that occurred at different stages in their life. One who fought well in battle may have become known by an appellation celebrating his bravery. A Meru of Kenya woman may have been referred to by her new husband as the daughter of so-and-so, rather than by her birth name. Another method for differentiating people—which is still fairly common today—was to assign a second name expressing the person's craft, workplace, or former village. For example, an Igbo wrestler named EJIOFO might have been known as EJIOFO DINGBA (Ejiofo, the master wrestler) and a Hausa man named YAKUBU originally from Lame, Nigeria, now living in Zaria could be locally known as YAKUBU LAME, or Yakubu from Lame.

These age-old naming traditions began shifting when Africans came into contact with western traders, explorers, missionaries, and colonialists in the nineteenth century. Especially in more urban areas, people began to take on Christian or European first names and applied their African names as surnames. Some Africans, under the influence of the church, through employment or personal liaisons, adopted both first and last names of European origin. The Ijaw of southern Nigeria, in particular, adopted European surnames during this early period, such as BROWN, CLARK, LAWSON, and DOUGLASS. Familiar western surnames heard in

Liberia and Sierra Leone, like WILLIAMS and JOHNSON, were carried back to these countries by freed American and British slaves. In southern Africa some families anglicized their indigenous names, for example converting the Basotho name TAU to its direct English translation LION or transforming the local name MOGANE to MORGAN. A popular family name in Burkina Faso is DIEUDONNÉ, taken straight from the French language and meaning "God given." Today Africans have largely embraced the western concept of family surnames, with governments encouraging this through both practice and edict.

By identifying trends in surnames from various African nations and cultures, a layman can make a passing guess at a person's ethnic origin. If a Kenyan's last name begins with o, sounding like ODERO or OUKO, it would be worth betting that they are Luo. In Guinea names ending with ou mean "of the land of" or "of the people of." Thus, the surname TAMBALOU means "of the Tamba people." Exceptionally long, twisty names beginning with b, n, s, and u—for instance BARANSARITSE, NGIRABATWARE, and UWILIYINGIYAMANA—should point one towards Rwanda or Burundi. Like Rwanda and Burundi, the island country of Madagascar produces some of Africa's lengthiest surnames, many starting with ra and andrian, as in ANDRIANANTENAINA and RAKOTOVOLOLONA. Names ending with the letter h, such as SALEH and BARREH of Djibouti, and those beginning with al, as in AL-RAZZAZ of Egypt, demonstrate Arabic influences. Surnames spelled with ou to produce an oo sound indicate a French bias, suggesting the person comes from a country that was once colonized by France or Belgium. Examples of this include the names CHOUKOU of Chad, SOULEYMANOU of Cameroon, and BOUNKOULOU of Congo. Those last names starting with double s, as in SSALI and SSEKITOLEKO, are likely Ugandan.

The following list of surnames may be useful for those endeavoring to change their family name to one of African origin. There are many appealing names on the next page that can be used as a person's given name as well, for example KABECA and NEDIA (Kenya), CINDI (Lesotho), BETIANA (Madagascar), KORSHEL (Somalia), and ASRAT, AWEKE, BISHAQA, IRENA, and TAMERAT (all of Ethiopia). In many cases these surnames were once, or are still, used as first names. Readers should bear in mind that African ethnic groups are not always confined within the borders of a single country, so surnames listed under one country may also be used by ethnic relatives in neighboring countries.

Algeria

Achoubi
Aziza (*ah*-ZEE-*zah*),
   Muslim, "precious"
Bahbouh
Belhadj (*behl*-HAHDJ)
Benachnhou
Benbitour
Benbouzid
Bensalem
Bouchair
Brahti
Cheikh, Muslim,
   "head, chief"
Cherif, Muslim,
   "noble"
Dembri
Ghozali
Hamiani
Hamrouche
Kaidoum
Kesdali
Lamouri
Laskri
Lebib
Madani
Meghlaoui
Mekhloufi
Rahmani, Muslim,
   "merciful"
Sakhri
Sifi
Teguia
Yacine
Zerhouni
Zeroual

Angola

Antunes
Assis
Craveiro
Dias
Dos Anjos
Epalanga
Liahuka (*lee-ah*-HOO-
   kah), Ovimbundu
Malungo
Manuvakola
Mbandi (*m*-BAHN-*dee*)
Moco
Neto, Portuguese,
   "vigor"
Rocha
Tjipilica
Tonha

Benin

Adahui
Ahoyo
Dossou
Dramane
Gbegan
Holo
Houessou
Kpatashi
Kpatokpa
Ladikpo
Mito-Baba
Osseni
Soglo
Tigri

Botswana

Balopi
Butale
Chiepe
Kedikilwe
Legwaila
Magang
Masire
Matome
Merafhe
Mogae
Mogwe
Molomo
Morake
Skelemani
Temane

Burkina Faso

Belombaogo
Bonkoungou
Diallo
Dieudonné (DEE-*ew-
   dohn*-NAY), "God
   given"
Kanidoua
Koutiebou
Larba
Ouedraogo
Sanou
Sawadogo
Somda
Somé, Dagara
Traoré
Yameogo

Burundi

Bakana
Bakevyumusaya
Barranyanka
Biha
Bukuru
Buyoya
Ciza
Fyiroko
Kabushemeye
Kanyenkiko
Manwangari
Minani
Nahimana
Ndadaye
Ndimurukundo
Ngendahayo
Ngendakumana
Nikobamye
Niyonkuru

Niyonsaba
Ntamobwa
Ntihabose
Nyamwana
Nzeyimana
Rugambarara
Rwagasore
Simbizi
Toyi

Cameroon

Abassa
Achu
Adjoudji
Bava
Bokam
Dairou
Edzoa
Ekindi
Emah
Endely
Esso
Kalla (KAH-*lah*)
Kodock
Kouomegni
Mbappe
Mbede
Mbila
Moutome
Ndiyam
Njawe
Ntsimi
Ondoua
Owona
Oyono
Samgba
Souleymanou
Souman
Takem
Tsoungui
Woum
Yaou
Yondo

**Central African
Republic**

Badekara
Bodemon
Dobanga
Dokouna
Gaba
Gbafolo
Goyemide
Koyara
Mandaba
Mazi
Mbosso
Ndodet
Odoufou
Ogbami
Patasse
Tchendo
Toumbona

Chad

Absakine
Alhabo
Bakit
Balaam
Barraka
Bolou
Bouchar
Choukou
Dé By
Djimasta
Garba
Garfa
Guelmodji
Habré
Haggar
Hamdane
Izo
Kebzabo
Laina
Lemohiban
Mandah

Marabaye
Nour
Pahimi
Regui
Romba
Seif
Thiam

Comoros

Attoumane
Bourhane
Hamidi
Hassanali
Houmadi
Idarousse
Islam
Issa
Kemal
Madi
Mirghane
Moumin
Moussa
Moustakim
Sagaf
Soilihi
Toybou

Congo

Bounkoulou
Dibindou
Doulou
Galibali
Gizenga
Itadi
Koyo
Massala
Matsika
Matsiola
Milongo
Mouamba
Ngouolali
Nkombo

Sinda
Tangui
Tchitchele
Tsomambet

Cote d'Ivoire

Akadje
Akele
Angoran
Atsain
Bombet
Coulibaly (*koo-lee*-BAH-
    lee)
Desbhy (*dehs*-BEE)
Epie
Essy
Fadika
Guikahue
Horan
Kipre
Koffi
Konan (KOH-*nan*)
Kone
Kouman
Molle
Morifere
Sangare
Tadjo
Tiapani
Touré
Wodie
Yadi
Zakpa
Zaourou

Djibouti

Abbas
Abdou
Barreh
Chehem
Dini
Farah

Haki (HAH-*kee*)
Hamadou
Humad
Olhaye
Robleh
Salah
Waberi

Egypt

Abaza
Al-Alfi
Al-Istambuli
Al-Razzaz
Al-Shazli
Amer
Ashour
Boutros-Ghali
Farouk (*fuh*-ROOK)
Gomah
Gouda
Husni
Maher
Mahgoub
Mahran
Mansur
Moussa
Mubarak (*moo*-BAHR-
    uhk)
Naguib
Nasser (NAH-*suhr*)
Osman (*ohs*-MAHN)
Radi
Sabri
Sadat (*suh*-DAHT)
Salim (*sah*-LEEM)
Sharif
Sidqi
Sulayman
Tantawi
Wali

Equatorial Guinea

Asangono

Asue
Bengono
Bileka
Congue
Mangue
Mba
Mifumu
Nanga
Ndongo
Nfube
Nfumu
Ngore
Nseng
Nvo
Obama
Ovono

Eritrea/Ethiopia

Abbadoyo
Abdella
Adula, Oromo
Adus
Alemu, Amharic/
    Ge'ez, "his world"
Aligaz
Alyu
Amaya
Amberber
Anebo
Ashame
Asrat, Ge'ez, "tithe"
Atero
Aweke (*ah*-WAY-*kay*)
Awoke (*ah*-WOH-*kay*)
Badebo
Bahobeshi
Bajinet
Balcha
Bali
Baraka (*bah*-RAH-*kah*),
    Barale, Oromo
    Oromo
Bedos
Begete

Bekele (*buh*-KUH-*luh*), Amharic, "he has grown"

Benti, Oromo

Beshada

Bilala, Oromo

Birru, Amharic, "silver"

Bishaqa

Bitawa

Bonga

Borga

Boru (BOH-*roo*), Oromo

Brehu

Bulbula

Bulcha

Bulli

Bulto

Buta, Oromo, "circumcision feast"

Chabo

Dafena

Dalkere

Dekebet

Delessa

Donsa

Dubale

Duki

Egeno

Ereg

Fenkebo

Fita

Gaaz

Gahir

Gayid

Gebissa

Gebremariam (GUH-*bruh*-MAH-*ree-ahm*), Ge'ez, "servant of Mary"

Gebreselase (GUH-*bruh-suh*-LAHS-*ee*), Ge'ez, "servant of

the Trinity"

Geded

Geger

Gelano

Gemechu

Geno

Gerima

Ghermazien

Gidey (*gi*-DAY), "my share"

Giedada

Girma

Gochi

Gulma

Hadito

Hagos (*hah*-GOHS), "happiness, joy"

Haile (HIGH-*lay*), Amharic/Ge'ez, "might"

Haymanot

Hayuti

Hordofa

Ingirda

Irena

Karat

Kebede, Amharic, "he is heavy"

Kello, Oromo

Keredin

Kesta

Keval

Kire

Kolase

Measho (*muh*-AH-*shoh*)

Megerssa

Mekete

Meri

Merne

Mesfin (*mehs*-FIN), "noble"

Mindase

Mita

Mondase

Mutela

Nata

Nawud

Nemera

Rafli

Rijiyo

Roba (ROH-*bah*), Oromo, "rain"

Sakika

Sebsibe, Amharic, "I have collected"

Seda

Selassie (*suh*-LAHS-*ee*), Ge'ez, "Trinity"

Shelis

Sherma

Shihimo

Shume

Simachew

Solomon

Sori

Tabor

Tadessa, Amharic, "he was renewed"

Tafa, Amharic, "ornamented shield"

Tamerat, Amharic, "miracles"

Tchebsi

Tchorka

Tedla, Ge'ez, "delight"

Temamo

Tersime

Tesfasion, Ge'ez, "promise of Zion"

Tessema (*tuh*-SUH-*mah*), Amharic, "he has been heard, people listen to him"

Totil (*toh*-TEEL)

Tullu, Oromo

Ubeshi
Urgesa
Warhu
Wari, Oromo,
 "midnight"
Watcho, Oromo
Wogaso
Wolde, Ge'ez, "my
 son"
Wordofa
Worku, Amharic, "his
 gold"
Yadete
Yifru, Amharic, "let
 them be afraid"
Yimamu
Yitbarek, Amharic,
 "may he be
 blessed"
Zeleke, Amharic, "he
 surpassed"
Zenawi
Zewde, Amharic,
 "my crown"

Gabon

Adiahenot
Bekale
Berre
Bike
Bouyiki
Dingombe
Mabila
Magouindi
Matoka
Mayaga
M'ba
Methogo
Missambo
Miyakou
Muetsa
Myboto
Ngari

Nzeng
Nziengui
Obiang
Ping
Toungui

Gambia

Bensouda
Bojan
Ceesay
Haidara
Jameh
Jow
Mbenga
N'gum
Sabally
Samateh
Singhateh
Sisay
Sonko
Tambedu
Touray

Ghana

Abbey, Ga
Addo, Ga
Addy, Ga
Adomako
Aidoo
Allotey, Ga
Amatsewe, Ga
Amoo, Ga
Ankrah, Ga, "he
 never bids
 goodbye"
Ansah
Armah
Asamoah
Ayele, Ga
Ayi, Ga
Ayikai, Ga
Ayite, Ga

Ayittey
Damte, Ga
Dede, Ga
Duah
Ekuban
Fosu
Guma
Korkor, Ga
Kpakpa, Ga, also
 spelled Papa, "good
 and strong"
Krote, Ga
Lalai, Ga
Laluah
Mensah
Nettey, Ga
Nunoo, Ga
Ohene
Okaija, Ga
Papafio (*pah*-PAH-*fee-
 oh*), Ga
Peprah
Quakyi
Sackey, Ga
Salia
Tetteh
Yaote, Ga

Guinea

Barry, Peul
Camara
Cisse
Conde
Conté
Diallo (*dee*-AH-*loh*),
 Peul, "bold"
Dorank
Fassou
Fofana
Gushein
Kaba (KAH-*buh*), Sous-
 sous
Kamara

Mara
Sako
Saloom
Sow (*soh*)
Sylla
Tambalou, forest
  region
Tolno
Zoumanigui

Guinea-Bisau

Balde
Cabral
Cardoso
Correia
Dias
Gomes
Lima
Manè
Mendes
Pereira
Pires
Procenca
Sanca
Sanha
Semedo
Viegas

Kenya

Adero (*ah*-DAIR-*oh*),
  Luo, "one who
  comes to make
  things better"
Adiel, Luo
Afundi, (*ah*-FOON-*dee*)
Anjere, Luhya
  Baraza (*bah*-RAH-
  zah), Swahili,
  "veranda, council
  house"

Chieng (*chee*-EHNG),
  Luo, "sun"
Darmani (*dahr*-MAH-
  nee)
Didi (DEE-*dee*)
Echakara
Gecau
Gichuru (*gih*-CHOO-
  roo), Kikuyu
Gogo (GOH-*goh*)
Imanyara (*ee-
  mahn*-YAHR-*ah*)
Iwebor, Luo
Kabaiko, Kikuyu
Kabeca (*kah*-BEHK-*uh*),
  Embu
Kamau (*kuh*-MOW),
  Kikuyu
Kapten
Karisa (*kahr*-IHS-*uh*)
Koinange (*koy*-NAHN-
  gay), Kikuyu
Leparleen (*lay-
  pahr*-LEEN),
  Samburu
Mataka (*mah*-TAH-*kah*),
  Swahili
Mathenge
  (*mah*-THEHN-*gay*),
  Kikuyu
Mathu, Kikuyu
Mboya (*m*BOY-*uh*)
Moi (*moy*), Kalenjin,
  "calves"
Mugo (*moo*-GOH),
  Kikuyu
Muhindi (*moo*-HEEN-
  dee)
Muigai (*mwee*-GIGH),
  Kikuyu
Muite (MWEE-*tay*),
  Kikuyu
Mungai (*moon*-GIGH),
  Kikuyu

Musyoka
Mwaniki (*mwah*-NEE-
  kee), Kikuyu and
  Embu
Nderi (*n*DAIR-*ee*),
  Kikuyu
Ndotto (*n*DOH-*toh*),
  Kamba
Nedia (NEH-*dee-uh*),
  Luo
Nkinda (*n*KIHN-*duh*),
  Meru, "the
  wrestlers"
Ntanta (*n*TAHN-*tah*),
  Maasai
Ntimama (*ntee*-MAH-
  mah), Maasai
Nzomo (*n*ZOH-*moh*)
Oburu (*oh*-BOOR-*oo*),
  Luo
Odhiambo (*oh-
  dee*-AHM-*boh*), Luo
Ogot, Luo
Okwach (*oh*-KWAHCH),
  Luhya
Ole Shunet, Maasai
Ole Surum, Maasai
Omtatah, Luo
Osieli (*oh-see*-EHL-*ee*),
  Luo
Osodo (*oh*-SOH-*doh*),
  Luo
Parsankul (*pahr-
  sahn*-KOOL), Maasai
Sankan (*sahn*-KAHN),
  Maasai
Sidi (SEE-*dee*)
Tapsubei, Nandi
Thiong'O (*thee*-OHN-
  goh)
Thuku (THOO-*koo*),
  Kikuyu
Toeri, Kisii
Towett (*toh*-WEHT),

Kipsigi
Wahome (*wah*-HOH-
    may)
Waiyaki (*wigh*-YAH-
    kee), Kikuyu
Warges (*wah*-RAH-
    gehs), Samburu

Lesotho

Buhali
Cindi
Didebe
Dlamini
Gwebu
Jelele
Khaketla
Khombelwako
Lekhanya
Madonsela
Mahlamba
Mahlobo
Makhanya
Makhobo
Makhubu
Maseko
Mashinini
Maxatshwa
Mdludlu
Mhlambi
Mhlophe
Mlangeni
Mngomezulu
Mokhehle
Msibi
Msika
Mtambo
Ncubuka
Ndlebe
Ngozo
Ngwenya
Nkosi
Nkutha
Ntobela

Nzimande
Phungwayo
Rameama
Rangoajane
Sekhonyana
Shiba
Shongwe
Sibanyoni
Sibeko
Sikhosana
Thabane
Thabede
Tshabangu
Vilakazi
Yika
Zimu

Liberia

Bara, Vai
Bestman
Carter
Dahn
Danquah
Dokie
Duclay, Vai
Gbasi, Vai
Gbon
Jayjay
Johnson
Kali, Vai
Kamara
Kanneh
Kekie
Koromah
Kpomakpor
Massaquoi, Vai
Moina
Mulbah
Nimely
Sawyer
Supuwood
Tabaku, Vai
Taylor

Tipoteh
Walker
Ware
Wesseh
Woeweiyu
Wolokolie
Zangai

Libya

Al-Badri
Al-Fezzani
Al-Hinshiri
Al-Mal
Al-Sid
Azwai
Badi
Dakhil
Fekini
Hifter
Huni
Khuaibah
Kikhia
Maatouq
Matar
Muntasser
Qadhafi (*kuh*-DAHF-*ee*)
Rabti
Shatwan
Swessi
Zentani

Madagascar

Andriamanjato
Andrianantenaina
Andrianasolo
Andrianbao
Anony
Beranto
Betiana
Fanony
Mahatovo
Marolahy

Nirina
Rabenirainy
Rabenja
Rabetsitonta
Rakotovahiny
Rakotovololona
Raliandimby
Ramaromisa
Raoefils
Raserijaona
Ratsimamanga
Ravony
Razafimahaleo
Razafindrazaka
Sylla

Malawi

Banda (BAHN-*dah*)
Chibambo
Chihana
Chilumpha
Chitalo
Chizumira
Fachi
Itimu
Kanyanya
Malewezi
Mbewe
Mpanje
Mpasu
Mtafu
Muluzi
Mwangazu
Nakanga
Nakumba

Mali

Berthe
Beye
Diabate
Diarra, "gift"
Diawara

Haidara
Kamissoko
Kone (KOO-*nay*)
Lamin (*lah*-MEEN)
Ouloguem
Sacko
Saidou
Samake
Sissoko
Sow (*soh*)
Sy
Tall
Thiam
Traore
Yambo

Mauritania

Aiche
Badi
Daddah (DAH-*dah*)
Hebeti
Kane
Kharcy
Killi
Lamar
Lehbib
Lekhal
M'Bareck
Moukmass
Moussa (MOO-*sah*)
Ould Jiddou
Ould Kharcy
Ould Mah (*ool* MAH)
Ould Saleh (*ool* SAH-
    lay)
Ould Sidi (*ool* SEE-*dee*)
Samba
Tagaddi
Yayia
Yessa

Morocco

Ahasbi

Ahizoun
Azziman
Basri
Belfkih
Bensaid
Berdugo
Cherif
Elmandjra
Filali
Harrouchi
Hassad
Jattou
Kabbaj
Montassem
Rabie
Sahil
Saidi
Senhaji
Sinasser
Tabet
Touali

Mozambique

Bordina
Catupa
Chipande
Chissano (*chi*-SAH-*noh*)
Comiche
Guebuza
Kachamila
Kamacho
Kavandame
Mabote
Machel (*mah*-SHEHL)
Machungo
Matsinhe
Mazula
Mocumbi
Mutota
Pachinaupa
Rebelo
Veloso
Zandamela

Namibia

Amathila
Angula
Gurirab
Hamutenya
Haraseb
Hausiku
Ithana
Iyambo
Kabajani
Kalangula
Kashe, Bushman
Kautima, Ovambo
Kerina
Kgosimang, Tswana
Majavero
Pohamba
Rukoro
Shipanga
Simasiku
Uazukuani

Niger

Abdoulaye
Anako
Bakary
Billo
Dayak
Effad
Foumakoye
Garba
Hama
Hassoumi
Ibba
Issouffou
Kandine
Kato
Kaziende
Koullou
Mamani
Oumarou
Sadikou

Sadio
Salissou
Seydou
Tahirou
Tandja
Taya
Waziri

Nigeria

Abacha (*ah*-BAH-*chah*),
 Kanuri
Abiola (*ah-bee*-OH-*lah*),
 Yoruba, "honor"
Adedeji (*ah-day*-DAY-
 jee), Yoruba
Adu (AH-*doo*), Bendel
 State
Agunwa (*ah*-GOON-
 wah), Igbo
Ajala (*ah*-JAH-*lah*),
 Yoruba
Ajose (*ah*-JOH-*say*),
 Yoruba
Akinkoye (*ah-*
 keen-KOY-*yay*),
 Yoruba
Akum (AH-*koom*)
Alkali (*ahl*-KAHL-*ee*),
 Hausa, "judge"
Amadiume (*ah-mah-*
 dee-OO-*may*)
Audu (OW-*doo*),
 Hausa, "the servant
 of"
Bamidele (*bah-*
 mee-DAY-*lay*), Yoruba
Bassey (BAH-*see*),
 Ibibio, "God"
Bature (*bah*-TOOR-*ay*),
 Hausa, "white
 person"
Dike (DEE-*kay*), Yoruba
Dingba (DEENG-*bah*),

Igbo, a praise name
 meaning "master
 wrestler"
Dipcharima (*dip-*
 chahr-EE-*mah*),
 Kanuri
Egunjobi (*eh-goon*-JOH-
 bee), Yoruba
Ekwuanu (*eh*-KWAH-
 noo)
Ekwueme (*eh*-KWAY-
 may), Igbo
Ezeogu (*eh*-ZEH-*goo*),
 Igbo, a praise name
 meaning "lord of
 battle"
Fasuyi (*fah*-SOO-*yee*)
Ifeajuna (*ee-fay-ah*-JOO-
 nah), Igbo
Isoun (EE-*soh-oon*)
Itsekiri (*eet-say*-KEER-
 ee), Ibuza
Junaidu (*joon*-IGH-*doo*),
 Hausa
Kalu (KAH-*loos*), Igbo
Kingibe (*keen*-GEE-
 bay), Kanuri
Madaki (MAH-*dahk-ee*),
 Hausa, traditional
 title for a chief's
 deputy
Madubuike (*mah-*
 doo-BWEE-*kay*), Igbo
Mba (*m*BAH), Igbo
Muhktar (MOOK-*tahr*),
 Hausa
Nsa (*n*SAH), Igbo
Ofurum (*oh-foor*-OOM)
Ogundipe (*oh-*
 goon-DEE-*pay*),
 Yoruba, "Ogun
 consoles me this"
Ojike (*oh*-JEE-*kay*),
 Yoruba

Okaome (*oh-kah-*OH-*mah*), Igbo, "he says and does as he said he would do"

Okon (*oh-*KOHN)

Okpuzu (*ohk-*POO-*zoo*), Igbo

Olajuwon (*oh-*LAH-*joo-wahn*), Yoruba

Omengboji (*oh-mehng-*BOH-*jee*), Igbo, "he demonstrates his richness when he is rich"

Omenka (*oh-*MAYN-*kah*), Igbo

Omenuko (*oh-*MEH-*noo-koh*), Igbo, "one who acts in time of scarcity"

Osagie (*oh-*SAH-*gee*), Yoruba

Oyegunle (*oy-*YAY-*goon-*LAY), Yoruba

Shagari (SHAH-*gahr-ee*), Hausa, name of a town

Shehu (SHAY-*hoo*), Hausa

Sofola (*soh-*FOH-*lah*), Yoruba

Sotubo (*soh-*TOO-*boh*), Yoruba

Ulasi (*oo-*LAH-*see*)

Were (WAIR-*ay*)

Yakubu (*yah-*KOO-*boo*), Hausa, "Jacob"

Yekini (*yay-*KEE-*nee*), Yoruba

Rwanda

Baransaritse

Bihozagara

Bizimungu (*bee-zee-*MOON-*goo*), "only God knows"

Buseruka (*boo-sair-*OOK-*uh*)

Hakizimana (*hah-kee-zee-*MAH-*nah*), "God is the savior"

Kagame

Kanyarengwe

Karemera

Mazimhaka

Mbarushimana

Mugenzi

Nayinzira

Ngirabatware

Nsanzimana

Ntamabyaliro

Nzayisenga

Rudasingwa

Rwanbuka

Rwigyema

Sendama (*sehn-*DAH-*mah*)

Sendashonga

Sendashonjwa

Twagiramungu (*twah-gee-rah-*MOON-*goo*)

Uwiliyingiyamana, "one who puts confidence in God."

Senegal

Bá (*bah*), Peul

Bathily

Binetu

Cisse

Condé (*kahn-*DAY), Malinke

Dansokho

Daour

Dieng

Diob

Diop (*dyahp*), Wolof, "ruler, scholar"

Diouf (*joof*)

Gueye, Wolof

Ka

Karamoko

Laye

Loum

Maissa

M'Backé

M'Baye (*uhm-*BAH-*ee*)

Mboup

Ndao

N'Dyare

Niang

Niasse

Paye

Sagna

Sarr

Seck, Wolof

Sene

Seye

Sidimé, Malinke

Sonko

Sow (*soh*), Peul

Sy

Tall, Peul

Thiam, Peul

Thiandoum

Tidjiani

Traoré

Wade

Yamar

Sierra Leone

Bangura (*bahn-*GOO-*ruh*), Susu, Temne, Mandingo

Bundu (BOON-*doo*), Susu, Temne, "dark-brown"

Fofana
Gibril
Jalloh (JAH-*loh*), Fula
Jumu
Kabia
Kalokoh
Kamara (*kah*-MAH-*rah*),
 Susu, Temne,
 Mandingo
Kanu (KAH-*noo*), Susu,
 Temne
Karbo
Khoryama
Koroma
Maligi
Sankoh (SAHN-*koh*),
 Temne
Sewah
Sillah (SEE-*lah*), Susu
 and Mandingo
Sisi (SEE-*see*), Also, a
 name of respect for
 an older sister
Sowa (SOH-*wah*),
 Temne
Turay

Somalia

Abdullahi (*ahb-*
 dool-AH-*hee*)
Adan
Addou
Ahmed
Aidid (*igh*-DEED)
Aliyow
Araye
Diriye (DEER-*ee-ay*)
Hagi-Dirie
Hamed
Hasean
Hashi
Hersi
Isaq (EE-*sahk*)

Jess (*jehs*)
Korshel
Noor
Soba (SOH-*bah*)

South Africa

Bookholane
Chikane
Coka, Zulu
Dhlamini (*lah*-MEE-
 nee)
Kwiri, Basotho,
 "spotted hyena"
Herero
Idube, Zulu, "zebra"
Ikokoni, Basotho,
 "wildebeest"
Impisi, Zulu,
 "spotted hyena"
Imvubo, Xhosa and
 Zulu,
 "hippopotamus"
Inci, Xhosa, "earth
 wolf"
Indhlovu, Xhosa and
 Zulu, "elephant"
 (also spelled
 NDHLOVU)
Ingonyama, Zulu,
 "lion" (also spelled
 IMBUBESI and
 IMBUBI)
Ingwe, Xhosa and
 Zulu, "leopard"
Insimba, Zulu,
 "genet"
Intini, Zulu, "otter"
Inzipone, Xhosa,
 "springhare"
Iputi, Basotho,
 "duiker"
Iqwara, Xhosa,
 "zebra"

Issel
Jabavu, Xhosa
Kadalie
Khumalo
Kompe
Kuzwayo
Leweng
Lisisi, Basotho, "civet
 cat"
Makanda, Xhosa,
 "porcupine"
Makwa, Sesuto,
 "zebra"
Mamkhala
Mantanzima, Xhosa,
 "heavy saliva"
Manzini
Mashinini
Mayeza, Xhosa
Mhlope, Xhosa
Mngoma
Mofokeng
Mogane
Mokhesi, Xhosa
Mompati
Mopheme, Basotho,
 "silver fox"
Moshesh, Basotho,
 "the shaver"
Motenda
Naidoo
Ndzanga
Ngcobo
Ngoyi
Ngulule, Zulu,
 "hunting leopard"
Nkosi
Nziki, Zulu,
 "reedbuck" (also
 spelled MZIKI)
Phandelani, Venda,
 "driven away"
Pincus, South African
 name of Egyptian

origin
Pofu, Basotho,
　"eland"
Poto, Xhosa, "long,
　slender stalk of
　corn"
Puti, Sechuana,
　"duiker"
Qubeka
Radebe, Zulu,
　"ancestor of the
　Amahlubi"
Ramotse
Sekoto
Shabalala, Xhosa,
　"decay" or "perish"
　(also spelled
　TSHABALALA)
Shangaan, Zulu
Shenxane
Shoshona,
　(shoh-SHOH-nah)
Sibeko
Sigakaka, Basotho,
　"hunting leopard"
Sikakane
Silinga
Sipejana, Swazi,
　"black rhinoceros"
Sisulu
Soga, Xhosa,
　"bachelor"
Takalani, Venda,
　"happiness"
Tau (TAH-oo),
　Sechuana and
　Basotho, "lion"
Thiagale
Tlali
Tshipa, Basotho,
　"genet"
Tsipi, Sechuana,
　"springbuck"
Tuku, Basotho, "earth

wolf"
Tuli, Zulu, "dust" or
　"silent person"
Tutla, Sechuana and
　Basotho, "giraffe"
Ukombe, Zulu,
　"rhinoceros"
Vilakazi (vee-lah-KAH-
　zee), Zulu
Vundla, Xhosa,
　"hare"
Zulu (ZOO-loo) Zulu,
　"heaven"

Sudan

Agoth (ah-GOHTH),
　southern Sudan
Bashir (bah-SHEER),
　northern Sudan
Bol (bohl), Dinka
Chol (chohl), Nuer
Deng (dehng), Dinka
Duku (DOO-koo),
　southern Sudan
El-Mufti, northern
　Sudan
Gai (guy), Nuer
Garang (guh-RANG),
　Dinka
Geneif, northern
　Sudan
Kassiano
Khelefi, northern
　Sudan
Kong, Nuer
Kulang, Nuer
Kwaje
Lam (lam), Nuer
Long (long), Nuer
Mabor (mah-BOR),
　southern Sudan
Machar (mah-CHAHR),
　Nuer

Marial (MAHR-ee-ahl),
　southern Sudan
Mustafa (moo-STAHF-
　ah), northern Sudan
Nuer (noo-AIR), Nuer
Oduho (oh-DOO-hoh),
　southern Sudan
Pidak, Nuer
Sabdarit, northern
　Sudan
Sahatini, Zande
Salih, northern
　Sudan
Sharfi, northern
　Sudan
Shura
Sidahemed, northern
　Sudan
Subek, Bari
Taha, northern Sudan
Yak (yak), southern
　Sudan

Swaziland

Dlamini
Khanya
Khoza
Lukhele
Magagula
Makhubu
Masuku
Nquku
Nxumalo
Phinda
Shabangu
Shongwe
Simelane
Sobhuza
Zwane

Tanzania

Amana (ah-MAH-nah),

Swahili, "pledge"
Duviyani (*doo-
vee*-YAH-*nee*),
Wagoni
Ikangaa (*ih*-KAHN-*guh*)
Kawawa
Kayamba
Khanga (KHAHN-*gah*)
Kilama (*kee*-LAH-*mah*)
Kinana (*kee*-NAH-*nah*)
Kiula
Kiwete
Mahundi (*mah*-HOON-
dee)
Makinda (*mah*-KIN-
duh)
Makwaia, Sukuma
Marando
Mbunga (*m*BOON-*guh*),
Wagoni
Mdoe
Mhina
Millinga, Wagoni
Mnubi
Mtikila
Njau (*n*JOW)
Nkoma (*n*KOH-*muh*)
Serwano
Tambwe (TAHM-*bway*)

Togo

Abalo
Agbobli
Akakpovie
Alassounouma
Amedome
Andjo
Boukpessi
Dadzie
Dagba
Felli
Gali
Jibidar (*jih-bee*-DAHR)

Kodjo
Komlavi
Mawussi
Seddoh
Sivomey
Yentchabre

Tunisia

Assad
Bousnina
Chaabane
Chaouch
Chebbi
Essid
Ghanouchi
Kallel
Karoui
Khelil
Lazreg
Moalla
Nabli
Kabah
Rejeb
Rouisi
Tlili
Yahia
Zenaidi
Zorgati
Zouari

Uganda

Adriko
Adyebo
Bito, early dynasty of
west-central
Uganda
Butegwa
Chwezi, early
dynasty of west-
central Uganda
Ejalu
Etolu

Kabonero (*kah-boh-
NYAIR-oh*),
Banyankole
Kaijuka
Kategaya
Kazibwe
Kisekka
Mayanja
Mutembi
Rukidi (*roo*-KEE-*dee*)
Sabagereka
Sebunya
Senkebejje
Ssali
Ssekitoleko
Ssemogerere
Tembuzi, early
dynasty of west-
central Uganda
Zirimu

Zaire

Babibangi
Bakafwa
Bolamba (*boh*-LAHM-
bah)
Dondo (DOHN-*doh*)
Eyenga
Gifudu
Kibassa
Kitenge
Kiziki
Koko (KOH-*koh*)
Longo (LOHN-*goh*)
Lumbi (LOOM-*bee*)
Makakula (*mah-
kah*-KOO-*lah*)
Massamba
Matambo
Mehele
Mokede
Mudima
Mukendi

Mulele (*moo*-LAY-*lay*)
Muyembe
Nguza
Nzanzu
Onawelho
Tshalwe
Tshisekedi

Zambia

Chiluba
Chongwe
Hambayi
Kamana
Kapinga
Kashita
Kavindele
Kayonga
Lewanika
Lupunga
Maka
Miyanda
Mukela (*moo*-KAY-*lah*)
Mushota

Mwila
Nawakwi
Penza
Sata
Shepande
Wina
Zimba
Zukas

Zimbabwe

Chakaipa
Chidyausiku
Chidzeru
Chihota
Dangarembga
Gonzo (GOHN-*zoh*)
Karimanzira
Katomeni (*kah-
   toh*-MAY-*nee*)
Lenneiye
Lesabe
Lieros
Mahachi

Mahoso (*mah*-HOH-
   soh)
Makhalisa, Ndebele
Maraire
Mazhindu
Midzi
Mombeshora
Mukonoweshuro
   (*moo-koh-noh-
   way*-SHOO-*roh*),
   Shona, "male
   rabbit"
Mungoshi (*moon*-GOH-
   shee), Shona
Nyamapfene
Nzenza
Rungano (*roon*-GAH-
   noh)
Sekeramayi
Shamuyarira
Tekere
Tungwarara
Zindoga (*zeen*-DOH-
   gah)

NOTE: The source for many of these surnames were the Cabinet Post listings found in *Political Handbook of the World 1994-1995*, edited by Arthur S. Banks, CSA Publications, State University of New York, Binghamton, New York, 1995.

São Tomé and Príncipe and Seychelles are not included because the last names found were almost exclusively of European origin (Portuguese for the former and French for the latter.)

APPENDIX C

REFERENCE GUIDE TO THE PEOPLES AND LANGUAGES OF AFRICA

Africa's cultural composition can be rather bewildering. Over 2,000 names are used for the continent's inhabitants and their languages. Ethnic groups range in size from a handful of kinsmen—like the Buso of Chad numbering only a few dozen—to several millions of people, such as the Hausa of West Africa, Oromo of Ethiopia and Kenya, and Xhosa and Zulu of South Africa.

All African countries house more than one, if not hundreds, of ethnic groups within their borders. An estimated 200 tribes live in Cameroon alone, a country slightly larger than the state of California. With a population made up almost entirely of ethnic Somalis, Somalia is one of Africa's most homogeneous nation, but even there clan divisions assume a life of their own to further distinguish and divide the populace.

The following list of peoples of Africa and their languages indicates in which countries the groups reside. Because African cultures tend to spill over the national boundaries that were arbitrarily drawn by European powers, there may be instances where not every country in which a certain tribe lives is mentioned; however, the primary countries of residence should be included. Although this list appears extensive it is only a survey of some of the more populous and well-known peoples. To illustrate this point, note that of Cameroon's approximately 200 different ethnic groups and Tanzania's 130 plus tribes less than two dozen of each are found below.

Abyssinians   former name for Ethiopians
Acholi   a people of northern Uganda and Sudan
Adal   see AFAR
Adja   a people and language of southern Benin and southern Togo
Adouma   a people of southeast Gabon
Afar   a people of Djibouti, southeast Eritrea, and eastern Ethiopia, also called ADAL and DANAKIL
Afrikaans   an official language of South Africa derived from Dutch

Afrikaner South Africans of European, especially Dutch, descent

Agni a language of southeast Cote d'Ivoire and Ghana, also called ANYI

Ahanta a dialect of AGNI

Aizo a language of Benin

Akan language of Ghana, includes TWI of the central region and FANTI, spoken around the coast; term is also used for members of Akan-speaking ethnic groups

Akus (Creoles) people of Gambia who are descendants of freed slaves

Alba a people of southwestern Ethiopia

Alur language and people of western Uganda and Zaire

Amarinya see AMHARIC

Ambo see OVAMBO

Amhara people of Ethiopia whose language is AMHARIC, also a province of northwest Ethiopia and a former kingdom

Amharic official language of Ethiopia, also called AMARINYA

Angolares a people of São Tomé and Príncipe

Antaimoro a people of Madagascar

Antaisaka a people of southeastern coastal Madagascar

Anufo a people of Ghana and Togo

Anyi see AGNI

Anyuak a people of southern Sudan and Ethiopia, also called ANYWAA

Arabs peoples of Arabian ancestry primarily living in Algeria, Central African Republic, Chad, Comoros, Djibouti, Egypt, Kenya, Libya, Morocco, Nigeria, Sudan, Tanzania, and Tunisia

Asante see ASHANTI

Ashanti a people of central Ghana, also called ASANTE, the Ashanti speak AKAN (TWI-FANTE)

Asians peoples of Asian ancestry, mainly from India, settled primarily in Botswana (approx. 15,000 as of mid-1980s), Kenya (some 78,000 as of 1979 census), Madagascar (24,000), South Africa (one million in 1993), Tanzania (approx. 40,000), and Zimbabwe (about 10,000 in 1986)

Asu a people of Tanzania

Azande see ZANDE

Baga a people of coastal Guinea

Baganda a people of southern Uganda, also called GANDA, their language is called LUGANDA and their former kingdom is called BUGANDA

Bagirmi a people of Chad

Bagisu a people living on the western slopes of Mt. Elgon in Kenya and Uganda, also called GISU and MASABA

Bahima see TUTSI

Bahutu see HUTU

Bajuni a people of coastal southern Somalia who speak a dialect of KISWAHILI

Bakitara see BANYORO
Bakoko a people of Cameroon
Bakongo see KONGO
Bakwele people of 1. Congo 2. southeast Nigeria
Balante people of central Guinea-Bissau and Senegal
Balengue a people of Equatorial Guinea, also spelled BALENGI
Balese a people of northeastern Zaire
Baluba see LUBA
Bamana see BAMBARA
Bambara a people and principal language of the upper Niger River valley, mainly found in central Mali as well as in Burkina Faso, Cote d'Ivoire, Guinea, southern Mauritania, and Senegal, also called BAMANA and MALEL
Bambuli see MBOLE
Bamileke a people of western Cameroon
Banda a people and language of Central African Republic
Bangala a people and trade language of northeastern Zaire
Banyankole see NYANKORE
Banyoro A people of Uganda, also called NYORO and BAKITARA
Bapounou a people of Gabon and Congo, also called PUNU
Bara a people of southwest Madagascar
Barambo a people of eastern Zaire and Sudan
Bargu see BARIBA
Bari a people and language of southern Sudan
Bariba a people and language of northern Benin, Nigeria, and northeast Togo, also called BARGU
Barotse see LOZI
Barwe a people of Mozambique
Basa a people of central Nigeria
Basarwa see BUSHMAN
Basoga see SOGA
Basotho see BASUTO
Bassa a people of Liberia
Bassari people of 1. northern Togo 2. Gambia, Guinea, and Senegal
Basters a mixed-race people of Namibia who speak Afrikaans, centered around Rehoboth, south of Windhoek
Basuto people of Lesotho (approx. 99 percent of the country's population) as well as South Africa and southern Zimbabwe, their language is SESOTHO
Bata see KIRDI
Batoro a people living in the Great Lakes region of Uganda, also called TORO
Batutsi see TUTSI

Batwa   see PYGMY
Baulé   one of the principal ethnic groups and a language of Cote d'Ivoire, also in Ghana
Bavili   a subgroup of the BAKONGO
Bedouin   traditionally nomadic Arab peoples of North Africa, they speak Arabic
Beja   language of the BENI AMER of Eritrea and Sudan, also called BEDAWIYE
Bella   a people of Liberia
Bemba   a people of northern Zambia and southeast Zaire
Beni Amer   a people of Eritrea and Sudan
Berba   a people of Togo
Berber   Moslem peoples spread across North Africa and their Hamitic language, also called ZANATA, includes the KABYLE, SHAWIYYAH (CHAOUIA), MZAB (MOZABITES), TUAREG, TUAT, and WARGLA (OUARGLA) peoples
Bergdama   see DAMARA
Beta Israel   see FALASHA
Bete   one of the principal ethnic groups and a language of Cote d'Ivoire
Beti   a people of Cameroon
Betsileo   a people of Madagascar's southern plateau of Indonesian descent
Betsimisaraka   the name of a principal city as well as a people of northeast Madagascar
Bilala   a people of Chad
Binga   see PYGMY
Bini   a people and language of southern Nigeria, also called EDO
Bioko   a people of Equatorial Guinea and Gabon, also called BUBI
Birifor   a people of Burkina Faso and northern Ghana
Birom   a people of Nigeria living in the region of Jos
Bissa   a people of Burkina Faso
Bobo   a people of southwest Burkina Faso and Mali
Boki   a people of southeastern Nigeria
Borana   a people of northern Kenya
Borobo   see PEUL
Bubi   see BIOKO
Bulom or Bullom   a people of Sierra Leone, also called SHERBRO
Bulu   a people of Cameroon
Buraka   a people of Central African Republic and Congo
Busa   a people of Benin, Burkina Faso, Ghana, and Nigeria
Bushman   traditionally nomadic people of the Kalahari Desert of southern Africa, mainly in Botswana (where they are also called BASARWA) and Namibia (SAN)

Chaga a people of Tanzania, also called WACHAGA and spelled CHAGGA
Chewa a people and principal language of southern Malawi and western Mozambique, they speak CHINYANJA
Chokwe a people of Angola, Zaire, and Zambia
Chopi a people of southern coastal Mozambique
Comorian main language of the Comoros, which is an Arabised dialect of Kiswahili
Coptic Afro-Asiatic language used today only for religious purposes of the Coptic Church—the Christian Church of Egypt
Copts refers to Egyptians of ancient Egyptian ancestry, as well as to members of the Coptic Church
Creoles people of mixed European and African ancestry and their languages living in West Africa and Indian Ocean countries
Dagari a people of Burkina Faso and Ghana
Dagomba a people and language of northern Ghana
Dahomeyans see FON
Dakakari a people of northern Nigeria
Dama see DAMARA
Damaqua see DAMARA
Damara a people of Namibia, also called BERGDAMA, DAMA, and DAMAQUA, their language is called NAMA
Dan a people of western Cote d'Ivoire and Liberia
Danakil see AFAR
De or Dey a people of Liberia, also called DEWOI
Dholuo the language of the Luo people of western Kenya
Dialonka a people of Guinea
Diawara a section of the SONINKE people
Dilling see NUBAN
Dinka a people and language of southern Sudan
Diola a people of Gambia, Senegal, also spelled DYOLA
Dioula see DYULA
Djerma-Songhai see ZARMA
Dogon a people of Mali and Burkina Faso
Douala a people of Cameroon
Dyula a people of Burkina Faso and Cote d'Ivoire, also called DIOULA and JULA
Ebrie a people of Cote d'Ivoire
Edo language of Nigeria, also called BINI
Efe a people of Togo and Benin; also see PYGMY
Efik a people and language of southern Nigeria
Embu a people of Kenya, their language is KIEMBU
Eshira a people of southwest Gabon
Eton a people of Cameroon

Europeans   Europeans reside throughout the continent, some of the larger concentrations include Algeria (approx. 75,000 southern Europeans in early 1980s), Angola (approx. 10,000 Portuguese), Central African Republic (approx. 3,000 French in 1993), Egypt (approx. 350,000 Greeks in 1990), Kenya (approx. 50,000 foreign residents), Madagascar (30,000), Morocco (est. 60,000 foreign citizens in 1992, mostly French, Spanish, Italian, and Algerian), Mozambique (about 10,000 in the mid-1980s, plus 35,000 mixed African-Europeans), Namibia (approx. 85,000 in 1991), South Africa (approx. 5 million as of 1993), Swaziland (some 11,000 in 1986), Zaire (est. 200,000 non-Africans in early 1990s, including Greeks, Belgians, Lebanese, and Indians), Zambia (about 17,000 in 1984), and Zimbabwe (approx. 150,000 in 1986)

Evalue   a people of southwest Ghana

Ewe   a language of Togo and eastern Ghana, also called POPO

Ewondo   a people of Cameroon

Falasha   Jewish Ethiopians, the majority of whom have emigrated to Isreal in recent years, also called BETA ISRAEL

Fang   a people and language of Cameroon, Equatorial Guinea, northern Gabon, and Congo, as well as the main ethnic group of São Tomé and Príncipe

Fante   see FANTI

Fanti   see AKAN

Fata   see KIRDI

Fernandinos   people of Equatorial Guinea of mixed ancestry (freed slaves from the mainland and Europeans, mostly Spaniards)

Fingo   a people of Cape Province, South Africa

Fon   a people of southern Benin, also called DAHOMEYANS, they speak an EWE dialect

Fula or Fulani   large group of people of West Africa found in Benin, Burkina Faso, northern Cameroon, Chad, Gambia, Guinea, Guinea-Bissau, Mali, Mauritania, Niger, Nigeria, Senegal, Sierra Leone, and Togo, also called the FULBE, PEUL, and TUKULOR, their language is called FULA and FULFULDE

Fur   a people of Chad and Sudan, also called KONJARA

Ga   a people and language of Ghana around the Accra area and of Benin and Togo, also called GAN

Gabbra   a people of northern Kenya

Gadabourssi   a Somali people of Djibouti

Galla   see OROMO (note: Galla is found in older documents, it is considered a derogatory term and should not be used today)

Ganda   see BAGANDA

Gbandi   a people of Liberia

Gbari   see GWARI

Gbaya   a people and language dialects of Central African Republic

Gikuyu a people originally from the central highlands of Kenya, their language is called KIKUYU—a term also used to refer to the people
Gio see DAN
Giriama a people of coastal Kenya
Gisu see BAGISU
Gogo a people of Tanzania
Gola a people of western Liberia and Sierra Leone
Gourmantché a people of Benin, eastern Burkina Faso, Togo, and Ghana, also called GURMA
Grebo a people of Liberia
Grusi peoples of northern Ghana and Burkina Faso, including the KASENA and ISALA
Guidar see KIRDI
Gur name for a group of people of West Africa that includes the DAGBANE, GURMA, and GRUSI
Gurage a people of Ethiopia
Gurma see GOURMANTCHÉ
Gusii a people of Kenya and Tanzania
Gwari a people of northwestern Nigeria, also called GBARI
Ha a people of northwest Tanzania, also called HAHA
Hausa one of Africa's largest ethnic groups, these people live mainly in northern Nigeria, southern Niger, and Benin, Hausa is an important trade language of the region (spoken by about 85 percent of the people in Niger)
Haya a people of western Tanzania
Hehe a people of Tanzania
Herero a people of Namibia
Hlengwe a people of southern Zimbabwe
Hottentot people and language of southern Africa, especially Botswana and Namibia, includes the BERGDAMA, also called KHOI
Hutu a people of Burundi and Rwanda, also called BAHUTU
Ibibio a people and language of southeastern Nigeria
Ibo a people and language of southeastern Nigeria, also called IGBO
Idoma a people of Nigeria
Igbo see IBO
Ijaw a people and language of southern Nigeria, also called IJO
Isala see GRUSI
Ishan a people of Nigeria
Issa a people of Djibouti who speak a dialect of Somali
Issaq a Somali people of Djibouti
Iteso see TESO
Jola a people of Gambia
Jula see DYULA
Kabre a people of northern Togo

Kabyle see BERBER

Kalanga a people and language of Botswana and western Zimbabwe (a subgroup of the SHONA)

Kalenjin a people and language group of Kenya

Kamba people of 1. Kenya 2. Congo

Kanuri a people and language of northern Nigeria and Niger

Kapsiki see KIRDI

Karamajong a people of northeast Uganda

Karanga a people and language of southern Zimbabwe (a subgroup of the SHONA)

Kasena see GRUSI

Kela a people of Zaire

Kgalagadi Botswana

Khoi see HOTTENTOT

Khoi-San a grouping of peoples and languages of southern Africa that includes HOTTENTOT (Khoi) and BUSHMAN (San)

Kiga a people of Uganda

Kikuyu a people originally from the central highlands of Kenya and their language

Kimbundu a people and language of Angola

Kinyarwanda the Bantu language of Rwanda spoken by virtually 100 percent of the population

Kirdi peoples of northern Cameroon and Nigeria, includes the KAPSIKI, FATA, BATA, MAFA, GUIDAR, and PODOKO

Kirundi the Bantu language of Burundi spoken throughout the country, also called RUNDI and IKIRUNDI

Kissi a people of Guinea, Liberia, and Sierra Leone

Kiswahili this important lingua franca of East and Central Africa is a Bantu-based language with heavy Arabic and some European language influences

Kongo a people of western Zaire, Angola, and southwestern Congo, also called BAKONGO, their language is called KIKONGO.

Konjara see FUR

Kono people of Sierra Leone

Koranko a people of Sierra Leone and Guinea

Kotokoli a TEM-speaking people of northern Togo, their name means "infidel"

Kpelle a people of Guinea and Liberia

Kran or Krahn a people of Cote d'Ivoire and Liberia

Kru language family of Cote d'Ivoire and Liberia, includes BASSA, KRU, KRAN, and GREBO

Kunama a people of southwest Eritrea

Kunda a people of Malawi, Mozambique, and Zambia

Kusasi a people of Burkina Faso and northern Ghana
Lala 1. a language family of Nigeria 2. a people and language of Zaire and Zambia 3. a people of South Africa
Lamba 1. a TEM-speaking people of Benin and Togo 2. a people and language of Zambia and Zaire
Lango people of 1. northern Uganda 2. southern Sudan speaking LOTUKO
Limba people of 1. Guinea, Sierra Leone 2. Cameroon
Lingala after French, the main language of central Zaire as well as parts of the Congo
Lobi a people of Burkina Faso, Cote d'Ivoire, and Ghana
Loma a people of Guinea and Liberia, also called TOMA
Lomwe a principal ethnic group of Mozambique
Lozi collective name for twenty-five tribes of Botswana and Zambia, also called BAROTSE
Luba a people and major language of southeastern Zaire, the people are also called BALUBA, they speak KILUBA and TSHILUBA
Luganda language of the Baganda people of Uganda
Lugbara a people of Uganda and Zaire
Luhya a people of western Kenya and Uganda
Lunda a people and language of Angola, Zaire, and Zambia
Luo a people of western Kenya, their language is called DHOLUO and LUO
Maasai traditionally pastoral people of Kenya and Tanzania
Mafa see KIRDI
Makonde a people of Tanzania and northern Mozambique
Makua a people and language of the Comoros and Mozambique
Malagasy people of Indonesian descent and an official language of Madagascar
Malel see BAMBARA
Mande West African peoples and language group that includes the MALINKE, BAMBARA, DYULA, and SUSU, also called MANDINGO (found in Guinea, Gambia, Burkina Faso, Mali, Liberia, Senegal, and Sierra Leone)
Mandjako a people of Guinea-Bissau
Mano a people of Liberia
Maravi collective name for the CHEWA, NSENGA, and NYANJA peoples of Malawi, Mozambique, and Zambia
Marka see SARAKOLLE
Masaba see BAGISU
Mashona see SHONA
Matabele see NDEBELE
Maures see MOORS
Mbede a people of Congo and Gabon, also called MBETE

Mbene   a people of Cameroon
Mbete   see MBEDE
Mbole   a people of Zaire, also called BAMBULI
Mboshi   a people of northwest Congo
Mbukushu   a people of Angola, Botswana, and Namibia
Mbundu   see OVIMBUNDU
Mbuti   see PYGMY
Mende   a people and language of southeastern Sierra Leone and Liberia
Merina   a people of Indonesian descent living on Madagascar's central
   plateau
Meroitic   refers to an early people of Sudan and their language, with a
   kingdom centered around MEROE, an ancient city on the Nile River
Meru   a people of the Mount Kenya area of Kenya who speak KIMERU
Mihavane   see NGURU
Mijikenda   coastal people of Kenya whose name means "nine towns"
Minya   a people of Cote d'Ivoire
Moors   Muslim people of mixed Arab and Berber ancestry of northwest
   Africa, especially Mauritania, also spelled MAURES
Mossi   a people and language of central Burkina Faso
Murle   a people of southern Sudan
Mvele   a people of Cameroon
Myéné   a people of Gabon
Mzab   see BERBER
Nama   see HOTTENTOT
Nandi   a people and language of western Kenya
Nawdemba   a TEM-speaking people of Togo
Ndebele   a people of Zimbabwe and South Africa, also known as
   MATEBELE, who speak SINDEBELE
Ngbandi   a people and language of northern Zaire
Ngoni   group of peoples and languages of southern and southeastern
   Africa, includes the Xhosa, Zulu, Ndebele, and Swazi, also called
   NGUNI
Nguru   people of Mozambique and Malawi, also called MIHAVANE
Nkore   see NYANKORE
Nsenga   a people of Zambia
Nuban   a people and language of southcentral Sudan, also called DILL-
   ING and NYIMA
Nubian   a people and language of northern Sudan and southern Egypt
Nuer   a people and language of southern Sudan
Nupe   a people and language of Nigeria
Nyamwezi   a people of Tanzania
Nyanja   a people of Malawi and Zambia
Nyankore   a people of Uganda, also called NKORE and BANYANKOLE

Nyima   see NUBAN
Nyoro   see BANYORO
Oromo   one of Africa's largest ethnic groups and their language, these people live in Ethiopia and northern Kenya
Ovambo   a people of northern Namibia, Angola, and Zambia, also called AMBO and WAMBO
Ovimbundu   a people of west-central Angola, also called MBUNDU and UMBUNDU
Pedi   a people of the Transvaal, South Africa
Pepel   a people of Guinea-Bissau
Peul   see FULANI
Podoki   see KIRDI
Popo   see EWE
Punu   see BAPOUNOU
Pygmy   a people of Burundi and Rwanda (where they are also called TWA or BATWA), southern Cameroon, Congo, southwestern Central African Republic (also called BINGA), eastern Gabon and Zaire (also called MBUTI and EFE)
Qwara   a people of the Lake Tana region of Ethiopia
Rashaida   a people of northwest Eritrea
Rendille   a people of northern Kenya
Sakalava   a people of western Madagascar
Samburu   a traditionally nomadic people of Kenya
Samo   a people of Burkina Faso
San   see BUSHMAN
Sango   1. a language spoken throughout Central African Republic   2. a people of Tanzania
Sao   a people of northern Cameroon
Sara   largest ethnic group of southern Chad, they speak BONGO-BAGIRMI languages
Sarakolle   a people of Senegal and Mali who speak SONINKE
Senufo   people and language of southwest Burkina Faso, northern Cote d'Ivoire, and Mali
Serahuli   a people of Gambia
Serer   a people of Senegal
Sesotho   Also spelled SESUTO, the language of the BASUTO people of southern Africa
Setswana   the national language of Botswana
Seychellois   the term for inhabitants of the Seychelles
Shangaan   see TSONGA
Shawiyya   see BERBER
Sherbro   see BULOM
Shilluk   a people of Upper Nile Province of southern Sudan

Shona a people and language group of Zimbabwe and central Mozambique, includes the dialects ZEZURU, KARANGA, MANYIKA, KOREKORE, NDAU, and KALANGA, the people are also called MASHONA

Sindebele language of the NDEBELE people

Siswati language of the SWAZI people

Soga a people of Uganda

Somali a traditionally nomadic people and language of Somalia, as well as southern Djibouti, eastern Ethiopia, and east and northeast Kenya

Somba see TAMBERMA

Songhai a people of Mali and Niger and trade language of the region

Soninké language spoken by peoples in Senegal, Gambia, Mali, Burkina Faso, and Mauritania, including the MARKA, SERAHULI, SARAKOLLE, GAJAGA, TUBAKAI, and ASWANIK

Sotho name for a people and language of Lesotho, South Africa, and southern Zimbabwe, the people are also called BASOTHO and BASUTO, the language is also called SESOTHO and SESUTO

Sukuma a people of Tanzania

Susu a people of southern Guinea, Sierra Leone, and Mali

Swahili coastal people of East Africa (mainly Kenya and Tanzania), their language is KISWAHILI, the name Swahili is derived from Arabic and means "belonging to the coast"

Swazi a people of Swaziland and South Africa, their language is called SWATI and SISWATI

Tamberma a people of Benin, also called SOMBA

Tanala a people of Madagascar

Temba a people of northern Togo who speak TEM

Temne a people and language of Sierra Leone

Teso a people and language group of northeastern Uganda and Kenya, also called ITESO

Tigre a Semitic language of Eritrea, Ethiopia, and eastern Sudan

Tigrinya a Semitic language of Eritrea as well as parts of Ethiopia and the Sudan

Tiv a people of Nigeria

Toma see LOMA

Tonga or Thonga a people of 1. Malawi 2. Mozambique 3. Zambia and Zimbabwe

Toro see BATORO

Toucouleur French variation of TUKULOR

Tsimihety a people of Madagascar

Tsonga a people and language of South Africa and Mozambique, including the dialect SHANGAAN

Tswana people and language of Botswana, Namibia, and South Africa

Tuareg traditionally nomadic Berber people of the western Sahara, including southwest Libya, northern Mali, and Niger, and their language

Tuat   see BERBER

Tukulor   name the FULANI use for themselves

Turkana   a people of northwestern Kenya

Tutsi   a people of Burundi and Rwanda, also called the BAHIMA, WATUTSI, WATUSI, and BATU

Twa   see PYGMY

Twi   see ASHANTI

Umbundu   see OVIMBUNDU

Urhobo   a people of Nigeria

Vai   a people and language of northern Liberia and Sierra Leone

Venda   a people and language of the Transvaal, South Africa, and southern Zimbabwe

Wachagga   see CHAGGA

Walamo   a people and language of southwestern Ethiopia

Wargla   see BERBER

Watusi   see TUTSI

Watutsi   see TUTSI

Wolof   a people and main language of Senegal, Gambia, and Mauritania

Xhosa   a large group of people of South Africa and their language, which uses many click sounds

Yao   a people of Malawi and northern Mozambique

Yoruba   a people and important language of Nigeria and Benin

Zanata   see BERBER

Zande   people of southern Sudan, Central African Republic, and Zaire, the plural form is AZANDE and their language is called Pa-Zande

Zaramo   a people and language of Tanzania

Zarma   a people of Niger and Nigeria

Zezeru   a people of central Zimbabwe and their language, which is a dialect of the Shona language

Zulu   people and important language of Natal Province, South Africa

Although this list was composed independently, it was verified by using the Guide to Peoples and Languages, found in the Franklin Watts' *Encyclopedia of Africa* (1976) and *The Statesman's Year Book (1994–1995)*, edited by Brian Hunter (St. Martin's Press, NY). For those wishing to research the peoples of Africa further, comprehensive information is available in the International African Institute's *Ethnographic Survey of Africa*, as well as the series on African languages that includes *Handbook of African Languages* (Andre/Basset), *Languages of West Africa* (D. Westermann and M. A. Bryan), *The Non-Bantu Languages of Northeastern Africa* (A. N. Tucker and M. A. Bryan), and *The Bantu Languages of Africa* (M. A. Bryan). Travel books, such as *Fielding's Africa South of the Sahara*, generally provide brief overviews of a country's ethnic composition.

ENGLISH LANGUAGE INDEX TO AFRICAN NAMES

Aaron, HARUNI

Abel, HABILI

abound, TWAMVULA

above all, BELAYNESH, BELAY

Abraham, BRAIMA, BURAHIMU

abundance, YALWA

advancer, MUKADAMU

accident, KOTSI, TSIETSI. See Introduction

accomplished, ATUM

active in the womb, KASAMBA

active in times of scarcity, OMENUKO. See surnames list, Nigeria

Adam, ADAMU, KAZIMUNTU

admire, ADUKE, ALAKE, AMOKE, APEKE, APINKE, JUMOKE

adore, YASSOUNGO

affairs of the heart, VISOLELA

affectionate, ADENIKE

afraid, MAHAVAVY, YIFRU. See surnames list, Eritrea/Ethiopia

ahead, ZULI

airplane, JIRGI

al-Ghazali, GAZALI

all, DUKA

alligator, POLO

allure, TAMANISHA

almighty, LAZIZI

amulet, HIRSI

Aminah, AMAN

ancestor of the Amahlubi, RADEBE. See surnames list, South Africa

anchored, ZINDZI

angel, MALAIKA. See Introduction

animal, CHEELO

ant, MULAHI, WONYE

anteater, BIKITA

antelope, ELE. See Introduction

Arab. See day of week names charts for BALARABE, BALARABA, and LARABA

arid, KAME

aristocrat, TATAU

ash, OBURU, WAMUHU

ashamed, TIJU-IKU

assistant, NASIRU

attack, HAAZITA

aunt, SHANGAZI

available, HAJANIKA

axe, EKUVA

Aziz, LAZIZI

Azriel, ZIRAILI

baby girl, ATITI, OTITI

bachelor, SOGA. See surnames list, South Africa

bad luck, MWENDALUBI

bad-maker, CHIVODZI

bag, OKE

balance, MIZAN

banished, DINGISWAYO

basket names, ADITA, ATONGA, AWITI, ODHERU, OWITI

Bashir, BASH

be known, JULIKANA

beans, CIWAKE

beautiful, ADUMADAN, ANYAWU,
APONBEPORE, EHOBIB, EZENMA,
HASANA, and HUSEINA, see twin
name charts HUSNA, ISABIS,
KARUNGI, KAZURI, KITOKO, LEWA,
SARAMA, SHESHE, WUBET, ZENE
beautiful child, OMOLEWA
beautiful eyes, MAHA
been through a lot, AHATAJANALE.
See Introduction
beer, BUKOKO, HATTABARI
before everyone else, SENDIBADA
before we die we shall have seen,
TAFATAONA
beginning, DAVU
begrude, ORILONISE
believe, SADIKI
bell, MULANGU. See Introduction
belly button, HAKUNYO, KUNYO
belongs to God, UWIMANA
belongs to the coast, SWAHILI. See
reference guide to peoples and
languages
beloved, AMADIKA, HABIBUNA,
MUDIWA, MUDIKANWA, THANDIWE
Benedictus, MUHISANI
benefactor, MUHISINI. See MUHISANI
bent, HADIIMANA
betrayal, BAMPORIKI, BANYANGIRIKI,
UWAMURENGEYE
betrothal, RITA
better life, RAHWA
big, DJITO
big building, RISHAN
big headed, GUNE. See twin name
charts
big place, BAKAU
big river, ASUBONTENG
big strides, NTIMBANJAYO
Bilal, BINA
bitterness, PANDASALA
black, BERKANE, IZIBILI
black magic, MUROGI, NDOKI
black rhinoceros, SIPEJANA. See

surnames list, South Africa
blade of a knife, MUCHESE
bleeding during pregnancy,
KAMBUNDU
blessed, KUDISAN, KIBWE, MUHISANI,
YITBAREK. See surnames list,
Eritrea/Ethiopia
blessings, BARKE, BARAKE,
KIBARAKE, TRHAAS
blind, KAMEKE. See Introduction
bliss, ANANDA
Blue Nile River, ABAY
bold, DIALLO
boogie man, AKOKO
born at Christmas, NATASHA. See
Introduction
born covered with ruptured
membrane, SALAKO, TALABI
born face downward, AJAYI. See
Introduction
born feet first, IGE, NAFUNA
born in a scotch cart, CHIKOCHI. See
Introduction
born in Baganda territory,
KABAGANDA. See Introduction
born in the bush, KOSENGE, USENGE
born while parent is on pilgrimage
to Mecca, MAKAWIYYU. See
Introduction
born without complications,
KAIJABWANGU. See Introduction
boss, MOKONZI, RUSSOM
bowlegged, OGWEL
brave, AKINYELE, MUGESI, ZOOB,
UKO. See Introduction
breath, HABILI
breech birth, IGE, NAFUNA
bright light, FANUS
brightest, ANWAR
brilliant, MOUNIR, ZULI
brings together, DAPO
brook, JAFARU
Bubastis, BAST
buffalo, KIAMBOGO

building, JENGO
bull, TWON
burnt, GUBAN
bush, KOSENGE, USENGE
buying, KAULA
by God, BEYLA
Caesarean birth, PASUA
Cain, KABILI
calabash, KURUMAN
calm, LUAM, NACALA, RIG'AT
calm world, YIRGA-ALEM
calves, MOI
came from above, WOREDE
cassava, ROGO
cattle kraal, CHIMPATI
cedar trees, TARAKWET
celebration, SHANGWE
chair, ENTEBBE
chance, BAHATISHA
chaste, TAYIBU
cheerful, TESHI
cherished, BARAMOUSSO
chicken, OGWENO. See time of day
and season name charts
chief, CAUNGULA, KAJOK-KOJI, MAI
ZARIA, MANGI MKUU, MASA,
MOKONZI, MWANI, SARKI, SID,
CHEIKH. See surnames list,
Algeria
chief of farmers, SARKIN NOMA. See
NOMA
chief's deputy, MADAKI. See
surnames list, Nigeria
child dies, CAIMILE, VONDILA,
VUMBA
child given to enemies, MPABAISI
and BALYESIMA. See Introduction
child of the air roots, NWAOGA. See
Introduction
childless, ESENJE, IZEFIA
chosen, HAREENA, MUTAFA
Christmas, ABIODUN
cinder, KAMIAPIULU

circumcision feast, BUTA. See
surnames list, Eritrea/Ethiopia
civet cat, LISISI. See surnames list,
South Africa
cleansing, NSANZYA. See
Introduction
clement, ALIMA
clever, IKID. See Introduction
clever idea, AKILI
cloaked one, MUDASHIRU
cold, OLEN KIJABE, UFWENUKA,
SERAME. See Introduction
collected, SEBSIBE. See surnames
list, Eritrea/Ethiopia
color of morning, NGULA. See
Introduction
comes from nowhere, KIONE
comes to make things better,
ADERO. See surnames list, Kenya
comes with her own things,
NTOZAKE
comforter, ABADEET, ABADI,
NONTUTUZELO
compassion, NOSENTE, RAIMI
confidence in God,
UWILIYINGIYAMANA. See
surnames list, Rwanda
conflict, MAKONDO
congratulations, BISSIRAT, YOHANA
console, ASHIETU, NONTUTUZELO
control anger, KASIM
council house, BARAZA. See
surnames list, Kenya
councilor, DIWANI
courage, VUMILIA
court case, MILANDU
court clerk, MABBALANI
courthouse, NTURANYENINKIKO
covenant, KIDANE
craftsman, MUCHESE
create, YIFTER
creator, CHI
creek, JAFARU

croaking frog, CHILILABOMBWE
cross, OKAL
crown, ADE, TADJ, ZEWDI
crown brings together, ADEDAPO.
    See DAPO
crown has a shadow, ADENIJI
crown is loving, ADENIKE
crown is peaceful, ADETUTU
crown remains in this house,
    ADEKUNLE
curly hair, DADA
customs differ, MBUNDU. See
    Introduction
Cyrus, KIROS
danger, KOTSI, ODUNEWU. See
    Introduction
dark-brown skin, BUNDU
dark-skinned, ADUMADAN, IZIBILI,
    DINKA. See Introduction
darkness, CHAUSIKU, DUKANA, and
    HADUKANA. See time of day and
    season charts
daughter of a warrior, NJERI
daughter of fortune, 'YAR ARZIKI
daughter of God, ADACHI. See CHI
daughter of Riji, NYARIJI
daughter of the oath, BATHSHEBA.
    See Introduction
daughter of the waters, LOSTRIS
daughters only, NTOMBIZODWA
dawn. See time of day and season
    name charts for DIRAM, DIRAMU,
    and BUCHEDO
days, MAZUBA. See time of day and
    season name charts
daytime, TARANA
dead, OKU
dead and awake, AKUJI
death, AYONDELA, KATAFWA,
    NOKOFA, NTAMPUHWE, VUMBA,
    LEFU. See Introduction
decay, SHABALALA. See surnames
    list, South Africa

December, KENDA
dedicated, IDIRISI
delight, TEDLA. See surnames list,
    Eritrea/Ethiopia
departure, ZOAN
descend, WOREDE, ZERU
descendent of Daniel, ZERU DANIEL.
    See ZERU
descent, OAFE
desire, WINTA
desolate, KAME
despair, CAIMILE, VONDILA, VUMBA
destiny, ORILONISE
determination, ABAY
development, MAJAMBERE
diamond, ALMAZ
did not find, SIBAJENE
dignity, RAFFET
diminishing, OTUHO
dimples, NABUNYA
discord in the family, BANGAMWABO
dispute, MILANDU, TWAAMBO
divination, LAORATU
document, HATI (see BAHATISHA),
    WARAKA
don't do harm, see Introduction for
    ABOKA, EMENE, IROEGBUNNE,
    IWEOBI, and MADUEKWENJO
don't go, MALOMO
don't interfere with another's
    course, NJAKUPITI. See
    Introduction
double-crossers, AOLA
dreadlocks, DADA
dress up, AWERO
driven away, PHANDELANI. See
    surnames list, South Africa
drought, CILANGA, MONYYAK. See
    Introduction
drummer, OGINGA
dry stalk of grain, SENWE
duck, BATA
duiker, IPUTI and PUTI. See

feigned sadness of a bride, HUSO
fertile, LEMLEM, ROGO
festivals, ONDEKU and ADEIKA. See
  Introduction
fibrous plant, ALGI
fields, MASIMONG. See twin name
  charts
fight, AJAMU, AJANI
finished, KAPERA, MANDIPEDZA,
  NTIRUSHIZE, OTUHO
firefly, MUTENITENI
first child, DIKKO
first daughter after many sons,
  KANDE
first son after many daughters,
  TANKO
first taste of the world, TAIWO and
  TAIYE. See Introduction and twin
  name charts
fish, IKOKO
fishermen, WALUWI
flight, HAJARI
flower, NAKIMULI, PALESA
follower, MUNACITONKWA
follows through, OKAOME. See
  surnames list, Nigeria
foolish, IYOYO
forefathers, MUSE, NAISER, OMEL,
  POLONGOMA, TAKA
forerunner, BASH, BASHIRU
forewarner, MUKADAMU
forgive, XOLANI
forgiver, MAHARI
forgotten, TIASSALE
forsaken, NTSHIUWA and MOSIUWA.
  See twin name charts
fort, EMBAYE
found one, FUMANE
fox, KONDO
free men, ORMA
freedom, NETSENET
freshness, BINA
friend/friendly, MACHARIA,
  RAMOSA, YASUMINI

friendly with strangers,
  MALIDOMA. See Introduction
frog, HARACHA, KAMBUNDU, RACH
fruitful, EPHREM
fulfilled, SEMIRA
full, KOSHI, SHIBA, JORE. See twin
  name charts
full of love, NONTANDO
funeral, MWENDALUBI, OBURU
future, KESHO
Gabriel, JIBURILI
Gabriel's wing, KENFA GABREEL. See
  KINFE
garden, CHILILI, JANINA, KIRUNDU
gatherings, LUK
generation, KIZAZI
generous, KERIMU, SAITOTI
genet, INSIMBA and TSHIPA. See
  surnames list, South Africa
gentle, ANANA
George, JORJ
ghost, CHEELO
gift, CHIPELO, CHIPO, EBUN, MPHO,
  see twin name charts, DIARRA.
  See surnames list, Mali
giraffe, TUTLA. See surnames list,
  South Africa
girl, NYAKO
give, CHIPEI
giver, MANANI
glad, FURAHA, GAMADA
glory, AZUKA, OPEYEMI
go beyond, OKAL
goat, ABBARE'E, ADIEL, BUZI, MULEYA
God, CHI, CHUKS, ERINLE, MOGAI.
  See surnames list, Nigeria
God answers prayers, CHINAZA
God bless, ALAMAKO, BARAKE
God does me honor, OLUSOLA
God gives, CHUKUMEKA, FABUNNI,
  MANANI, NYAMEKYE, OLUJIMI
God has granted this child,
  EFUNSETAN
God has power over me,

IYAKAREMYE
God heals, SUKUAKUECE. See
Introduction
God helps me stand, OLUMOROTI
God I don't dispute, CAPOPIA
God is able, YIKEALO
God is mighty, OLUTOBI
God is the saviour, HAKIZIMANA.
See surnames list, Rwanda
God is worthy of worship,
OLUWATOYIN
God knows, BIZIMANA, NIYIBIZI,
BIZIMUNGU. See surnames list,
Rwanda
God lied, VATUKEMBA
God loves me, OLUFEMI
God loves us, MBARUSHIMANA
God made, CHIMELU
God makes one have a child,
HABYARIMANA
God of strength, CHIKE. See CHI
God of wealth, CHIAKU. See CHI
God will decide, NAHIMANA
God will help us, ALATANGA
God-given, DIEUDONNE. See
surnames list, Burkina Faso
God-like, MIKAILI
God's beloved, HABIBULAI
God's fruit, FREZGHI
God's gift, KIRABO
God's grace, AMARACHI. See
Introduction
God's help, ZIRAILI
God's hope, TESFAZGHI
God's light, IHECHI. See
Introduction
God's plan, ELOCHUKWU. See
Introduction
God's will is inescapable,
CAIMBASUKU. See Introduction
God's word, KAL'AB
going, AMWENDO
gold, WORKU. See surnames list,
Eritrea/Ethiopia

golden, ZARINA
golden mouth, AFEWERKI, AFEWARK.
See Introduction
good, CITALALA, DARA,
FIANARANTSOA, NYABERA, TAYIBU
good cheer, BASHASHA
good child, OMODARA
good news/good tidings, BISSIRAT,
BOSEDE, BASHIRI, ZENAWI
good ones die, MFON NK PANA. See
Introduction
good times, NAFASI
gossip, BARAYAGWIZA, BAYAVUGE
grace, HANETU, KISAKYE, MELITTE
granary loft, NYIRABIGEGA
grandfathers, WAGULO
grandmother, MAIKULU, SIMINI
grandmother dies, ABIBA, IYABODE,
YETUNDE
grandmother moon, KOKO-MWEZI
grape, WEYNEE
grape seed, FREWEYNEE
grass, ILUNMUN. See Introduction
gratefulness, MISGANNA,
MODUPEOLA
gratified, THABISO. See twin name
charts)
gratitude to God, ADOGHE. See
Introduction
green, ALEMASH, CITALALA, LEMLEM
greet, SALIMU
grieve, MAHLOMOLA. See
Introduction
grinds millet, GAKEE
grown, BEKELE. See surnames list,
Eritrea/Ethiopia
guess, BAHATISHA
guests, BEENZU
guardian of the fire, MALIKI
guide, KARANJA
Hafsah, AFISHETU
Hagar, HAJARI
hair, MASUSU
hairlip, FAHRU

hairy, ISSAY
Halima, ALIMA
handsome, ALASAN, HASSAN, HUSAYN, and HUSSEINI. See twin name charts
Hannah, HANETU
happiness, ANANDA, FURAHA, FISSEHA, HAGOSA, MAKENNA, THANAYI, THABANG, and NTHABISENG, see twin name charts; HAGOS, see surnames list, Eritrea/Ethiopia; TAKALANI. See surnames list, South Africa
happy hill, SAKEGAMADA
happy occasion, TAMASHA
hardship, SHIDA, TUAYUNGE. See Introduction
hardworking man, KAZI
hardworking woman, NIELENI
hare, KANDIMBA, VUNDLA. See surnames list, South Africa
harmattan, AKARIKA. See Introduction
harvest, MAPOPWE
Hasan, ALASAN
hate, BANOBA. See Introduction
hate without reason, KAVOVO
hawk, ENYAMA, HORUS
he was born, TEWELDE
head of the house, BABA-ILE
head up, UFWENUKA
headman, MANGI MKUU, MEQUANENT, MOKONZI, MUGAMBI, RUSSOM, CHEIKH . See surnames list, Algeria
healing one, MAHAJANGA
healthy girl, EZELAOBA. See Introduction
heart, ZAMOYONI
heaven, ZULU. See surnames list, South Africa
heavenly, SAMAWATI
heavy, DIDINGA, DJITO, KEBEDE. See surnames list, Eritrea/Ethiopia

heir, HADGU, IZEFIA
helper, NASIRU, SAIDI
her place, SAFARA
herbs, MICHELO
heritage, OAFE
hero, AKINYELE, MFUMU
hidden, AMUN
high rank, RAFFET
hill, KIA
hippopotamus, NGEVE, see CILOMBO; IMVUBO. See surnames list, South Africa)
Hitler, ITILA. See Introduction
honest, AMINI, LAMIN
honor, FOLA, see FOLASADE; LADIPO, ABIOLA. See surnames list, Nigeria
honor bestows a crown, FOLASADE
honor increases, OLABISI
honor is full of troubles, LANIYONU
honored, MUTIA
hope, SUUBI, TUMAINI, TESFU, TSHEPO. See twin name charts
horn, PIIPI
hospital (mother doesn't arrive at the hospital in time for the delivery), AOKO, HANZILA, NZILA, OOKO
hot, HAM
human, MOTU
humane, ALIMA
humming bird, KANJONJO. See Introduction
hunger, AKECH, SHANGWA, UFWENUKA, MWAJANANZALA. See Introduction
hunter/hunting, HANYAMA, ILEGA, KACELA, LOLEGA, ORINGO, SIAJU, SISHOKWE, MUTEYE. See Introduction
hurry, JIRGI, SARDA
hyena, SUNTWE, KWIRI, and IMPISI. See surnames list, South Africa
I am here, NIKO

I have said, AWACHO
illuminated, ANWAR
impatience, NGAYABARAMBIRWA
important, TWON
increase, YOSEFU
induced pregnancy, MIYANDA,
  MICHELO
inevitability of death, AYONDELA
infertility, AHORISHAKIYE, ADESINA
infidel, KOTOKOLI. See reference
  guide to peoples and languages
inheritor, GADDO. See twin name
  charts)
insect, MUUKA
inspired, MABILI
inspirer, DUMI
intelligence, AKILI, SUDETU
interfering, KANJONJO. See
  Introduction
invincible people, BETSILEO
irreplaceable, VONDILA
Isaiah, ISAYAS
island, KERKENNA
Jacob, YAKUBU
Jafar, JAFARU
Jasmine, YASUMINI
jealousy, EHIOZE, MONA
Jeremiah, YEREMIYA
jewel, SERWA
Joseph, YOSEFU
journey, ABIONA, LEETO, LWEENDO,
  MWIINDE, SENGENDO
joy, ANISA, AYODELE, AYOKA,
  FISSEHA, HAGOSA, THABO. See
  twin name charts; HAGOS. See
  surnames chart, Eritrea/Ethiopia
judge, ALKALI. See surnames list,
  Nigeria
junior, MOKE
Jupiter, MUSHITARA
just, ADILA
Kano, BAKANO
Kareem, KERIMU
key of mercy, MUFTAU

kicker, KASAMBA
Kikuyu ancestors. See Introduction
  for GIKUYU, MUMBI, WANJERI,
  WANJIRU, WAMBUI, WANGUI,
  WANGECHI, WAMBURA, WANJIKU,
  WANGARI, WAMUYU, and WAIRIMU
kind, MLULAMI
king, KIROS, MALIKI, MUGABE,
  MUKAMA, MWAMI
kingly, EZENWA
kings, AKWAY CAM, BENHAZIN,
  CHITIMUKULU, JUNJU, KARAN,
  MUKAMUTALA
king's word, ENOBAKHARE
kite (the bird), ACHWIL. See twin
  name charts
know one another, JUANA
knowledge, SHAIHI, TSABO
lady, SADATINA
lags behind, KEHINDE. See
  Introduction and twin name
  charts
lake, MAYANJA
lame, HADIIMANA
lanky, DOGO, MULEFU
lantern, FANUS
large, RAHAB
last child, KODA, TWAMVULA
last daughter, AUDI, MANDIPEDZA
lasting friend, MACHARIA
late, OMOPE
law, MAAT
lazy, MULELE
leader, CAUNGULA, MFUMU,
  MUGAMBI, TESHOME
left behind, CHISHALE SHALE, KONO,
  VATUSIA
left-handed, GURE
leopard, KANGWE, SILUWE. See
  surnames list, South Africa, for
  INGWE, NGULULE, and SIGAKAKA
let us go, TUYENI
letter, WARAKA
liberal, KERIMU

liberator, FATIU
life, ASHA, HAWAKULU, HEEWAN,
HIWOT, MO
light, MUZWENGE. See time of day
and season name charts
light of God, IHECHI. See CHI
Light was born, TEWELDE BERHAN.
See TEWELDE
light-skinned, APONBEPORE,
BATURIYA, BAGULE, GBOLI,
MAMAGULE, ARAB. See
Introduction
like very much, MAKADISA
lion, AGU, DIATA, HOSI (see twin
name charts), LENCHO, SHANGE,
WAHRAN, ZAKI. See surnames
list, South Africa for
INGONYAMAM and TAU
lioness, AFISHETU, TIARET
lit what was gloomy, ABRAHA
little, BULUS, MOKE
little blessings, KIBARAKE
little man, KIBWANA
live in the future, UZABAKILIHO
live near the courthouse (or
border), NTURANYENINKIKO
lives by medicine, KAIHEMBA
living image of Amun,
TUTANKHAMUN
locusts, CHISONZI. See Introduction
long, DOGO
long face, EIBARAB. See
Introduction
long pregnancy, MUHONGO, OMOPE,
SHEKARAU
long wait (for a child), BITON,
CHILALA, CHIPEGO, GAMADA,
HABYARIMANA, YIKEALO
Lord (title), KHEDIVE, MAULANA,
MWANI, SID, UBA. See
Introduction for GETAHUN,
GETACHAW, and GETANAH
Lord be praised, TOLULOPE
Lord hath heard, SEM'ON

Lord is with you, MUNASHE
lord of battle, EZEOGU. See
surnames list, Nigeria
lost, HASWEEKA
Lot, LUTU
lovable, KAI, NALO
love, IFE, LERATO, NONTANDO,
UPENDO
love excels all, IFETAYO
love is beautiful, LOLONYO
love is sweet, LOLOVIVI
loved, ADUKE, KENDI, MAHABUBA,
MAHABUBU, THANDEKA, EDIMA.
See Introduction
loving, ADENIKE
luck/lucky, BAHATI. See BAHATISHA,
CHOOLWE, MBARUSHIMANA,
MUGISHA, ORILONISE, RABO,
TADELESH
lucky hill, KUBI AYANA
luminous, MOUNIR
lush, LEMLEM
magic, MUROGI
magnanimous, MUHISINI. See
MUHISANI
maiden, MBOPPO. See Introduction
maize, MAPOPWE
make known, JULISHA
making of a woman, MAHAVAVY
male child, HINDOLO
man from the east, SHAMSHUNI
man from Tibesti, TOUBOU
man of God, JIBURILI
man without a chief, GAMAEMBI
many, BANJI
many enemies, SINZABAKWIRA
Mariyah, MARIATU
market, NYIRAGERERO
market day, EDET. See Introduction
Mary, MARIAMU, MERIA
Mary's place, SAFARA
master of the house, BABA-ILE
mayor, DIWANI
meaningless, CHEELO

meat, HANYAMA, ORINGO
medicines, KAIHEMBA
medicine man, JABILO
medicinal tree, AWACHO
meeting place for the elders, KULAL
men of men, NAMAQUA
menstruation, ILORI, OKUMU
mercy, LUSUNGU, MAHARI, MUFTAU,
RAMOTA, RAMOSA, TSITSI,
RAHMANI. See surnames list,
Algeria
merriment, NYAKALLO
messenger, BUNZI, JAKADA,
LAKWENA
Michael, MIKAILI
midnight, ODUOR, see time of day
and season name charts; WARI.
See surnames list, Eritrea/
Ethiopia
might, HAILE. See surnames list,
Eritrea/Ethiopia
migration, AMWENDO, GODANA,
HAGODANA, KONO
milking a cow, ELLEMA
million, MILLIYON. See Introduction
miracles, TAMERAT. See surnames
list, Eritrea/Ethiopia
mirror, TALA-TALA
mischievous, MONAFIKI, AGWO. See
Introduction
miser, GOHA
misery (bring out of), MERHAWEET
mobile, SUNTWE. See Introduction
for MATAKAIRA and KOSALE
mock, KASEKO
Mohammed, MOMO
moisture, BINA
moon, ARAWET
moon God, KHENSU
moonlight, MUKAMWEZI
Monday born, TENEN
money, NAVO, SIKA
money is sweet, GAVIVI
monkey, KAFELO, NAKAFELO,

NAMPELO
morning. See time of day and
season name charts for OMONDI,
AMONDI, OKINYI, AKINYI,
ONYANGO, ANYANGO, OLUOCH,
and ALUOCH. See Introduction
for EWIE
Moses, MUSSIE
Mosque minister, IMAMU
mother, IYA, see IYABODE; UMMI. See
Introduction for UM, MAMA, and
EKA
mother of a king, CHANDAMUKULU
mother of compassion, NOSENTE
mother of death, NOKOFA
mother of soldiers, MASCARA
mother returns, IYABODE, YETUNDE
mother's family, OLUINA
mother's image, YEJIDE
mother's pet, KODA
mountaineer, HARUNI
mountains, EMBAYE, ITIENI, KULAL,
LESIOLO, MOGAI, SATIMA,
TARAKWET
mushuku juice, VEMBO
Mustafa, MUTAFA
my coming opens the way, ADESINA
mystery, ELUMBU, KUSH
mystic, RABI
namesake, NATORMA, NFATORMA
Narcissus, NARIGISI
Nasir, NASIRU
nation, TAIFA, ZWELITHINI
neglected, CAPUKULUA. See
Introduction
never bids goodbye, ANKRAH. See
surnames list, Ghana
new arrival is gold, ENGEDA WARK.
See Introduction
new world, ZWELITSHA
New Year, ABIODUN
Nica people, MANICA
nice, SARAMA
night, CHAUSIKU. See also time of

day and season name charts for
BUSIKU, OTIENO, and ATIENO
nightingale, SHORI
Nile River, ANUKIS, NALUBALE
nine, KENDA
nine towns, MIJIKENDA. See
reference guide to peoples and
languages
no hope, NDOTONYI. See
Introduction
no more hoe, KOSOKO
no more rags, AKISATAN. See
Introduction
no problem, SIAPOLE
Noah's Ark, SAFINA
Noah's Sea, NAKIMA
noble, MESFIN, CHERIF. See
surnames list, Algeria
noise maker, CHIYOBEKA
noise of the market, UDEAFO. See
Introduction
northeast wind, DUMI
northwest wind, KUNZI
nose, SANKA. See Introduction
nothing to be thankful for,
BASIMAKI. See Introduction
numerous, TWAMVULA
oath, BILKI
Ogun consoles me this, OGUNDIPE
oil, MAFUTA
old man, CHISHALE SHALE,
HADIIMANA
old mother, MAIKULU
older sister, SISI. See surnames list,
Sierra Leone
only child, KONTAR
only daughter, DELU
only son, IGGI
open, DJIBOLA, FATIU
opportunity, NAFASI
original, ASLI
orphan, MACIA
orphan boy, KILEKEN
ostrich, SEGHEN

Othman, SUMANA
otter, INTINI. See surnames list,
South Africa
Our Lord God, RABANA
outside, AOKO, OOKO
outsmart, TIBLETZ
overtaken, MWIINDE
owner, MALIKI
owner of cattle, ABALONI
owner of frogs, ABARACHA
owner of Zaria, MAI ZARIA
pageant, TAMASHA
palace, RISHAN
parent dies, GASIGWA
parrot, ICHOKU. See Introduction
paths, DANDU, HANZILA, NZILA
patience, UWITONZE, VUMILIA
Paul, BULUS, PAULO
payer, MOLEFI. See twin name
charts
payment, TEFO
peace/peaceful, AKWE, BEM,
KISERIAN, LUAM, MIREMBE,
NACALA, RIG'AT, SULEMANI,
KGOTSO. See Introduction
peacemaker, UWAMAHORO
pearl, MAKULA
people listen to him, TESSEMA. See
surnames list, Eritrea/Ethiopia
people of the caves, TURKANA
people of the rock, ANTANKARA
people who die of old age,
KARAMOJONG
perish, SHABALALA. See surnames
list, South Africa
permanence of the eyebrow,
ZAMANGIRRA
perplex, TATA
person, MOTU
pet (admired), ADUKE, ALAKE,
AMOKE, APEKE, APINKE
pilgrim, ALHAJI, HIJA
pillar, ANDE
pillar of Mary, ANDE MARIAM

pitiless, NTAMPUHWE
pity, CILINGOHENDA
plan together, AJAKOTA. See
   Introduction
planning, CETEWAYO
pleasant, ABDELLATIF
pleased, GAMADA
pleases Aton, IKHNATON
pleasure, ANISA, GENET
pledge, AMANA. See surnames list,
   Tanzania
plenty, YALWA
pointed lips, AMGOSEB. See
   Introduction
pollen of the grape plant,
   TSEGEWEINI, see WEYNEE
porcupine, MAKANDA. See
   surnames list, South Africa
possession, KABILI
poverty, ABARACHA, BAKUNDUKIZE,
   BUKENE, KAVUTA, see
   Introduction for ANTUBAM,
   BASIMAKI, and TIBEITA
power/powerful, AGU, AJAMU,
   AJANI, AMANDLA, HAILE, KUSH,
   LAZIZI, SEKHMET
power of blood, MANJAKAZE
praise, WUDASSE
praise God, OLUWATOYIN,
   TOCHUKWU
praised one, MOMO
precious, AZIZA, see surnames list,
   Algeria; CHIBEKWABEKWA. See
   Introduction
precious child, GINIKANWA
precious water, SHASA
precursor, BASH, BASHIRU
pregnant one, WAHU
premature baby, ELUMBU
present, NEO. See twin name charts
presenter, MUKADAMU
pretty, HASHOBA. See Introduction
   for SEPONONO and NNEYEN
prevent worry, HANAZULLUMI

previous children have died, ADITA,
   AKUJI, ATONGA, AWITI, BARMANI,
   CAIMILE, CEYAVALI, CHILALA,
   CHEELO, GHIDAY, HARACHA,
   IGBEKOYI, JUJI, KAPERA, KOSOKO,
   MOSELE, MUUKA, MAHU, MALOMO,
   MULAHI, NTIRUSHIZE, OKU,
   ODHERU, OWITI, RACH, TIJU-IKU,
   WONYE. See Introduction for
   AKISATAN, UDENE, and
   NKPAKUGHA
pride, HABEN, REZENE
prince, AMIRI, AVONGARA,
   GALADIMA, HYKSOS, L'UUL,
   MULANGIRA, SID
princely, MABILI
princess, MUMBEJA, SAYIDANA,
   SHAHRAZAD
princess sunrise, MATALAI SHAMSI
problems, FATUKOBIRI
professor, SHAIHUN MALLAMI. See
   SHAIHI
promise, TSHEPISO. See twin name
   charts
promise of Zion, TESFASION. See
   surnames list, Eritrea/Ethiopia
prone to laughter, TESHI
prophet, ARIANHDIT, LAIBON, WAL
prophetess, NEBYAT
propagate, XINAVANE
prosper/prosperous, ABALONI,
   MONONO, RISKU, YALWA, YILMA,
   ABAYIE, and MAIWADA. See
   Introduction
protection, NZALI
prowess, ZAKI
pumpkin, CHITANGA
pupil of an eye, BILEN
pure, ASLI, MARIATU, SEFIYETU
pure gold, TERUWARK
quarrel, CHIYOBEKA, TWAAMBO
queen, MALIKIYA, NANTEZA, THEMA,
   KWINI. See Introduction
Queen Nzinga's sisters, KIFUNJI,

MUKUMBU
queen of beauty, EZENMA
Queen of Sheba, BILKI
queen of the universe, MAWU
rabbit, MUKONOWESHURO. See
surnames list, Zimbabwe
Rabiyah, RABIA
radiance, MOUNIR
Rahim, RAIMI
Rahmah, RAMOTA
Ramadan, ALHAJI, HIJA,
RAMADHANI, HAJI. See
Introduction
Ramlah, LAORATU, REMI
rain, HALWIINDI, LWIINDI, MARKA,
MPULA, NASHA, NOMVULA. Also
see time of day and season name
charts for AKOTH, OKOTH,
MAINZA, HAMVULA, SHAVULA,
PULE, PULANE, PULENG, ROBA,
HAROBA
rainbow, MUSOKE, NAMUSOKE
rainmaker, MUGESI
raisin, ZEBIB
rank, DARAJA
ready, TAYARI
Rebecca, RIMKA
rebellious, MARIAMU, MERIA
reconciliation, PATANISHA
red, MASHAVA
red earth, ADAMU
reddish-skin, APONBEPORE, BAGULE,
JENGO, MAMAGULE
reedbuck, NZIKI. See surnames list,
South Africa
refuse, LEHANA
rejoicing, SHANGWE, SHEREHE
related, JIRA
renewed, TADESSA. See surnames
list, Eritrea/Ethiopia
replace, TEKIE
reptile, MUUKA
reputation, CINAWENDELA,
YENDELELA

resin, LUBNA
respect the winner, NKEJUWIMYE
resting place, PAULO
restless, WIGASI
restrainer, KASIM
restricted, HULILAPI. See
Introduction
returned, CHEPTO
revenge, ABOKA. See Introduction
rhinoceros, UKOMBE. See surnames
list, South Africa
ricefields, FARAFENNI
rich/riches, HABTOM, OLANIYONU,
OLATUNDE
ridicule, KASEKO
rightly guided, MAHDI, RASHID
river, ASUBONTENG, ZAIRE
river spirit, MALEK, TIASSALE
road, HANZILA, MAZILA, NZILA
roadside camp, CILOMBO
rock, APATA, see ADENIJI, TIASSALE
roots, HIDI, MIYANDA, MICHELO
Rose, ROZI
royal, ADE, ADEDAPO, MESFIN,
OYEWOLE, RETH
rubbish heap, JUJI
ruler, DIOP. See surnames list,
Senegal
ruler of foreign lands, HYKSOS
rumors, DIPUO. See twin name
charts
Ruqiyyah, RUKIA
rush, SARDA
sad, MAKIADI
Sadiq, SADIKI
saffron, ZAAFARANI
Safiyyah, SEFIYETU
saliva, MANTANZIMA. See surnames
list, South Africa
salt/salty, DUKE, HADA, SAUTU
salvation of Jehovah, ISAYAS
Samson, SHAMSHUNI
sandy, KEI
satisfied, KOSHI, SHIBA, SIKOLIWE

save me, YOMI
saved from the water, MUSSIE
saviour, MEDHIN
saviour of the nation, AGYEMANG
saviour was born, TEWELDE
  MEDHIN, see TEWELDE
scary creature, AKOKO
scholar, DIOP. See surnames list,
  Senegal
sea, BAHARI
second born son, MORLAI
second wife, NYEKI
secrets are not for sale, EWANISHA
seed of Mary, ZARA MARYAM
seer, MORATHI
select birth, ASABI
selected, MUTAFA
selfishness, RAMONA
self-sufficient, KARIKOGA, NZITUNGA
Senegal, ZENAGA
senseless, IYOYO
sent away, AWITI, OWITI
serpent man, KARI KAI
servant, UMI, AUDU. See surnames
  list, Nigeria
servant of Mary, GEBREMARIAM. See
  surnames list, Eritrea/Ethiopia
servant of the Trinity, GEBRESELASE.
  See surnames list, Eritrea/
  Ethiopia
setting sun, LIBBILA. See time of
  day and season name charts
settled, RIG'AT
share, ANYWAA, GHIDAY,
  SINZABAKWIRA, GIDEY. See
  surnames list Eritrea/Ethiopia
shaver, MOSHESH. See surnames
  list, South Africa
Sheba, BILKI
shelter, DINA, OGBE
shield, WALTA, TAFA. See surnames
  list, Eritrea/Ethiopia
ship, MERKAB
shop, COKOVENDA, DUKA, KAULA

shortcut, TAKABA
short-horned cow, GUMEL
short man, GENDEME, TUMBUI
short-tempered, CHAMUCIMA
shout, POPOTA
show, TAMASHA
shows wealth, OMENGBOJI. See
  surnames list, Nigeria
shrine for rain, HALWIINDI, LWIINDI
shrub, MAHAJANGA
Shuhdah, SUDETU
sibling died, TEKIE
sickly, KATAFWA, CHILWALO. See
  Introduction
sight for sore eyes, CILOMBO
silent person, TULI. See surnames
  list, South Africa
silver, BIRRU. See surnames list,
  Eritrea/Ethiopia
silver fox, MOPHEME. See surnames
  list, South Africa
Simon, SEM'ON
Sinbad, SENDIBADA
sister, UHUTI
sit down, BANJOKO, MAGARA
sky, NUT, SEMAINESH
sky blue, SAMAWATI
slander, BARAYAGWIZA, BAYAVUGE,
  SINUMVAYABO
slender, OPELENGE, SENWE
sleeping, CHILALA
small, DOGO, HADIKETI, KAZURI,
  KANIINI, KATITO
small bird, CISENGU
small boy, BORBOR
small girl, DIKETI
small thing, CHECHE
small wide one, OKAHANDJA
smile, BASHASHA, BESMA
smile to mask vengeance,
  AJERIAKHILI. See Introduction
smoke, MESI. See twin name charts
snake, NYOKA, AGWO. See
  Introduction

soft, ANANA, RAKAYA
Solomon, SULEMANI
son, MODU, YARO
son of Bassa, OZIANIVASSA. See
  Introduction
son of David, WOLDE DAWIT. See
  WOLDE'AB
son of God, WOLDE'AB
son of enjoyment, DAN MORE
son of Kano, DAN KANO
son of Mariam, WOLDE MARIAM. See
  WOLDE'AB
son of the Light, WOLDE BERHAN.
  See WOLDE'AB
sorcerer, NDOKI
sorghum, HAKANKONE
sorrow, BYAGO, EKUNDAYO, MAKIADI
southeast wind, BUNZI
spare time, NAFASI
spared, TIRFE, YEHDEGA
spear, KIPKARREN, SHOPO
spiritual leader, IMAMU, ZO
split, PAOUA
spoiled, CHIBEKWABEKWA. See
  Introduction
spoiler, MESSINA
spread, XINAVANE
sprightly, KOSALE. See Introduction
spring, RABIA
springbuck, TSIPI. See surnames
  list, South Africa
springhare, INZIPONE. See
  surnames list, South Africa
squinty eyes, KAMEKE. See
  Introduction
squirrel, KAIKURA
stable, ZINDZI
stalk of maize, LUSATI, POTO. See
  surnames list, South Africa
stands apart, ITIENI
star, ASTER, MANYELETI, NAJMA
stay, BANJOKO, MAGARA, NACALA
steady rain, MARKA
steps, DARAJA

stockade, KEFFI
storax, LUBNA
stories, DEKAT
stride, TAKABA
strong, AGU, AJAMU, AJANI,
  AKINYELE, ANDE, GHE'LE, JENGO,
  TWON, ZOOB, KPAKPA. See
  surnames list, Ghana
sturdy, ANDE
stutterer, GIIGLE
substance of life, MO
substitute, TEKIE
successful, FAUZIYA
sultan, MWAMI
sun, ANYAWU, ASIS, SHAMSA,
  CHIENG. See surnames list, Kenya
sun-born, RAMSES
Sunday (born on), SONDO
sunlike, SHAMSHUNI
sunny, see time of day and season
  name charts for OCHIENG and
  ACHIENG
superior, BELAYNESH, BELAY, RUKIA
supper (born during), DARFN TUWO
supplanter, YAKUBU
support, AZUKA, OAFETALO
surpassed, ZELEKE. See surnames
  list, Eritrea/Ethiopia
sustenance, RIZIKI
sweet, PALELEY, YASUMINI
sweet potatoes, CHIMBWALI. See
  Introduction
sweetheart, MAHABUBA, MAHABUBU
swift, ELE. See Introduction
tail end of the ricefields, FARAFENNI
tail of the dog, MOSELE
talk, LOBA, DIPUO. See twin name
  charts
talkative, POPOTA, SIMWATALANA,
  TWAAMBO. See Introduction for
  MULANGU, ICHOKU, and
  MUSHOSHOMU
tall, DOGO, MULEFU, UROWO, GAXUB.
  See Introduction

tall man, MOIVUMBA, PAJONGA
tall messenger, DOGON JAKADA
tangle, TATA
tastes nice, MEAZA
Tayyib, TAYIBU
teacher, MWALIMU
tear, PASUA
tender bonds, RIMKA
thank God, MODUPEOLA (see DUPE),
    MATONDO
thanks, DUPE, JENDAYI, KURON,
    NAGODE
there is God, HABIMANA
thicket, DENHERE, KADENERE
think first, LIVANGA
thirst, MARWE
thorny, OKUTHE
threaten, TISHA. See BAHATISHA
thriving, ZAKWANI
throne, ZUFAN
throw away, AYASHE, ABASHE
tired, MULELE
tithe, ASRAT. See surnames list,
    Eritrea/Ethiopia
title enters the house, OYEWOLE,
    TESHOME
tomorrow, HAJUNZA, KESHO, LOBI,
    JUNZA. See time of day and
    season name charts
too much, TWAMVULA
tortoise, KURUMAN, IKID. See
    Introduction
train, JIRGI, TAZARA
tranquility, NACALA
travel, CINAWENDELA, HAJUNZA,
    HACEMPETA, JARAMOGI, MAZILA,
    MOTSAMAI, SHEKARAU,
    SIBBILISHOKWE, YENDELELA,
    ZIMANAKWANGWA
treasure, HAZINA
treated badly, NZIRUBUSA
tree, BAMUTHI, CHITIMUKULU,
    DUAH, LOIYENGALANI, LESIOLO
trials, IYAPO, NOMZAMO

tribe, TAIFA
Trinity, SELAS, SELASSIE. See
    surnames list, Eritrea/Ethiopia
triumphant rejoicing, SHEREHE
trouble, DAMBUDSO, KATAHALI,
    MERHAWEET, MASHAKA, MATATA,
    SHIDA, TAABU, NAHIMANA,
    NIYIBIZI, NTAMPUHWE
troubled pregnancy, ORWA
troublesome, SHUMPA
trust in God, UWIZEYE
trusted/trustworthy, AMAN, AMINI,
    LAMIN, THEMBA, THEMBEKA,
    TSHEPO. See twin name charts
truth, MAAT, SADIKI
turn, GHIDAY
twelfth son, ADEBEN. See
    Introduction
twin dies, MULIINDA
two baobobs, YAKA LAMAN
ultimate, AZANA
umbilical cord, HAKUNYO, KUNYO,
    OWINO
unexpected birth, SIKUJWA
unexpected pregnancy, KIWANUKA,
    NABAWANUKA
unjust treatment, NZIRUBUSA
unknown, KUSH
unripe fruit, BUNZE
unto you, WAIYAKI
unwavering, ANDE
urge primeval, HAWAKULU, HEEWAN
urged, CITONKWA, MUNACITONKWA
vapor, HABILI
vegetable, TOPWE
veil, LUTU
Venus, KILEKEN
veranda, BARAZA. See surnames
    list, Kenya
veteran, MUSEVENI
victorious, FAUZIYA
vigor, NETO. See surnames list,
    Angola
village headman, MEQUANENT

visitors, BEENZU
vow, KIDANE
vulture, UDENE. See Introduction
wake up and pray, BYUKUSENGE
walk, CHIMIWENDA
wanderer, HACEMPETA
want, TAKA
war, HAAZITA, MAKONDO, MIJOGA
war general, BALOGUN
warlike, MIJOGA
warlord, KAURA
warrior, AKINYELE, LUANDA MAGERE
wash and dress up, AWERO
water, AKIPPI, SHASA
waterfalls, VISOLELA
way, HANZILA
wealth, HABTOM, SUMANA
weaned, FATIMETU
weekend, SATI. See time of day
names charts
well-behaved, NSOMI
when it happens it happens,
AHORISHAKIYE
where, ANA
whirlwind, KAMBIHI
white, KEI
white person, BATURE. See
surnames list, Nigeria
wide, IFE
wild tobacco, KURUMAN
wildebeest, IKOKONI. See surnames
list, South Africa
willful, IDOWU. See Introduction

and twin name charts
wind, KINFE, MOPEPE
wisdom, AKILI, MAWU
wise, MORATHI, MOHLALEFI. See
Introduction
wish, TIMNEET
wondering, MAKALO
work, CINAKAVALI, CISANGANDA,
KAZIJA, KAZI, YENGE
work for the king, KALEI
work for the Lord, BATIRAISHE
world, ALEM, YIRGA-ALEM,
ZWELITSHA, ZWELITHINI, ALEMU.
See surnames list, Eritrea/
Ethiopia
worn out welcome, KATEKE
worry, HANAZULLUMI
wrestlers, NKINDA, see surnames
list, Kenya; DINGBA. See
surnames list, Nigeria
writer, MABBALANI
yesterday, LOBI
young bull calf, SATIMA
young lioness, AFISHETU
young man, YIGO, IKPE. See
Introduction
youth, UJANA
Zalikha, ZULI
Zaynab, ZENE
zebra. See surnames list, South
Africa, for IDUBE, IQWARA, and
MAKWA

APPENDIX E

PERIODICALS ON AFRICA

The following is a selected list of periodicals on subjects related to Africa. Most of these publications should be available in larger public libraries or at university libraries. A subscription to one of these publications may make a unique gift for those curious to learn more about Africa, complimenting an existing interest of a relative or friend. For instance, Christian friends may enjoy receiving *Action Africa* or *African Christian* to read about what is happening in the Christian community in Africa. There are several publications that might appeal to entrepreneurs working with African products and companies, or persons planning to enter this field, such as *African Business, Africa–North America Business Register,* and *New African.* Those looking for career opportunities related to Africa— especially of an academic nature—could try the *Tuesday Bulletin* or *African Studies Association News,* which regularly lists employment opportunities. For general reading on Africa best bets are *Africa Events, African Concord, Focus on Africa,* and *New African.* Prices given are approximate annual prices.

Action Africa, free quarterly in tabloid-format covers Christian missions in Africa: Africa Evangelical Fellowship, P.O. Box 100, 4 Morgan St., Kingsgrove, N.S.W. 2208 Australia.

Africa Confidential, fortnightly newsletter covering African political and economic issues: Miramoor Publications Ltd., 73 Farringdon Rd., London EC1M 3JB, England ($90 students).

Africa Events, monthly consumer magazine covering politics, business, arts, and sports: Dar Es Salaam Ltd., 55 Banner St., London EC1Y 8PX, England ($50).

Africa Insider, twice-monthly report on U.S.–African political and foreign affairs: Matthews Associates, Box 53398 Temple Heights Sta., Washington, D.C. 20009, (301) 897-3243 ($37.50 to individuals).

Africa Journal of International Affairs and Developments, semi-annual articles on African foreign relations and world affairs: College Press, 27 Are Ave., New Bodija, Secretariat, P.O. Box 30678, Ibadan, Nigeria ($35.95 to individuals).

Africa News, an on-line service that covers politics and social movements:

Africa News Service, P.O. Box 3851, 720 9th Street, Durham, NC, 27702, (919) 286-0747 ($48).

Africa–North America Business Register, annual directory includes trade opportunities, financial, trade, and demographic data, trade shows and exhibits, key ministries, etc.: Secton Group International, P.O. Box 264, Stn. P, Toronto, ON, M5S 2S8, Canada ($50).

Africa South of the Sahara, yearly book of African affairs, includes information on regional organizations and facts and figures: Europa Publications Ltd., London, England (available in reference sections of libraries).

Africa Today, quarterly academic journal covering current affairs, includes book reviews: Lynne Rienner Publishers, 1800 30th St., Suite 314, Boulder, CO, 80301, (303) 444-6684 ($25 to individuals).

Africa Update, semi-annual newsletter of the Africa Travel Association: 347 Fifth Ave., Ste. 610, New York, NY, 10016, (212) 447-1926 ($10).

Africa Watch, news from human rights organization on observance of internationally accepted human rights in Africa: Human Rights Watch, Africa Watch, 485 Fifth Ave., New York, NY, 10017-6104, (212) 972-8400 ($40).

African Affairs, quarterly academic journal, forum for discussing African writing by Africans and non-Africans: Oxford University Press, Inc., 2001 Evans Rd., Cary, NC, 27513, (919) 677-0977 ($108).

African Arts, illustrated quarterly magazine includes film and book reviews: University of California at Los Angeles, James S. Coleman African Studies Center, Los Angeles, CA, 90024, (310) 825-1218 ($47 to individuals).

African Business, monthly business magazine for executives working in or trading with Africa: 7 Coldbath Square, London EC1R 4LQ, England ($90).

African Christian, fortnightly information on church news and developments in Africa: African Church Information Service, P.O. Box 14205, Nairobi, Kenya.

African Concord, weekly pan-African magazine: Concord Ltd., Aare Abiola House, 26–32 Whistler St., London N5 INJ, England ($182).

African Economic History, annual journal: African Studies Center, Boston University, 270 Bay State Rd., Boston, MA, 02215 ($15 to individuals).

African Herald, monthly newspaper with news on Africa and African Americans: Good Hope Enterprises Inc., Box 2394, Dallas, TX 75221-2394, (214) 823-7666 ($15).

African Identity, monthly consumer magazine: Afrimedia Communications, 236 Albion Rd., Ste. 1910, Rexdale, ON M9W 6A6, Canada, (416) 743-1900 ($20.40).

African Interpreter, monthly journal of African and Arab affairs: African Interpreter Publishing Co., Radergguertel 11, 50968 Cologne, Germany ($45).

African Languages and Cultures, semi-annual academic publication on African linguistic and cultural subjects, including art, music, and literature: Oxford University Press, Inc., 2001 Evans Rd., Cary, NC, 27513, (919) 677-0977 ($30).

African Literature Association (ALA) Bulletin, quarterly: African Literature Association, Comparative Literature and Film Studies Department, University of Alberta, Edmonton, AB T6G 2E6, Canada, (403) 492-5535 (price varies).

African Music, approx. annual newsletter: International Library of African Music, Institute of Social and Economic Research, Rhodes University, Grahamstown 6140, South Africa ($22).

African Recorder, fortnightly digest of current events culled from African and other newspapers: Asian Recorder & Publications (Private) Ltd., A-126, Niti Bagh, New Delhi 110 049, India ($136).

African Rural and Urban Studies, thrice-yearly academic journal: African Studies Center, Michigan State University, 100 Center for International Programs, East Lansing, MI, 48824-1035, (517) 353-1700 ($30 · to individuals).

African Studies, bi-annual scholarly journal with articles covering topics in anthropology, history, sociology, literature, and languages: Witwatersrand University Press, Wits 2050, South Africa ($35).

African Studies Association (ASA) News, quarterly newsletter for members: African Studies Association, Emory University, Credit Union Bldg., Atlanta, GA, 30322, (404) 329-6410.

African Studies Review, thrice-yearly scholarly journal: African Studies Association, Emory University, Credit Union Bldg., Atlanta, GA, 30322, (404) 329-6410 (with membership).

African Trade, free irregular publication with intra-African trade information: United Nations Economic Commission for Africa, P.O. Box 3001, Addis Ababa, Ethiopia.

African Trader, quarterly: Association of Chambers of Commerce, P.O.B. 91267, Auckland Park 2006, South Africa.

African Wildlife, bi-monthly magazine of the Wildlife Society of Southern Africa: Wildlife Society of Southern Africa, Northwards, 21 Rockridge Rd., Parktown 2193, South Africa (R.88).

African Woman, monthly women's interest: Ring Rd. West, P.O.B. 1496, Accra, Ghana.

Africanus, twice-yearly academic journal of development alternatives: University of South Africa, Department of Development Administration, P.O. Box 392, Pretoria 0001, South Africa ($6).

APRI Journal, bi-monthly newsletter analyzes peace issues, including environment, disarmament, violent conflict, and foreign debt: African Peace Research Institute, P.O. Box 51757, Falomo, Ikoyi, Lagos, Nigeria ($40).

Focus on Africa, magazine of the British Broadcasting Corporation covering current events, arts, and culture: BBC African Service, Bush House, P.O. Box 78, Strand, London WC2B 4PH, England.

International Journal of African Historical Studies, quarterly academic journal covering African history from Stone Age to present: Boston University, African Studies Center, 270 Bay State Rd., Boston, MA, 02215, (617) 353-3673 ($35 to individuals).

Issues: A Journal of Opinion, occasional: African Studies Association, Emory University, Credit Union Bldg., Atlanta, GA, 30322, (404) 329-6410.

Journal of African History, thrice-yearly scholarly journal covering African History up to about 1960: Cambridge University Press, Journals Dept., 40 W. 20th St., New York, NY 10011-0495, (212) 924-3900 ($57 to individuals).

Journal of Modern African Studies, quarterly survey of politics, economics, and related topics of contemporary Africa: Cambridge University Press, Journals Dept., 40 W. 20th St., New York, NY 10011-0495, (212) 924-3900 ($61 to individuals).

Netsebraq Eritrea ("Reflections" Eritrea), quarterly Eritrean Newsletter with majority of stories written in Tigrinya: Tsegai Negash, editor, P.O. Box 871, Louisville, CO, 80027, (303) 665-1005.

New African, monthly current affairs magazine includes financial analysis: I.C. Publications Ltd., 7 Coldbath Square, London EC1R 4LQ, England ($90).

New African Yearbook, annual directory includes major fact and figures of all countries: I.C. Publications Ltd., 7 Coldbath Square, London EC1R 4LQ, England ($80).

Northeast African Studies, thrice-yearly journal covering the Horn of Africa: African Studies Center, Michigan State University, 100 Center for International Programs, East Lansing, MI, 48824-1035, (517) 353-1700 ($30 to individuals).

Panamerican/Panafrican Association (PPA) Notes, quarterly newsletter: Panamerican/Panafrican Association, P.O. Box 143, Baldwinsville, NY, 13027, (315) 635-6318.

Studies in African Linguistics, thrice-yearly academic journal with articles on African languages and linguistics: University of California at Los Angeles, Department of Linguistics, Los Angeles, CA, 90024-1310, (310) 825-3686 ($16 to individuals).

Transafrica Forum, quarterly journal of opinion on Africa and the Caribbean: Transaction Periodicals Consortium, Dept. 3092, Rutgers University, New Brunswick, NJ, 08903, (908) 932-2280 ($32 to individuals).

Tuesday Bulletin, weekly newsletter of seminars, programs, classes, publications, and career opportunities related to Africa: Michigan State University, African Studies Center, 100 International Center, East Lansing, MI 48824-1035.

World Today Series: Africa, annual academic publication on economic and
    social problems of the continent: Stryker-Post Publications, P.O. Drawer
    1200, Harpers Ferry, WV, 25425, (800) 995-1400 ($8.50).

INFORMATION SERVICES

Africa News Service, P.O. Box 3851, Durham, NC, 27702
The African-American Institute, 833 UN Plaza, New York, NY, 10017
African Imprint Library Services, 410 W. Falmouth Hwy., Box 350, West
    Falmouth, MA, 02574
African Newspapers Currently Received by American Libraries, pamph-
    let listing 276 newspapers received in U.S. libraries: African Studies
    Center, 10 Lenox St., Brookline, MA, 02146

NOTE: The majority of the entries above were found in the *Guide to
International Education in the United States* (Gale Research, Detroit, MI) and
Ulrich's International Periodicals Directory 1994–95.

SOURCE NOTES FOR APPENDIX A

DAY OF THE WEEK NAMES

1. Embassay of Cote d'Ivoire.
2. Kosi Gbediga. "What Is in an African Name?," *The African* (November 1994).
3. Ibid.
4. F.W.H. Migeod. "Personal Names Among Some West African Tribes," *Journal of the Royal African Society* 17 (October 1917).
5. Ibid.
6. Ibid.
7. A. B. Quartey-Papafio. "The Use of Names Among the Gas or Accra People of the Gold Coast," *Journal of the African Society* 13 (January 1914).
8. Ibid.
9. Ebo Ubahakwe. *Igbo Names: Their Structure and Their Meanings.* Ibadan, Nigeria: Daystar Press, 1981.
10. Z. I. Oseni. *A Guide to Muslim Names.* Lagos, Nigeria: Islamic Publications Bureau, 1981. Additional information from Aminu Yakubu.
11. Embassy of Mali.

TIME OF DAY AND SEASON NAMES

1. Dan Omondi Oburu of Kenya and Dishon Opiyo, Embassy of Kenya.
2. Mwizenge S. Tembo. *What Does Your African Name Mean? The Meanings of Indigenous Names Among the Tonga of Southern Zambia.* Lusaka, University of Zambia: Institute of African Studies, 1989.
3. Dr. Hillary Kelly.
4. Dan Omondi Oburu, op. cit.
5. Mwizenge S. Tembo, op. cit.
6. Ihechukwu Madubuike. *A Handbook of African Names.* Washington, D.C.: Three Continents Press, 1976.
7. Paulus M. Mohome. "Naming in Sesotho: Its Sociocultural and Linguistic Basis," *Names* 20 (September 1972).

ORDER OF BIRTH NAMES

1. G. O. Whitehead. "Personal Names Among the Bari," *Man* (March 1947).
2. Ibid.

3. R. Cornevin. "Names Among the Bassari," *Southwest Journal of Anthropology* 10 (summer 1954).

4. Ibid.

5. Ibid.

6. Ibid.

7. F.W.H. Migeod. "Personal Names Among Some West African Tribes," *Journal of the Royal African Society* XVII (October 1917).

8. Ihechukwu Madubuike. *A Handbook of African Names*. Washington, D.C.: Three Continents Press, 1976.

9. Mary McVey and Lamin Sillah.

TWINS AND CHILDREN BORN NEAR TWINS

1. Samuel Johnson. *The History of the Yorubas: From the Earliest Times to the Beginning of the British Protectorate*. Westport, Connecticut: Negro University Press, 1970.

2. Percy G. Harris. "Some Conventional Hausa Names," *Man* (December 1931). Additional information from Aminu Yakubu.

3. G. O. Whitehead. "Personal Names Among the Bari," *Man* (March 1947).

4. Ibid.

5. Francis Mading Deng. *The Dinka of the Sudan*. Illinois: Waveland Press, Inc., 1972.

6. Ibid.

7. Ihechukwu Madubuike. *A Handbook of African Names*. Washington, D.C.: Three Continents Press, 1976.

8. Ibid.

9. Dan Omondi Oburu of Kenya and Dishon Opiyo, Embassy of Kenya.

10. Chikodi Nnanyelu Ezegwui Anigbogu. *Authentic African Names*. Kenya: Kalajine Foundation, 1992.

11. Paulus M. Mohome. "Naming in Sesotho: Its Sociocultural and Linguistic Basis," *Names* 20 (September 1972).

12. Embassy of Uganda.

BIBLIOGRAPHY

Anigbogu, Chikodi Nnanyelu Ezegwui. *Authentic African Names*. Kenya: Kalajine Foundation: 1992.

Ayot, Henry Okello. *A History of the Luo-Abasuba of Western Kenya*. Nairobi: Kenya Literature Bureau, 1979.

Beattie, J.H.M. "Nyoro Personal Names," *Uganda Journal* 21 (March 1957).

Canning, John, editor. *100 Great Kings, Queens and Rulers of the World*. London: Souvenir Press, Century Books, Ltd., 1973.

Chesaina, C. *Oral Literature of the Kalenjin*. Nairobi: Heinemann Kenya, Ltd., 1991.

Clark, Paul. *The Mountains of Kenya: A Walker's Guide*. Nairobi: Mountain Club of Kenya, 1989.

Cornevin, R. "Names Among the Bassari," *Southwestern Journal of Anthropology* 10 (summer 1954).

Deng, Francis Mading. *The Dinka of the Sudan*. Illinois: Waveland Press, Inc., 1972.

Ennis, Elisabeth Logan. "Women's Names Among the Ovimbundu of Angola," *African Studies* 4: No. 1 (March 1945).

Gbediga, Kosi. "What Is in an African Name?," *The African* (November 1994).

Hanbly, Wilfrid D. *The Ovimbundu of Angola*. Chicago: Field Museum of Natural History, 1934.

Harris, Percy G. "Some Conventional Hausa Names," *Man* 31 (December 1931).

Indiana Black Expo's African Symposium Committee. *An Afrikan Naming Book*, 1979.

Johnson, Samuel. *The History of the Yorubas: From the Earliest Times to the Beginning of the British Protectorate*. Westport, Connecticut: Negro University Press, 1970.

Kidd, Dudley. *Savage Childhood*. New York: Negro University Press, 1906.

Migeod, F.W.H. "Personal Names Among Some West African Tribes," *Journal of the Royal African Society* 17, (October 1917).

Mohome, Paulus M. "Naming in Sesotho: Its Sociocultural and Linguistic Basis," *Names* 20 (September 1972).

Mwaniki, H.S. Kabeca. *Embu Historical Texts*. Nairobi: East African Literature Bureau, 1974.

Mwaniki, H.S.K. *The Living History of the Embu and Mbeere*. Nairobi: Kenya Literature Bureau, 1973.

Okojie, Dr. Xto G. *What Is in a Name?* Lagos, Nigeria: Alumese Palmer, 1980.

Oseni, Z. I. *A Guide to Muslim Names.* Lagos, Nigeria: Islamic Publications Bureau, 1981.

Penwill, D. J. *Kamba Customary Law.* Nairobi: Kenya Literature Bureau, 1951.

Quartey-Papafio, A. B. "The Use of Names Among the Gas or Accra People of the Gold Coast," *Journal of the African Society* 13 (January 1914).

Raper, P. E. and G. S. Nienaber. *Hottentot (Khoekhoen) Place Names.* Durban/ Pretoria: Butterworth Publishers, 1983.

Room, Adrian. *African Place Names.* Jefferson, North Carolina: McFarland & Company, Publishers, 1994.

Rosenthal, Eric. *South African Surnames.* Cape Town: Howard Timmins, 1965.

Sankan, S. S. *The Maasai.* Nairobi: Kenya Literature Bureau, 1971.

Sofala, J. A. "What's in a Name?" *The Sociological Uses of Names and Naming Among the Yoruba and Ibo Ethnic Groups of Nigeria Ibadan* 28 (July 1970) pp. 43–48.

Spear, Thomas T. *The Kaya Complex, A History of the Mijikenda Peoples of the Kenyan Coast to 1900.* Nairobi: Kenya Literature Bureau, 1978.

Sweeney, Philip, editor. *Insight Guides: The Gambia and Senegal.* APA Publications (HK) Ltd., 1990.

Talbot, P. A. "Ibibio Customs and Beliefs," *Journal of the African Society* 13: 51 (April 1914) p. 241.

Tembo, Mwizenge S. *What Does Your African Name Mean? The Meanings of Indigenous Names Among the Tonga of Southern Zambia.* Lusaka, Zambia: Institute for African Studies, 1989.

Ubahakwe, Ebo. *Igbo Names: Their Structure and Their Meanings.* Ibadan, Nigeria: Daystar Press, 1981.

U.S. Central Intelligence Agency. *Amharic Personal Names.* Washington, D.C., 1965.

Werner, A. "The Galla of the East African Protectorate," *Journal of the African Society* 13: 50 (January 1914) p. 121.

Wescott, Roger W. "Bini Names in Nigeria and Georgia," *Linguistics* 124 (March 15, 1974).

Whitehead, G. O. "Personal Names Among the Bassari," *Man* (March 1947).

Wieschoff, Heinz. "Names and Naming Customs Among the Mashona in Southern Rhodesia," *American Anthropologist* 39 (July– Sept. 1937).

Wieschoff, Heinz A. "The Social Significance of Names Among the Ibo of Nigeria," *American Anthropologist* 43 (April–June 1941).